D1190089

WILLIAM WORDSWORTH

WITH AN
INTRODUCTION
BY
VISCOUNT GREY
OF FALLODON

THOMAS NELSON & SONS LTD
LONDON & EDINBURGH

CONTENTS

Contents

Contents

Contents

PART IV—ODES

PART V—SELECTIONS FROM " THE PRELUDE "

PART VI—SELECTIONS FROM "THE EXCURSION"

INTRODUCTION

[William Wordsworth was born on April 7, 1770, at
Cockermouth, in Cumberland, and was educated at Hawks-
head Grammar School. In October 1787 he entered St.
John's College, Cambridge, where, in January 1791, he
took his degree without distinction. In the following
November, filled with enthusiasm for the French Revolu-
tion, he went to France, where he spent nearly a year at
Orleans and Blois. While there he fell in love with a
young Frenchwoman, who by him became the mother of
the child to whom he wrote one of his best-known sonnets,
the one beginning—

" It is a beauteous evening, calm and free."

Finding his supplies from home cut off during the Reign
of Terror, he returned to England, and in 1793 published *An
Evening Walk* and *Descriptive Sketches*, the former dealing
with the Cumberland landscape, and the latter with his
continental travels. His revolutionary opinions were now
shaken, and at last overthrown, by the rise of Napoleon and
his progress towards complete imperialism. In 1795 a legacy
of £900 made him sufficiently independent to devote himself
entirely to literature. He went with his sister to live in
Dorsetshire, and afterwards, in 1797, to Alfoxden, in the
Quantocks, where he had S. T. Coleridge for his neighbour and
intimate friend. In 1798 the two poets published at Bristol
their famous volume of *Lyrical Ballads*, a landmark in the
history of modern English poetry. After a winter spent in
Germany, Wordsworth and his sister settled finally in the
Lake District, first at Grasmere, then at Allan Bank, and
lastly at Rydal Mount. In 1802 Wordsworth married Mary
Hutchinson, and spent the rest of his long and quiet life
in writing and publishing poetry which found but a small
public and few favourable critics. But his reputation grew
steadily, and he gradually attained the pre-eminence for

which he was destined. Late in life he was honoured with University degrees and a Civil List pension; at the age of seventy-three he became Poet Laureate in succession to Robert Southey. He died on March 23, 1850. Of his poems perhaps the most famous are the Patriotic Sonnets, the shorter lyrics, the *Ode on Intimations of Immortality*, and *Lines composed near Tintern Abbey*. The longer poems, *The Prelude* and *The Excursion*, are less often read, though they abound in passages of great magnificence, and are indispensable to the understanding of Wordsworth's character and philosophy. *The Prelude* stands alone as a poetical autobiography. It was written between 1799 and 1805, but was not published until after Wordsworth's death. In certain particular respects it is an incomplete record, and needs for supplement a detailed account of Wordsworth's relation to his sister Dorothy, his friend Coleridge, and to Annette Vallon, the love of his youth; but it contains a full, interesting, and convincing account of the growth of his mind, his view of the world of nature and of men, and the system of poetical philosophy which is his greatest bequest to the literature of his country.]

FIRST of all, let me say that, like many lovers of Wordsworth, I not only find *The Prelude* very interesting, but every time I read it the interest to be found in it grows wider and deeper and more intense, so that it ranks very high indeed in Wordsworth's work. This estimate of *The Prelude* is by no means universal. I once possessed —I am glad to say that I possess it no longer—a copy of an edition of Wordsworth in one volume, in which I was disappointed not to find *The Prelude*. On turning to the Preface I found it stated that the volume contained all the poems of Wordsworth which were of real value, and that the only omissions were of poems such as *The Prelude*, which were by general consent not up to the mark ; I have even found myself an object of pity to at least one literary friend for reading *The Excursion* or *The Prelude* at all. I once heard a distinguished man describe the speeches of another man, also distinguished, whose speeches were full of learning, but more copious than inspiring, as being like a magnum of soda water that had stood uncorked for a week.

To some people, I fear, *The Prelude* and *The Excursion* appear dreary and flat. As against their depreciation, I will quote an appreciation of *The Prelude* from a very unexpected quarter:—" When I came in after years to read *The Prelude* I recognized, as if it were my own history which was being told, the steps by which the love of the country boy for his hills and moors grew into poetical susceptibility for all imaginative presentations of beauty in every direction." The words are those of Mark Pattison. You may set that unexpected appreciation of *The Prelude* against much depreciation of it ; Mark Pattison says here just what makes many of us feel Wordsworth a special poet, the sense that in him we find our own experiences reproduced. As we read him we constantly find ourselves saying : " I know that I have felt that." And sometimes he reveals to us what we have not been previously conscious of, so that we say : " I have felt that without knowing it." Thus to those of us who have the same sort of susceptibility that Wordsworth had to all the aspects of natural beauty, his poetry becomes something not to be measured merely by poetic merit, but something which reproduces, interprets, and reveals to us our own experiences, and is therefore not like something outside appealing to our admiration, but like something which is akin to us, part of ourselves, part of our lives. Therefore, in speaking especially of *The Prelude*, I am not going to talk of its poetic merit or speak of it as a poem, though it has passages which seem to me of the highest poetical beauty. I want to speak of it as what it really is : an autobiography, a document of real authentic human interest. It begins with a description of Wordsworth's childhood and school-times, and as you read on in *The Prelude* you realize, or at least I realize, especially four things about Wordsworth : his extraordinary independence of spirit ; his resentment at any restraint ; his deep and unflinching love of liberty for himself and for the world ; and, finally, his firm conviction that it is not through knowledge that we grow—unless that knowledge be accompanied by feeling—that great, pure, exalted thoughts are due not to knowledge, but to right and elevated feeling. Those four things I find coming out again and again in *The Prelude*. First, take his childhood. His childhood really was incredibly free. At five years old he was making " one long bathing of a summer's day " in a small mill-race separated from the main stream. At ten years old he was out half the night in the late autumn or the early winter, alone on the hills, scudding from snare to snare which he had set for woodcocks, taking the woodcocks from his own snares, and sometimes taking those that were not in his snares but were caught in the snares set by another boy. That act he knew was wrong. He tells us how the consciousness of wrongdoing wrought on him ; he says :

> " . . . and when the deed was done
> I heard among the solitary hills
> Low breathings coming after me, and sounds
> Of undistinguishable motion, steps
> Almost as silent as the turf they trod."

I will take one more passage parallel to that. Again he does something that he feels to be wrong. He finds a boat tied to a willow tree on a moonlit night. He looses the boat and rows himself out on to the lake in it. It was, he says, an act of stealth. As he rowed, taking pride in his rowing, rising on his oars, he fixed his eyes on a bare ridge above which was nothing visible but the sky ; as he rowed farther, gradually there opened up the view of a high, dark peak behind the ridge, and as he rowed on the peak grew in height until it seemed to be something great and immense that was stalking after him. His conscience smote him, he took the boat back to the willow tree, and he went home, but after that, his conscience working in him, he was haunted by the vision he had seen of the peak.

> " . . . for many days my brain
> Worked with a dim and undetermined sense
> Of unknown modes of being ; o'er my thoughts
> There hung a darkness, call it solitude
> Or blank desertion.   No familiar shapes
> Remained, no pleasant images of trees,
> Of sea or sky, no colours of green fields ;
> But huge and mighty forms, that do not live
> Like living men, moved slowly through the mind
> By day, and were a trouble to my dreams."

I quote these passages to make this observation.   You can observe that on both occasions he thought in himself that the acts he had done were wrong.   There is no trace that he felt any fear of being found out, no trace that he dreaded human censure or punishment by his guardians or those who looked after him, or by any human agency ;   no trace of his caring for what others might think of his conduct.   His own conscience finds the reproof in what he thinks he sees in the aspects of Nature ;   and so you will find throughout *The Prelude* an almost abnormal indifference to human censure ;   he is never depressed by blame nor elated by praise, but constantly worked upon by his susceptibility to the outward aspects of Nature.   In that alone he found his education and discipline.   He goes on to describe various things in childhood—all examples of a wonderfully free life—in words that bring home to us the experience of our own boyhoods ;   things like his climbing cliffs for the raven's nest on a precipice so steep that he seemed hardly to be supported by foothold or handhold, but almost to be suspended in air ;   and then he says :—

> " With what strange utterance did the loud dry wind
> Blow through my ear ! the sky seemed not a sky
> Of earth—and with what motion moved the clouds ! "

Passages like that abound, and as you read on and turn
the pages you see " School-time," " School-time,"
" School-time " all through two books at the top of
every page ; and in the text not a single mention of his
once entering a school, having any lessons or teaching
or discipline, any rewards or any punishment; and he
sums up at last by a passage in which he says that he
and his companions loved sitting up late at night till
all other lights were out, scampering over the country
in the daytime, leading a life of sheer pleasure so far
as we can judge from *The Prelude*, innocent but uninter-
rupted perpetual pleasure : and then there is this other
touch, that though he sat up with his companions late
at night he would get up for his own pleasure early in
the morning, sometimes going five miles around the
lake before school-time, sometimes sitting alone in
the wood in the early morning or on some promontory;
and then there came to him these feelings even as a boy,
which we find so constant in his poetry afterwards : the
feeling as if bodily eyes were utterly forgotten. Finally
comes this touching tribute in blank verse to the place
where the days of his childhood were spent :

> " Dear native Regions, wheresoe'er shall close
> My mortal course, there will I think on you ;
> Dying, will cast on you a backward look ;
> Even as this setting sun (albeit the Vale
> Is nowhere touched by one memorial gleam)
> Doth with the fond remains of his last power
> Still linger, and a farewell lustre sheds
> On the dear mountain-tops where first he rose."

I quote that because Wordsworth did what I have not
known an instance of another poet having done. He
afterwards wrote it in rhyme and published it separately :

> " Dear native Regions, I foretell,
> From what I feel at this farewell,
> That, wheresoe'er my steps may tend,
> And whensoe'er my course shall end,

If in that hour a single tie
Survive of local sympathy,
My soul will cast the backward view,
The longing look alone on you.

Thus, while the sun sinks down to rest,
Far in the regions of the West,
Though to the vale no parting beam
Be given, not one memorial gleam,
A lingering light he fondly throws
On the dear hills where first he rose."

You can read these two passages for yourselves, the one in blank verse, and the other in rhyme, and consider at leisure which you think the best of the two.

When Wordsworth parts from school, when his school-time is over, he pays a tribute, not as we mostly do to masters or to the spirit of the school ; he says that he left school with his heart pure, free from low desires, and that this was due to the country in which he lived.

Now I pass from his school-time to his time at Cambridge. With that independent spirit of his he did not seem to find his entry into the University formidable. We, most of us, who have been to universities, in our first days or weeks have found the beginning rather formidable. There is no trace that Wordsworth found it so. But he did not get much good out of the University. He says he felt that he " was not for that time or for that place." One splendid tribute he pays to the statue of Newton :

" Newton with his prism and silent face,
The marble index of a mind for ever
Voyaging through strange seas of Thought alone."

A tribute he pays also to Milton ; but connected with the name of Milton there is an incident in *The Prelude* of a lighter kind. He drank wine in Milton's rooms with some friends, and he poured out libations to that famous memory until his head grew dizzy with the fumes of wine : he is careful to tell us that this never happened before or since. About this incident I must relate the story of an admirer of Wordsworth arguing with some one who did not admire Wordsworth. The former found himself confronted with the argument that Wordsworth was a prig without any natural weaknesses. I suppose if he had known the phrase the critic would have said, " Without one redeeming vice." The admirer of Wordsworth in defence said, " Well, at any rate, he got drunk once." " Yes," said the other, " I know he says so, but I am afraid his standard of intoxication was lamentably low." I put that on record as a lighter touch. Wordsworth proceeds to say, in justice to Cambridge, that if he got little good from it the fault was his own, and not that of any one else, and, having thus satisfied his conscience by blaming himself, he then goes on to say how unedifying he found the place. He said of the Dons : " They served to set our minds on edge and did no more." You can compare that with Gibbons's more flippant statement about his tutor at Oxford : " He remembered he had a salary to receive ; he only forgot he had a duty to perform." You cannot read *The Prelude* without feeling that the strictures on the University had at any rate some truth in them in those days, but let me say at once that nothing of that kind is true to-day. If the universities of the eighteenth century were dead, it is true of them to-day that they are living parts of the nation, that those who are most concerned in their teaching are most careful to keep in touch with the political, economic, and social thought of the day, and Oxford and Cambridge, with other universities, are to-day living parts of the nation's life. Wordsworth closes his description of Cambridge with an extraordinarily powerful passage describing what he felt not only about those in authority but about the undergraduates as well :

" Idleness halting with his weary clog,
And poor misguided Shame, and witless Fear,
And simple Pleasure foraging for Death;
Honour misplaced, and Dignity astray;
Feuds, factions, flatteries, enmity, and guile,
Murmuring submission, and bald government,
(The idol weak as the idolater),
And Decency and Custom starving Truth,
And blind Authority beating with his staff
The child that might have led him; Emptiness
Followed as of good omen, and meek Worth
Left to herself unheard of and unknown."

And so he parts from Cambridge.

I have now spent much time, and I have not got beyond his University life. I must pass over the part about his summer vacation, although it has that very important and interesting passage in it where, in the presence of a splendid sunrise, alone after a night of revelry, he feels that he is ever afterwards to be a dedicated spirit, and having said that and described that experience, he says :

" . . . on I walked
In thankful blessedness, which yet survives."

I want you to notice those last three words : " which yet survives."

The Prelude was written not in extreme youth but when he was in the thirties, in the prime of his poetic gifts and power, and that emotion of his early youth still survived. Most of us have these moments of great emotion under peculiarly favourable conditions of outward circumstance. We all recognize, or at least most of us must recognize, having felt amongst particularly grand or beautiful aspects of Nature what Wordsworth felt on the occasion of that memorable sunrise ; but with most of us the emotions are like a breeze upon a lake, making its ripple at the time and then leaving the lake as it was before. With most of us it is not so much that we are incapable of these great moments of great emotions as that they are, as far as we are concerned, rather like writing in water. With Wordsworth it was not so; they lasted. The substance of which he was made was something so tenacious that when these great moments of emotion came they wrote indelibly upon his personality; their effect was cumulative, they built him up and made him the great poet that he was, and those words " which yet survives " would apply no doubt to many of those great moments in his life. It seems to me that one of the special characteristics of Wordsworth in his youth was this combination of extreme susceptibility with great tenacity. That was a quality in Wordsworth which I think accounts for very much of the poetic excellence of what he wrote and for the power which his poetry has.

I come now to the next book, which is headed " Books," and I would observe two points about it, which are : (1) that he states absolutely and without qualification that for the young there should be complete liberty in reading; there should be no restraint upon their choice of books. I know that this must be a very controversial subject; personally, I side with Wordsworth. He takes the homely simile of a hen with her chickens, and he applies that to the supervision over the reading of the young. He says :

> " Behold the parent hen amid her brood ;
> Yet doth she little more
> Than move with them in tenderness and love."

I would observe, however, on this simile that, although it is absolutely true to the life of what some birds do, or appear to do, as regards their young, when the young are able to feed themselves the mother bird does lead the young where the best food is to be found, and I think a fair summary of Wordsworth's view of reading for young people is that they should be put in the way of the best literature, and should then be left to choose for themselves what they like best. (2) The other point is that knowledge got from reading will not do us good unless it produces real feeling ; that emotion must accompany knowledge. He pays a great tribute to what he owed to books, but he says he got from them knowledge with continually increasing joy, " knowledge not purchased with the lack of power," and he has a long passage, and an exceedingly good one, in which he expresses his scorn of the prig who reads merely in order to acquire knowledge without thereby growing in feeling and sensitiveness. Here are a few lines of it :

> " . . . he sifts, he weighs ;
> All things are put to question ; he must live
> Knowing that he grows wiser every day
> Or else not live at all, and seeing too
> Each little drop of wisdom as it falls
> Into the dimpling cistern of his heart :
> For this unnatural growth the trainer blame,
> Pity the tree.—Poor human vanity,
> Wert thou extinguished, little would be left
> Which he could truly love. . . ."

And then comes a burst of enthusiasm and contrast at the end :

> " Oh ! give us once again the wishing-cap
> Of Fortunatus, and the invisible coat
> Of Jack the Giant-Killer, Robin Hood,
> And Sabra in the forest with St. George !
> The child whose love is here, at least, doth reap
> One precious gain, that he forgets himself."

Well, that has wisdom in it for all of us who are in search either of knowledge or pleasure. We get neither in their highest form unless we seek them in such a way, with such enthusiasm, with such feeling that we forget ourselves. It is true that we find ourselves thereby, but we find ourselves by forgetting ourselves. That inability to forget one's self stands more almost than anything else in the way of the use people make of knowledge or of gifts, and stands often in their way even when they are trying to find pleasure. The ending of that passage :

> " . . . doth reap
> One precious gain, that he forgets himself,"

is one of far-reaching interest and wisdom.

I think one of the saddest things, as you reflect on the history of the world, is the mischief which has been done, the opportunities which have been missed, by men with great powers in great place being unable to forget themselves. It is a natural failing. The greater a man's powers, the more difficult it is for him to forget himself, and it is only when you come to the very great men of the world, whose greatness of soul and strength of moral purpose were greater even than their great powers, that you find the men who in public affairs have had great opportunities and risen to the full height of them, and done all they might for the world.

GREY OF FALLODON.

By kind permission of Messrs. Macmillan and Co., Ltd.
the Text used in this collection is that of the
Globe Edition of Wordsworth's Poems

PART I

MISCELLANEOUS POEMS

POEMS OF WORDSWORTH

MISCELLANEOUS POEMS

" IF THOU INDEED DERIVE THY LIGHT FROM HEAVEN "

If thou indeed derive thy light from Heaven,
Then, to the measure of that heaven-born light,
Shine, Poet ! in thy place, and be content :—
The stars pre-eminent in magnitude,
And they that from the zenith dart their beams,
(Visible though they be to half the earth,
Though half a sphere be conscious of their brightness)
Are yet of no diviner origin,
No purer essence, than the one that burns,
Like an untended watch-fire on the ridge
Of some dark mountain ; or than those which seem
Humbly to hang, like twinkling winter lamps,
Among the branches of the leafless trees.
All are the undying offspring of one Sire :
Then, to the measure of the light vouchsafed,
Shine, Poet ! in thy place, and be content.

" MY HEART LEAPS UP WHEN I BEHOLD "

My heart leaps up when I behold
    A rainbow in the sky :
So was it when my life began ;
So is it now I am a man ;

So be it when I shall grow old,
        Or let me die !
The Child is father of the Man ;
And I could wish my days to be
Bound each to each by natural piety.

TO A BUTTERFLY

STAY near me—do not take thy flight !
A little longer stay in sight !
Much converse do I find in thee,
Historian of my infancy !
Float near me ; do not yet depart !
Dead times revive in thee :
Thou bring'st, gay creature as thou art !
A solemn image to my heart,
My father's family !

Oh ! pleasant, pleasant were the days,
The time, when, in our childish plays,
My sister Emmeline and I
Together chased the butterfly !
A very hunter did I rush
Upon the prey :—with leaps and springs
I followed on from brake to bush ;
But she, God love her, feared to brush
The dust from off its wings.

CHARACTERISTICS OF A CHILD THREE
YEARS OLD

LOVING she is, and tractable, though wild ;
And Innocence hath privilege in her
To dignify arch looks and laughing eyes ;
And feats of cunning ; and the pretty round
Of trespasses, affected to provoke
Mock-chastisement and partnership in play.

And, as a faggot sparkles on the hearth,
Not less if unattended and alone
Than when both young and old sit gathered round
And take delight in its activity ;
Even so this happy Creature of herself
Is all-sufficient, solitude to her
Is blithe society, who fills the air
With gladness and involuntary songs.
Light are her sallies as the tripping fawn's
Forth-startled from the fern where she lay couched ;
Unthought-of, unexpected, as the stir
Of the soft breeze ruffling the meadow-flowers,
Or from before it chasing wantonly
The many-coloured images imprest
Upon the bosom of a placid lake.

ADDRESS TO A CHILD

DURING A BOISTEROUS WINTER EVENING

By my Sister

WHAT way does the wind come ?   What way does he go ?
He rides over the water, and over the snow,
Through wood, and through vale ; and, o'er rocky height
Which the goat cannot climb, takes his sounding flight ;
He tosses about in every bare tree,
As, if you look up, you plainly may see ;
But how he will come, and whither he goes,
There's never a scholar in England knows.

He will suddenly stop in a cunning nook
And ring a sharp 'larum ;—but, if you should look,
There's nothing to see but a cushion of snow
Round as a pillow, and whiter than milk,
And softer than if it were covered with silk.
Sometimes he'll hide in the cave of a rock,
Then whistle as shrill as the buzzard cock ;

—Yet seek him,—and what shall you find in the place ?
Nothing but silence and empty space ;
Save, in a corner, a heap of dry leaves,
That he's left, for a bed, to beggars or thieves !
As soon as 'tis daylight to-morrow, with me
You shall go to the orchard, and then you will see
That he has been there, and made a great rout,
And cracked the branches, and strewn them about ;
Heaven grant that he spare but that one upright twig
That looked up at the sky so proud and big
All last summer, as well you know,
Studded with apples, a beautiful show !

Hark ! over the roof he makes a pause,
And growls as if he would fix his claws
Right in the slates, and with a huge rattle
Drive them down, like men in a battle :
—But let him range round ; he does us no harm,
We build up the fire, we're snug and warm ;
Untouched by his breath see the candle shines bright,
And burns with a clear and steady light ;
Books have we to read,—but that half-stifled knell,
Alas ! 'tis the sound of the eight o'clock bell.
—Come now we'll to bed ! and when we are there
He may work his own will, and what shall we care ?
He may knock at the door,—we'll not let him in ;
May drive at the windows,—we'll laugh at his din ;
Let him seek his own home wherever it be ;
Here's a *cozie* warm house for Edward and me.

TO H. C. (HARTLEY COLERIDGE)

SIX YEARS OLD

O THOU ! whose fancies from afar are brought ;
Who of thy words dost make a mock apparel,
And fittest to unutterable thought
The breeze-like motion and the self-born carol ;

Thou faery voyager ! that dost float
In such clear water, that thy boat
May rather seem
To brood on air than on an earthly stream ;
Suspended in a stream as clear as sky,
Where earth and heaven do make one imagery ;
O blessed vision ! happy child !
Thou art so exquisitely wild,
I think of thee with many fears
For what may be thy lot in future years.
   I thought of times when Pain might be thy guest,
Lord of thy house and hospitality ;
And Grief, uneasy lover ! never rest
But when she sate within the touch of thee.
O too industrious folly !
O vain and causeless melancholy !
Nature will either end thee quite ;
Or, lengthening out thy season of delight,
Preserve for thee, by individual right,
A young lamb's heart among the full-grown flocks.
What hast thou to do with sorrow,
Or the injuries of to-morrow ?
Thou art a dew-drop, which the morn brings forth,
Ill fitted to sustain unkindly shocks,
Or to be trailed along the soiling earth ;
A gem that glitters while it lives,
And no forewarning gives ;
But, at the touch of wrong, without a strife
Slips in a moment out of life.

INFLUENCE OF NATURAL OBJECTS

IN CALLING FORTH AND STRENGTHENING THE IMAGINATION IN BOYHOOD AND EARLY YOUTH

WISDOM and Spirit of the universe !
Thou Soul, that art the Eternity of thought !
And giv'st to forms and images a breath

And everlasting motion ! not in vain,
By day or star-light, thus from my first dawn
Of childhood didst thou intertwine for me
The passions that build up our human soul ;
Not with the mean and vulgar works of Man ;
But with high objects, with enduring things,
With life and nature ; purifying thus
The elements of feeling and of thought,
And sanctifying by such discipline
Both pain and fear,—until we recognise
A grandeur in the beatings of the heart.
　　Nor was this fellowship vouchsafed to me
With stinted kindness. In November days,
When vapours rolling down the valleys made
A lonely scene more lonesome ; among woods
At noon ; and 'mid the calm of summer nights,
When, by the margin of the trembling lake,
Beneath the gloomy hills, homeward I went
In solitude, such intercourse was mine :
Mine was it in the fields both day and night,
And by the waters, all the summer long.
And in the frosty season, when the sun
Was set, and, visible for many a mile,
The cottage-windows through the twilight blazed,
I heeded not the summons : happy time
It was indeed for all of us ; for me
It was a time of rapture ! Clear and loud
The village clock tolled six—I wheeled about,
Proud and exulting like an untired horse
That cares not for his home.—All shod with steel
We hissed along the polished ice, in games
Confederate, imitative of the chase
And woodland pleasures,—the resounding horn,
The pack loud-chiming, and the hunted hare.
So through the darkness and the cold we flew,
And not a voice was idle : with the din
Smitten, the precipices rang aloud ;
The leafless trees and every icy crag

Tinkled like iron ; while far-distant hills
Into the tumult sent an alien sound
Of melancholy, not unnoticed while the stars,
Eastward, were sparkling clear, and in the west
The orange sky of evening died away.
   Not seldom from the uproar I retired
Into a silent bay, or sportively
Glanced sideway, leaving the tumultuous throng,
To cut across the reflex of a star ;
Image, that, flying still before me, gleamed
Upon the glassy plain : and oftentimes,
When we had given our bodies to the wind,
And all the shadowy banks on either side
Came sweeping through the darkness, spinning still
The rapid line of motion, then at once
Have I, reclining back upon my heels,
Stopped short ; yet still the solitary cliffs
Wheeled by me—even as if the earth had rolled
With visible motion her diurnal round !
Behind me did they stretch in solemn train,
Feebler and feebler, and I stood and watched
Till all was tranquil as a summer sea.

THE SPARROW'S NEST

BEHOLD, within the leavy shade,
Those bright blue eggs together laid !
On me the chance-discovered sight
Gleamed like a vision of delight.
I started—seeming to espy
The home and sheltered bed,
The Sparrow's dwelling, which, hard by
My Father's house, in wet or dry
My sister Emmeline and I
    Together visited.

She looked at it and seemed to fear it ;
Dreading, tho' wishing, to be near it :
Such heart was in her, being then
A little Prattler among men.
The Blessing of my later years
Was with me when a boy :
She gave me eyes, she gave me ears ;
And humble cares, and delicate fears ;
A heart, the fountain of sweet tears ;
 And love, and thought, and joy.

TO A BUTTERFLY

I'VE watched you now a full half-hour,
Self-poised upon that yellow flower ;
And, little Butterfly ! indeed
I know not if you sleep or feed.
How motionless !—not frozen seas
More motionless ! and then
What joy awaits you, when the breeze
Hath found you out among the trees,
And calls you forth again !

This plot of orchard-ground is ours ;
My trees they are, my Sister's flowers ;
Here rest your wings when they are weary ;
Here lodge as in a sanctuary !
Come often to us, fear no wrong ;
Sit near us on the bough !
We'll talk of sunshine and of song,
And summer days, when we were young :
Sweet childish days, that were as long
As twenty days are now.

POEMS ON LUCY

STRANGE fits of passion have I known :
And I will dare to tell,
But in the Lover's ear alone,
What once to me befell.

When she I loved looked every day
Fresh as a rose in June,
I to her cottage bent my way,
Beneath an evening-moon.

Upon the moon I fixed my eye,
All over the wide lea ;
With quickening pace my horse drew nigh
Those paths so dear to me.

And now we reached the orchard-plot ;
And, as we climbed the hill,
The sinking moon to Lucy's cot
Came near, and nearer still.

In one of those sweet dreams I slept,
Kind Nature's gentlest boon !
And all the while my eyes I kept
On the descending moon.

My horse moved on ; hoof after hoof
He raised, and never stopped :
When down behind the cottage roof,
At once, the bright moon dropped.

What fond and wayward thoughts will slide
Into a Lover's head !
" O mercy ! " to myself I cried,
" If Lucy should be dead ! "

SHE dwelt among the untrodden ways
    Beside the springs of Dove,
A Maid whom there were none to praise
    And very few to love :

A violet by a mossy stone
    Half hidden from the eye !
—Fair as a star, when only one
    Is shining in the sky.

She lived unknown, and few could know
    When Lucy ceased to be ;
But she is in her grave, and, oh,
    The difference to me !

———

I TRAVELLED among unknown men,
    In lands beyond the sea ;
Nor, England ! did I know till then
    What love I bore to thee.

'Tis past, that melancholy dream !
    Nor will I quit thy shore
A second time ; for still I seem
    To love thee more and more.

Among thy mountains did I feel
    The joy of my desire ;
And she I cherished turned her wheel
    Beside an English fire.

Thy mornings showed, thy nights concealed
    The bowers where Lucy played ;
And thine too is the last green field
    That Lucy's eyes surveyed.

———

THREE years she grew in sun and shower,
Then Nature said, " A lovelier flower
On earth was never sown ;
This Child I to myself will take ;
She shall be mine, and I will make
A Lady of my own.

" Myself will to my darling be
Both law and impulse : and with me
The Girl, in rock and plain,
In earth and heaven, in glade and bower,
Shall feel an overseeing power
To kindle or restrain.

" She shall be sportive as the fawn
That wild with glee across the lawn,
Or up the mountain springs ;
And hers shall be the breathing balm,
And hers the silence and the calm
Of mute insensate things.

" The floating clouds their state shall lend
To her ; for her the willow bend ;
Nor shall she fail to see
Even in the motions of the Storm
Grace that shall mould the Maiden's form
By silent sympathy.

" The stars of midnight shall be dear
To her ; and she shall lean her ear
In many a secret place
Where rivulets dance their wayward round,
And beauty born of murmuring sound
Shall pass into her face.

" And vital feelings of delight
Shall rear her form to stately height,
Her virgin bosom swell ;

Such thoughts to Lucy I will give
While she and I together live
Here in this happy dell."

Thus Nature spake—The work was done—
How soon my Lucy's race was run!
She died, and left to me
This heath, this calm, and quiet scene;
The memory of what has been,
And never more will be.

———

A SLUMBER did my spirit seal;
    I had no human fears:
She seemed a thing that could not feel
    The touch of earthly years.

No motion has she now, no force;
    She neither hears nor sees;
Rolled round in earth's diurnal course,
    With rocks, and stones, and trees.

THE CHILDLESS FATHER

" UP, Timothy, up with your staff and away!
Not a soul in the village this morning will stay;
The hare has just started from Hamilton's grounds,
And Skiddaw is glad with the cry of the hounds."

—Of coats and of jackets grey, scarlet, and green,
On the slopes of the pastures all colours were seen;
With their comely blue aprons, and caps white as snow,
The girls on the hills made a holiday show.

Fresh sprigs of green boxwood,* not six months before,
Filled the funeral basin at Timothy's door ;
A coffin through Timothy's threshold had past ;
One Child did it bear, and that Child was his last.

Now fast up the dell came the noise and the fray,
The horse and the horn, and the hark ! hark away !
Old Timothy took up his staff, and he shut
With a leisurely motion the door of his hut.

Perhaps to himself at that moment he said ;
" The key I must take, for my Ellen is dead."
But of this in my ears not a word did he speak ;
And he went to the chase with a tear on his cheek.

TO THE DAISY

" Her divine skill taught me this,
That from every thing I saw
I could some instruction draw,
And raise pleasure to the height
Through the meanest object's sight.
By the murmur of a spring,
Or the least bough's rustelling ;
By a Daisy whose leaves spread
Shut when Titan goes to bed ;
Or a shady bush or tree ;
She could more infuse in me
Than all Nature's beauties can
In some other wiser man."—G. WITHER.

* When I was a child at Cockermouth, no funeral took place without
a basin filled with sprigs of boxwood being placed upon a table covered
with a white cloth in front of the house. The huntings on foot, in
which the old man is supposed to join as here described, were of common, almost habitual, occurrence in our vales when I was a boy ; and
the people took much delight in them. They are now less frequent.

In youth from rock to rock I went,
From hill to hill in discontent
Of pleasure high and turbulent,
        Most pleased when most uneasy ;
But now my own delights I make,—
My thirst at every rill can slake,
And gladly Nature's love partake,
        Of Thee, sweet Daisy !

Thee Winter in the garland wears
That thinly decks his few grey hairs ;
Spring parts the clouds with softest airs,
        That she may sun thee ;
Whole Summer-fields are thine by right ;
And Autumn, melancholy Wight !
Doth in thy crimson head delight
        When rains are on thee.

In shoals and bands, a morrice train,
Thou greet'st the traveller in the lane ;
Pleased at his greeting thee again ;
        Yet nothing daunted,
Nor grieved if thou be set at nought :
And oft alone in nooks remote
We meet thee, like a pleasant thought,
        When such are wanted.

Be violets in their secret mews
The flowers the wanton Zephyrs choose ;
Proud be the rose, with rains and dews
        Her head impearling,
Thou liv'st with less ambitious aim,
Yet hast not gone without thy fame ;
Thou art indeed by many a claim
        The Poet's darling.

If to a rock from rains he fly,
Or, some bright day of April sky,

Imprisoned by hot sunshine lie
    Near the green holly,
And wearily at length should fare ;
He needs but look about, and there
Thou art !—a friend at hand, to scare
    His melancholy.

A hundred times, by rock or bower,
Ere thus I have lain couched an hour,
Have I derived from thy sweet power
    Some apprehension ;
Some steady love ; some brief delight ;
Some memory that had taken flight ;
Some chime of fancy wrong or right ;
    Or stray invention.

If stately passions in me burn,
And one chance look to Thee should turn,
I drink out of an humbler urn
    A lowlier pleasure ;
The homely sympathy that heeds
The common life, our nature breeds ;
A wisdom fitted to the needs
    Of hearts at leisure.

Fresh-smitten by the morning ray,
When thou art up, alert and gay,
Then, cheerful Flower ! my spirits play
    With kindred gladness :
And when, at dusk, by dews opprest
Thou sink'st, the image of thy rest
Hath often eased my pensive breast
    Of careful sadness.

And all day long I number yet,
All seasons through, another debt,
Which I, wherever thou art met,
    To thee am owing ;

An instinct call it, a blind sense ;
A happy, genial influence,
Coming one knows not how, nor whence,
     Nor whither going.

Child of the Year ! that round dost run
Thy pleasant course,—when day's begun
As ready to salute the sun
     As lark or leveret,
Thy long-lost praise thou shalt regain ;
Nor be less dear to future men
Than in old time ;—thou not in vain
     Art Nature's favourite.

THE GREEN LINNET

BENEATH these fruit-tree boughs that shed
Their snow-white blossoms on my head,
With brightest sunshine round me spread
     Of spring's unclouded weather,
In this sequestered nook how sweet
To sit upon my orchard-seat !
And birds and flowers once more to greet,
     My last year's friends together.

One have I marked, the happiest guest
In all this covert of the blest :
Hail to Thee, far above the rest
     In joy of voice and pinion !
Thou, Linnet ! in thy green array,
Presiding Spirit here to-day,
Dost lead the revels of the May ;
     And this is thy dominion.

While birds, and butterflies, and flowers,
Make all one band of paramours,
Thou, ranging up and down the bowers,
     Art sole in thy employment :

A Life, a Presence like the Air,
Scattering thy gladness without care,
Too blest with any one to pair ;
    Thyself thy own enjoyment.

Amid yon tuft of hazel trees
That twinkle to the gusty breeze,
Behold him perched in ecstasies,
    Yet seeming still to hover ;
There ! where the flutter of his wings
Upon his back and body flings
Shadows and sunny glimmerings,
    That cover him all over.

My dazzled sight he oft deceives,
A Brother of the dancing leaves ;
Then flits, and from the cottage-eaves
    Pours forth his song in gushes ;
As if by that exulting strain
He mocked and treated with disdain
The voiceless Form he chose to feign,
    While fluttering in the bushes.

TO THE SMALL CELANDINE *

PANSIES, lilies, kingcups, daisies,
Let them live upon their praises ;
Long as there's a sun that sets,
Primroses will have their glory ;
Long as there are violets,
They will have a place in story :
There's a flower that shall be mine,
'Tis the little Celandine.

* Common Pilewort.

Eyes of some men travel far
For the finding of a star ;
Up and down the heavens they go,
Men that keep a mighty rout !
I'm as great as they, I trow,
Since the day I found thee out,
Little Flower !—I'll make a stir,
Like a sage astronomer.

Modest, yet withal an Elf
Bold, and lavish of thyself ;
Since we needs must first have met
I have seen thee, high and low,
Thirty years or more, and yet
'Twas a face I did not know ;
Thou hast now, go where I may,
Fifty greetings in a day.

Ere a leaf is on a bush,
In the time before the thrush
Has a thought about her nest,
Thou wilt come with half a call,
Spreading out thy glossy breast
Like a careless Prodigal ;
Telling tales about the sun,
When we've little warmth, or none.

Poets, vain men in their mood !
Travel with the multitude :
Never heed them ; I aver
That they all are wanton wooers ;
But the thrifty cottager,
Who stirs little out of doors,
Joys to spy thee near her home ;
Spring is coming, Thou art come !

Comfort have thou of thy merit,
Kindly, unassuming Spirit !

Careless of thy neighbourhood,
Thou dost show thy pleasant face
On the moor, and in the wood,
In the lane ;—there's not a place,
Howsoever mean it be,
But 'tis good enough for thee.

Ill befall the yellow flowers,
Children of the flaring hours !
Buttercups, that will be seen,
Whether we will see or no ;
Others, too, of lofty mien ;
They have done as worldlings do,
Taken praise that should be thine,
Little, humble Celandine !

Prophet of delight and mirth,
Ill-requited upon earth ;
Herald of a mighty band,
Of a joyous train ensuing,
Serving at my heart's command,
Tasks that are no tasks renewing,
I will sing, as doth behove,
Hymns in praise of what I love !

TO THE SAME FLOWER

PLEASURES newly found are sweet
When they lie about our feet :
February last, my heart
First at sight of thee was glad ;
All unheard of as thou art,
Thou must needs, I think, have had,
Celandine ! and long ago,
Praise of which I nothing know.

I have not a doubt but he,
Whosoe'er the man might be,
Who the first with pointed rays
(Workman worthy to be sainted)
Set the sign-board in a blaze,
When the rising sun he painted,
Took the fancy from a glance
At thy glittering countenance.

Soon as gentle breezes bring
News of winter's vanishing,
And the children build their bowers,
Sticking 'kerchief-plots of mould
All about with full-blown flowers,
Thick as sheep in shepherd's fold !
With the proudest thou art there,
Mantling in the tiny square.

Often have I sighed to measure
By myself a lonely pleasure,
Sighed to think, I read a book
Only read, perhaps, by me ;
Yet I long could overlook
Thy bright coronet and Thee,
And thy arch and wily ways,
And thy store of other praise.

Blithe of heart, from week to week
Thou dost play at hide-and-seek ;
While the patient primrose sits
Like a beggar in the cold,
Thou, a flower of wiser wits,
Slipp'st into thy sheltering hold ;
Liveliest of the vernal train
When ye all are out again.

Drawn by what peculiar spell,
By what charm of sight or smell,

Does the dim-eyed curious Bee,
Labouring for her waxen cells,
Fondly settle upon Thee
Prized above all buds and bells
Opening daily at thy side,
By the season multiplied ?

Thou art not beyond the moon,
But a thing " beneath our shoon : "
Let the bold Discoverer thrid
In his bark the polar sea ;
Rear who will a pyramid ;
Praise it is enough for me,
If there be but three or four
Who will love my little Flower.

THE REDBREAST CHASING THE BUTTERFLY

ART thou the bird whom Man loves best,
The pious bird with the scarlet breast,
    Our little English Robin ;
The bird that comes about our doors
When Autumn-winds are sobbing ?
Art thou the Peter of Norway Boors ?
    Their Thomas in Finland,
    And Russia far inland ?
The bird, that by some name or other
All men who know thee call their brother,
The darling of children and men ?
Could Father Adam * open his eyes
And see this sight beneath the skies,
He'd wish to close them again.
—If the Butterfly knew but his friend,
Hither his flight he would bend ;

---

* See *Paradise Lost*, Book XI., where Adam points out to Eve the ominous sign of the Eagle chasing " two birds of gayest plume," and the gentle Hart and Hind pursued by their enemy.

And find his way to me,
Under the branches of the tree :
In and out, he darts about ;
Can this be the bird, to man so good,
That, after their bewildering,
Covered with leaves the little children,
        So painfully in the wood ?
What ailed thee, Robin, that thou could'st pursue
        A beautiful creature,
That is gentle by nature ?
Beneath the summer sky
From flower to flower let him fly ;
'Tis all that he wishes to do.
The cheerer Thou of our in-door sadness,
He is the friend of our summer gladness :
What hinders, then, that ye should be
Playmates in the sunny weather,
And fly about in the air together !
His beautiful wings in crimson are drest,
A crimson as bright as thine own :
Would'st thou be happy in thy nest,
O pious bird ! whom man loves best,
Love him, or leave him alone !

THE KITTEN AND FALLING LEAVES

THAT way look, my Infant,* lo !
What a pretty baby-show !
See the Kitten on the wall,
Sporting with the leaves that fall,
Withered leaves—one—two—and three—
From the lofty elder-tree !
Through the calm and frosty air
Of this morning bright and fair,

* The infant was Dora (Wordsworth).

Eddying round and round they sink
Softly, slowly : one might think,
From the motions that are made,
Every little leaf conveyed
Sylph or Faery hither tending,—
To this lower world descending,
Each invisible and mute,
In his wavering parachute.
——But the Kitten, how she starts,
Crouches, stretches, paws, and darts !
First at one, and then its fellow
Just as light and just as yellow ;
There are many now—now one—
Now they stop and there are none.
What intenseness of desire
In her upward eye of fire !
With a tiger-leap half-way
Now she meets the coming prey,
Lets it go as fast, and then
Has it in her power again :
Now she works with three or four,
Like an Indian conjurer ;
Quick as he in feats of art,
Far beyond in joy of heart.
Were her antics played in the eye
Of a thousand standers-by,
Clapping hands with shout and stare,
What would little Tabby care
For the plaudits of the crowd ?
Over happy to be proud,
Over wealthy in the treasure
Of her own exceeding pleasure !
　'Tis a pretty baby-treat ;
Nor, I deem, for me unmeet ;
Here, for neither Babe nor me,
Other play-mate can I see.
Of the countless living things,
That with stir of feet and wings

(In the sun or under shade,
Upon bough or grassy blade)
And with busy revellings,
Chirp and song, and murmurings,
Made this orchard's narrow space,
And this vale so blithe a place ;
Multitudes are swept away
Never more to breathe the day :
Some are sleeping ; some in bands
Travelled into distant lands ;
Others slunk to moor and wood,
Far from human neighbourhood ;
And, among the Kinds that keep
With us closer fellowship,
With us openly abide,
All have laid their mirth aside.

　　Where is he that giddy Sprite,
Blue-cap, with his colours bright,
Who was blest as bird could be,
Feeding in the apple-tree ;
Made such wanton spoil and rout,
Turning blossoms inside out ;
Hung—head pointing towards the ground—
Fluttered, perched, into a round
Bound himself, and then unbound :
Lithest, gaudiest Harlequin !
Prettiest Tumbler ever seen !
Light of heart and light of limb ;
What is now become of Him ?
Lambs, that through the mountains went
Frisking, bleating merriment,
When the year was in its prime,
They are sobered by this time.
If you look to vale or hill,
If you listen, all is still,
Save a little neighbouring rill,
That from out the rocky ground
Strikes a solitary sound.

Vainly glitter hill and plain,
And the air is calm in vain ;
Vainly Morning spreads the lure
Of a sky serene and pure ;
Creature none can she decoy
Into open sign of joy :
Is it that they have a fear
Of the dreary season near ?
Or that other pleasures be
Sweeter even than gaiety ?
    Yet, whate'er enjoyments dwell
In the impenetrable cell
Of the silent heart which Nature
Furnishes to every creature ;
Whatsoe'er we feel and know
Too sedate for outward show,
Such a light of gladness breaks,
Pretty Kitten ! from thy freaks,—
Spreads with such a living grace
O'er my little Dora's face ;
Yes, the sight so stirs and charms
Thee, Baby, laughing in my arms,
That almost I could repine
That your transports are not mine,
That I do not wholly fare
Even as ye do, thoughtless pair !
And I will have my careless season
Spite of melancholy reason,
Will walk through life in such a way
That, when time brings on decay,
Now and then I may possess
Hours of perfect gladsomeness.
—Pleased by any random toy ;
By a kitten's busy joy,
Or an infant's laughing eye
Sharing in the ecstasy ;
I would fare like that or this,
Find my wisdom in my bliss ;

Keep the sprightly soul awake,
And have faculties to take,
Even from things by sorrow wrought,
Matter for a jocund thought,
Spite of care, and spite of grief,
To gambol with Life's falling Leaf.

TO THE DAISY

WITH little here to do or see
Of things that in the great world be,
Daisy! again I talk to thee,
    For thou art worthy,
Thou unassuming Common-place
Of Nature, with that homely face,
And yet with something of a grace,
    Which Love makes for thee!

Oft on the dappled turf at ease
I sit, and play with similies,
Loose types of things through all degrees,
    Thoughts of thy raising:
And many a fond and idle name
I give to thee, for praise or blame,
As is the humour of the game,
    While I am gazing.

A nun demure of lowly port;
Or sprightly maiden, of Love's court,
In thy simplicity the sport
    Of all temptations;
A queen in crown of rubies drest;
A starveling in a scanty vest;
Are all, as seems to suit thee best,
    Thy appellations.

A little cyclops, with one eye
Staring to threaten and defy,
That thought comes next—and instantly
  The freak is over,
The shape will vanish—and behold
A silver shield with boss of gold,
That spreads itself, some faery bold
  In fight to cover !

I see thee glittering from afar—
And then thou art a pretty star ;
Not quite so fair as many are
  In heaven above thee !
Yet like a star, with glittering crest,
Self-poised in air thou seem'st to rest ;—
May peace come never to his nest,
  Who shall reprove thee !

Bright *Flower !* for by that name at last,
When all my reveries are past,
I call thee, and to that cleave fast,
  Sweet silent creature !
That breath'st with me in sun and air,
Do thou, as thou art wont, repair
My heart with gladness, and a share
  Of thy meek nature !

TO THE SAME FLOWER

BRIGHT Flower ! whose home is everywhere,
Bold in maternal Nature's care,
And all the long year through the heir
  Of joy or sorrow ;
Methinks that there abides in thee
Some concord with humanity,
Given to no other flower I see
  The forest thorough !

Is it that Man is soon deprest ?
A thoughtless Thing ! who, once unblest,
Does little on his memory rest,
          Or on his reason,
And Thou would'st teach him how to find
A shelter under every wind,
A hope for times that are unkind
          And every season ?

Thou wander'st the wide world about,
Unchecked by pride or scrupulous doubt,
With friends to greet thee, or without,
          Yet pleased and willing ;
Meek, yielding to the occasion's call,
And all things suffering from all
Thy function apostolical *
          In peace fulfilling.

TO A SKY-LARK

Up with me ! up with me into the clouds !
          For thy song, Lark, is strong ;
Up with me, up with me into the clouds !
          Singing, singing,
With clouds and sky about thee ringing,
          Lift me, guide me till I find
That spot which seems so to thy mind !

I have walked through wildernesses dreary
And to-day my heart is weary ;
Had I now the wings of a Faery,
Up to thee would I fly.

* I have been censured for the last line but one—" thy function
apostolical "—as being little less than profane. How could it be
thought so ? The word is adopted with reference to its derivation,
implying something sent on a mission ; and assuredly this little flower,
especially when the subject of verse, may be regarded, in its humble
degree, as administering both to moral and to spiritual purposes.—
The Author.

There is madness about thee, and joy divine
In that song of thine ;
Lift me, guide me high and high
To thy banqueting-place in the sky.

   Joyous as morning
Thou art laughing and scorning ;
Thou hast a nest for thy love and thy rest,
And, though little troubled with sloth,
Drunken Lark ! thou would'st be loth
To be such a traveller as I.
Happy, happy Liver,
With a soul as strong as a mountain river
Pouring out praise to the Almighty Giver,
   Joy and jollity be with us both !

Alas ! my journey, rugged and uneven,
Through prickly moors or dusty ways must wind ;
But hearing thee, or others of thy kind,
As full of gladness and as free of heaven,
I, with my fate contented, will plod on,
And hope for higher raptures, when life's day is done.

STRAY PLEASURES *

" ——*Pleasure is spread through the earth*
In stray gifts to be claimed by whoever shall find."

   By their floating mill,
   That lies dead and still,

* Suggested on the Thames by the sight of one of those floating mills
that used to be seen there. This I noticed on the Surrey side between
Somerset House and Blackfriars Bridge. Charles Lamb was with me
at the time ; and I thought it remarkable that I should have to point
out to *him*, an idolatrous Londoner, a sight so interesting as the happy
group dancing on the platform. Mills of this kind used to be, and
perhaps still are, not uncommon on the Continent. I noticed several
upon the river Saone in the year 1799, particularly near the town of
Chalons, where my friend Jones and I halted a day when we crossed
France ; so far on foot : there we embarked, and floated down to
Lyons.—*The Author.*

Behold yon Prisoners three,
The Miller with two Dames, on the breast of the Thames!
The platform is small, but gives room for them all ;
And they're dancing merrily.

　　From the shore come the notes
　　To their mill where it floats,
To their house and their mill tethered fast :
To the small wooden isle where, their work to beguile,
They from morning to even take whatever is given :—
And many a blithe day they have past.

　　In sight of the spires,
　　All alive with the fires
Of the sun going down to his rest,
In the broad open eye of the solitary sky,
They dance,—there are three, as jocund as free,
While they dance on the calm river's breast.

　　Man and Maidens wheel,
　　They themselves make the reel,
And their music's a prey which they seize ;
It plays not for them,—what matter ? 'tis theirs ;
And if they had care, it has scattered their cares,
While they dance, crying, " Long as ye please ! "

　　They dance not for me,
　　Yet mine is their glee !
Thus pleasure is spread through the earth
In stray gifts to be claimed by whoever shall find ;
Thus a rich loving-kindness, redundantly kind,
Moves all nature to gladness and mirth.

　　The showers of the spring
　　Rouse the birds, and they sing ;
If the wind do but stir for his proper delight,
Each leaf, that and this, his neighbour will kiss ;
Each wave, one and t' other, speeds after his brother ;
They are happy, for that is their right !

"THERE WAS A BOY"

THERE was a Boy; ye knew him well, ye cliffs
And islands of Winander!—many a time,
At evening, when the earliest stars began
To move along the edges of the hills,
Rising or setting, would he stand alone,
Beneath the trees, or by the glimmering lake;
And there, with fingers interwoven, both hands
Pressed closely palm to palm and to his mouth
Uplifted, he, as through an instrument,
Blew mimic hootings to the silent owls,
That they might answer him.—And they would shout
Across the watery vale, and shout again,
Responsive to his call,—with quivering peals,
And long halloos, and screams, and echoes loud
Redoubled and redoubled; concourse wild
Of jocund din! And, when there came a pause
Of silence such as baffled his best skill:
Then, sometimes, in that silence, while he hung
Listening, a gentle shock of mild surprise
Has carried far into his heart the voice
Of mountain-torrents; or the visible scene
Would enter unawares into his mind
With all its solemn imagery, its rocks,
Its woods, and that uncertain heaven received
Into the bosom of the steady lake.
This boy was taken from his mates, and died
In childhood, ere he was full twelve years old.
Pre-eminent in beauty is the vale
Where he was born and bred: the church-yard hangs
Upon a slope above the village-school;
And, through that church-yard when my way has led
On summer-evenings, I believe, that there
A long half-hour together I have stood
Mute—looking at the grave in which he lies!

TO THE CUCKOO

O BLITHE New-comer ! I have heard,
I hear thee and rejoice,
O Cuckoo ! shall I call thee Bird,
Or but a wandering Voice ?

While I am lying on the grass
Thy twofold shout I hear,
From hill to hill it seems to pass,
At once far off, and near.

Though babbling only to the Vale,
Of sunshine and of flowers,
Thou bringest unto me a tale
Of visionary hours.

Thrice welcome, darling of the Spring !
Even yet thou art to me
No bird, but an invisible thing,
A voice, a mystery ;

The same whom in my school-boy days
I listened to ; that Cry
Which made me look a thousand ways
In bush, and tree, and sky.

To seek thee did I often rove
Through woods and on the green ;
And thou wert still a hope, a love ;
Still longed for, never seen.

And I can listen to thee yet ;
Can lie upon the plain
And listen, till I do beget
That golden time again.

O blessèd Bird ! the earth we pace
Again appears to be
An unsubstantial, faery place ;
That is fit home for Thee !

YEW-TREES

THERE is a Yew-tree, pride of Lorton Vale,
Which to this day stands single, in the midst
Of its own darkness, as it stood of yore ;
Not loth to furnish weapons for the bands
Of Umfraville or Percy ere they marched
To Scotland's heaths ; or those that crossed the sea
And drew their sounding bows at Azincour,
Perhaps at earlier Crecy, or Poictiers.
Of vast circumference and gloom profound
This solitary Tree ! a living thing
Produced too slowly ever to decay ;
Of form and aspect too magnificent
To be destroyed.   But worthier still of note
Are those fraternal Four of Borrowdale,
Joined in one solemn and capacious grove ;
Huge trunks ! and each particular trunk a growth
Of intertwisted fibres serpentine
Up-coiling, and inveterately convolved ;
Nor uninformed with Phantasy, and looks
That threaten the profane ;—a pillared shade,
Upon whose grassless floor of red-brown hue,
By sheddings from the pining umbrage tinged
Perennially—beneath whose sable roof
Of boughs, as if for festal purpose, decked
With unrejoicing berries—ghostly Shapes
May meet at noontide ; Fear and trembling Hope,
Silence and Foresight ; Death the Skeleton
And Time the Shadow ;—there to celebrate,
As in a natural temple scattered o'er

With altars undisturbed of mossy stone,
United worship ; or in mute repose
To lie, and listen to the mountain flood
Murmuring from Glaramara's inmost caves.

NUTTING

————————————It seems a day
(I speak of one from many singled out)
One of those heavenly days that cannot die ;
When, in the eagerness of boyish hope,
I left our cottage-threshold, sallying forth
With a huge wallet o'er my shoulders slung,
A nutting-crook in hand ; and turned my steps
Tow'rd some far-distant wood, a Figure quaint,
Tricked out in proud disguise of cast-off weeds
Which for that service had been husbanded,
By exhortation of my frugal Dame—
Motley accoutrement, of power to smile
At thorns, and brakes, and brambles,—and, in truth,
More raggèd than need was !   O'er pathless rocks,
Through beds of matted fern, and tangled thickets,
Forcing my way, I came to one dear nook
Unvisited, where not a broken bough
Drooped with its withered leaves, ungracious sign
Of devastation ; but the hazels rose
Tall and erect, with tempting clusters hung,
A virgin scene !—A little while I stood,
Breathing with such suppression of the heart
As joy delights in ; and, with wise restraint
Voluptuous, fearless of a rival, eyed
The banquet ;—or beneath the trees I sate
Among the flowers, and with the flowers I played ;
A temper known to those, who, after long
And weary expectation, have been blest
With sudden happiness beyond all hope.

Perhaps it was a bower beneath whose leaves
The violets of five seasons re-appear
And fade, unseen by any human eye ;
Where fairy water-breaks do murmur on
For ever ; and I saw the sparkling foam,
And—with my cheek on one of those green stones
That, fleeced with moss, under the shady trees,
Lay round me, scattered like a flock of sheep—
I heard the murmur and the murmuring sound,
In that sweet mood when pleasure loves to pay
Tribute to ease ; and, of its joy secure,
The heart luxuriates with indifferent things,
Wasting its kindliness on stocks and stones,
And on the vacant air.   Then up I rose,
And dragged to earth both branch and bough, with
    crash
And merciless ravage : and the shady nook
Of hazels, and the green and mossy bower,
Deformed and sullied, patiently gave up
Their quiet being : and, unless I now
Confound my present feelings with the past ;
Ere from the mutilated bower I turned
Exulting, rich beyond the wealth of kings,
I felt a sense of pain when I beheld
The silent trees, and saw the intruding sky—
Then, dearest Maiden, move along these shades
In gentleness of heart ; with gentle hand
Touch—for there is a spirit in the woods.

" SHE WAS A PHANTOM OF DELIGHT "

SHE was a Phantom of delight
When first she gleamed upon my sight ;
A lovely Apparition, sent
To be a moment's ornament ;

Her eyes as stars of Twilight fair ;
Like Twilight's, too, her dusky hair ;
But all things else about her drawn
From May-time and the cheerful Dawn ;
A dancing Shape, an Image gay,
To haunt, to startle, and way-lay.

I saw her upon nearer view,
A Spirit, yet a Woman too !
Her household motions light and free,
And steps of virgin-liberty ;
A countenance in which did meet
Sweet records, promises as sweet ;
A Creature not too bright or good
For human nature's daily food ;
For transient sorrows, simple wiles,
Praise, blame, love, kisses, tears, and smiles.

And now I see with eye serene
The very pulse of the machine ;
A Being breathing thoughtful breath,
A Traveller between life and death ;
The reason firm, the temperate will,
Endurance, foresight, strength, and skill ;
A perfect Woman, nobly planned,
To warn, to comfort, and command ;
And yet a Spirit still, and bright
With something of angelic light.

"O NIGHTINGALE ! THOU SURELY ART"

O Nightingale ! thou surely art
A creature of a " fiery heart " :—
These notes of thine—they pierce and pierce ;
Tumultuous harmony and fierce !
Thou sing'st as if the God of wine
Had helped thee to a Valentine ;

A song in mockery and despite
Of shades, and dews, and silent night ;
And steady bliss, and all the loves
Now sleeping in these peaceful groves.
I heard a Stock-dove sing or say
His homely tale, this very day ;
His voice was buried among trees,
Yet to be come at by the breeze :
He did not cease ; but cooed—and cooed ;
And somewhat pensively he wooed :
He sang of love, with quiet blending,
Slow to begin, and never ending ;
Of serious faith, and inward glee ;
That was the song—the song for me !

"I WANDERED LONELY AS A CLOUD"

I WANDERED lonely as a cloud
That floats on high o'er vales and hills,
When all at once I saw a crowd,
A host, of golden daffodils ;
Beside the lake, beneath the trees,
Fluttering and dancing in the breeze.

Continuous as the stars that shine
And twinkle on the milky way,
They stretched in never-ending line
Along the margin of a bay :
Ten thousand saw I at a glance,
Tossing their heads in sprightly dance.

The waves beside them danced ; but they
Out-did the sparkling waves in glee :
A poet could not but be gay,
In such a jocund company :
I gazed—and gazed—but little thought
What wealth the show to me had brought :

For oft, when on my couch I lie
In vacant or in pensive mood,
They flash upon that inward eye
Which is the bliss of solitude ;
And then my heart with pleasure fills,
And dances with the daffodils.

WRITTEN IN MARCH

WHILE RESTING ON THE BRIDGE AT THE FOOT OF BROTHER'S WATER

THE Cock is crowing,
The stream is flowing,
The small birds twitter,
The lake doth glitter,
The green field sleeps in the sun ;
The oldest and youngest
Are at work with the strongest ;
The cattle are grazing,
Their heads never raising ;
There are forty feeding like one !

Like an army defeated
The snow hath retreated,
And now doth fare ill
On the top of the bare hill ;
The ploughboy is whooping—anon—anon :
There's joy in the mountains ;
There's life in the fountains ;
Small clouds are sailing,
Blue sky prevailing ;
The rain is over and gone !

"YES, IT WAS THE MOUNTAIN ECHO"

YES, it was the mountain Echo,
Solitary, clear, profound,
Answering to the shouting Cuckoo
Giving to her sound for sound!

Unsolicited reply
To a babbling wanderer sent;
Like her ordinary cry,
Like—but oh, how different!

Hears not also mortal Life?
Hear not we, unthinking Creatures!
Slaves of folly, love, or strife—
Voices of two different natures?

Have not *we* too?—yes, we have
Answers, and we know not whence;
Echoes from beyond the grave,
Recognised intelligence!

Such rebounds our inward ear
Catches sometimes from afar—
Listen, ponder, hold them dear;
For of God,—of God they are.

TO A SKY-LARK

ETHEREAL minstrel! pilgrim of the sky!
Dost thou despise the earth where cares abound?
Or, while the wings aspire, are heart and eye
Both with thy nest upon the dewy ground?
Thy nest which thou canst drop into at will,
Those quivering wings composed, that music still!

Leave to the nightingale her shady wood ;
A privacy of glorious light is thine ;
Whence thou dost pour upon the world a flood
Of harmony, with instinct more divine ;
Type of the wise who soar, but never roam ;
True to the kindred points of Heaven and Home !

FRENCH REVOLUTION

AS IT APPEARED TO ENTHUSIASTS AT ITS COMMENCEMENT.
REPRINTED FROM " THE FRIEND "

OH ! pleasant exercise of hope and joy !
For mighty were the auxiliars which then stood
Upon our side, we who were strong in love !
Bliss was it in that dawn to be alive,
But to be young was very heaven !—Oh ! times,
In which the meagre, stale, forbidding ways
Of custom, law, and statute, took at once
The attraction of a country in romance !
When Reason seemed the most to assert her rights
When most intent on making of herself
A prime Enchantress—to assist the work,
Which then was going forward in her name !
Not favoured spots alone, but the whole earth,
The beauty wore of promise, that which sets
(As at some moment might not be unfelt
Among the bowers of paradise itself)
The budding rose above the rose full blown.
What temper at the prospect did not wake
To happiness unthought of ?   The inert
Were roused, and lively natures rapt away !
They who had fed their childhood upon dreams,
The playfellows of fancy, who had made
All powers of swiftness, subtilty, and strength
Their ministers,—who in lordly wise had stirred

Among the grandest objects of the sense,
And dealt with whatsoever they found there
As if they had within some lurking right
To wield it ;—they, too, who, of gentle mood,
Had watched all gentle motions, and to these
Had fitted their own thoughts, schemers more mild,
And in the region of their peaceful selves ;—
Now was it that both found, the meek and lofty
Did both find, helpers to their heart's desire,
And stuff at hand, plastic as they could wish ;
Were called upon to exercise their skill,
Not in Utopia, subterranean fields,
Or some secreted island, Heaven knows where !
But in the very world, which is the world
Of all of us,—the place where in the end
We find our happiness, or not at all !

LINES

COMPOSED A FEW MILES ABOVE TINTERN ABBEY, ON
    REVISITING THE BANKS OF THE WYE DURING A
    TOUR.

FIVE years have past ; five summers, with the length
Of five long winters ! and again I hear
These waters, rolling from their mountain-springs
With a soft inland murmur.*—Once again
Do I behold these steep and lofty cliffs,
That on a wild secluded scene impress
Thoughts of more deep seclusion ; and connect
The landscape with the quiet of the sky.
The day is come when I again repose
Here, under this dark sycamore, and view
These plots of cottage-ground, these orchard-tufts,
Which at this season, with their unripe fruits,

* The river is not affected by the tides a few miles above Tintern.

Are clad in one green hue, and lose themselves
'Mid groves and copses.   Once again I see
These hedge-rows, hardly hedge-rows, little lines
Of sportive wood run wild : these pastoral farms,
Green to the very door ; and wreaths of smoke
Sent up, in silence, from among the trees !
With some uncertain notice, as might seem
Of vagrant dwellers in the houseless woods,
Or of some Hermit's cave, where by his fire
The Hermit sits alone.

            These beauteous forms,
Through a long absence, have not been to me
As is a landscape to a blind man's eye :
But oft, in lonely rooms, and 'mid the din
Of towns and cities, I have owed to them
In hours of weariness, sensations sweet,
Felt in the blood, and felt along the heart ;
And passing even into my purer mind,
With tranquil restoration :—feelings too
Of unremembered pleasure : such, perhaps,
As have no slight or trivial influence
On that best portion of a good man's life,
His little, nameless, unremembered acts
Of kindness and of love.   Nor less, I trust,
To them I may have owed another gift,
Of aspect more sublime ; that blessed mood,
In which the burthen of the mystery,
In which the heavy and the weary weight
Of all this unintelligible world,
Is lightened :—that serene and blessed mood,
In which the affections gently lead us on,—
Until, the breath of this corporeal frame
And even the motion of our human blood
Almost suspended, we are laid asleep
In body, and become a living soul :
While with an eye made quiet by the power
Of harmony, and the deep power of joy,
We see into the life of things.

If this
Be but a vain belief, yet, oh ! how oft—
In darkness and amid the many shapes
Of joyless daylight ; when the fretful stir
Unprofitable, and the fever of the world,
Have hung upon the beatings of my heart—
How oft, in spirit, have I turned to thee,
O sylvan Wye ! thou wanderer thro' the woods,
How often has my spirit turned to thee !

   And now, with gleams of half-extinguished thought,
With many recognitions dim and faint,
And somewhat of a sad perplexity,
The picture of the mind revives again :
While here I stand, not only with the sense
Of present pleasure, but with pleasing thoughts
That in this moment there is life and food
For future years.   And so I dare to hope,
Though changed, no doubt, from what I was when first
I came among these hills ; when like a roe
I bounded o'er the mountains, by the sides
Of the deep rivers, and the lonely streams,
Wherever nature led : more like a man
Flying from something that he dreads, than one
Who sought the thing he loved.   For nature then
(The coarser pleasures of my boyish days,
And their glad animal movements all gone by)
To me was all in all.—I cannot paint
What then I was.   The sounding cataract
Haunted me like a passion : the tall rock,
The mountain, and the deep and gloomy wood,
Their colours and their forms, were then to me
An appetite ; a feeling and a love,
That had no need of a remoter charm,
By thought supplied, nor any interest
Unborrowed from the eye.—That time is past,
And all its aching joys are now no more,
And all its dizzy raptures.   Not for this
Faint I, nor mourn nor murmur ; other gifts

Have followed ; for such loss, I would believe,
Abundant recompense. For I have learned
To look on nature, not as in the hour
Of thoughtless youth ; but hearing oftentimes
The still, sad music of humanity,
Nor harsh nor grating, though of ample power
To chasten and subdue. And I have felt
A presence that disturbs me with the joy
Of elevated thoughts ; a sense sublime
Of something far more deeply interfused,
Whose dwelling is the light of setting suns,
And the round ocean and the living air,
And the blue sky, and in the mind of man ;
A motion and a spirit, that impels
All thinking things, all objects of all thought,
And rolls through all things. Therefore am I still
A lover of the meadows and the woods,
And mountains ; and of all that we behold
From this green earth ; of all the mighty world
Of eye, and ear,—both what they half create,
And what perceive ; well pleased to recognise
In nature and the language of the sense,
The anchor of my purest thoughts, the nurse,
The guide, the guardian of my heart, and soul
Of all my moral being.
                              Nor perchance,
If I were not thus taught, should I the more
Suffer my genial spirits to decay :
For thou art with me here upon the banks
Of this fair river ; thou my dearest Friend,
My dear, dear Friend ; and in thy voice I catch
The language of my former heart, and read
My former pleasures in the shooting lights
Of thy wild eyes. Oh ! yet a little while
May I behold in thee what I was once,
My dear, dear Sister ! and this prayer I make,
Knowing that Nature never did betray
The heart that loved her ; 'tis her privilege,

Through all the years of this our life, to lead
From joy to joy : for she can so inform
The mind that is within us, so impress
With quietness and beauty, and so feed
With lofty thoughts, that neither evil tongues,
Rash judgments, nor the sneers of selfish men,
Nor greetings where no kindness is, nor all
The dreary intercourse of daily life,
Shall e'er prevail against us, or disturb
Our cheerful faith, that all which we behold
Is full of blessings.   Therefore let the moon
Shine on thee in thy solitary walk ;
And let the misty mountain-winds be free
To blow against thee : and, in after years,
When these wild ecstasies shall be matured
Into a sober pleasure ; when thy mind
Shall be a mansion for all lovely forms,
Thy memory be as a dwelling-place
For all sweet sounds and harmonies ; oh ! then,
If solitude, or fear, or pain, or grief,
Should be thy portion, with what healing thoughts
Of tender joy wilt thou remember me,
And these my exhortations !   Nor, perchance—
If I should be where I no more can hear
Thy voice, nor catch from thy wild eyes these gleams
Of past existence—wilt thou then forget
That on the banks of this delightful stream
We stood together ; and that I, so long
A worshipper of Nature, hither came
Unwearied in that service : rather say
With warmer love—oh ! with far deeper zeal
Of holier love.   Nor wilt thou then forget,
That after many wanderings, many years
Of absence, these steep woods and lofty cliffs,
And this green pastoral landscape, were to me
More dear, both for themselves and for thy sake !

AT THE GRAVE OF BURNS

SEVEN YEARS AFTER HIS DEATH

I SHIVER, Spirit fierce and bold,
At thought of what I now behold :
As vapours breathed from dungeons cold,
    Strike pleasure dead,
So sadness comes from out the mould
    Where Burns is laid.

And have I then thy bones so near,
And thou forbidden to appear ?
As if it were thyself that's here
    I shrink with pain ;
And both my wishes and my fear
    Alike are vain.

Off weight—nor press on weight !—away
Dark thoughts !—they came, but not to stay ;
With chastened feelings would I pay
    The tribute due
To him, and aught that hides his clay
    From mortal view.

Fresh as the flower, whose modest worth
He sang, his genius " glinted " forth,
Rose like a star that touching earth,
    For so it seems,
Doth glorify its humble birth
    With matchless beams.

The piercing eye, the thoughtful brow,
The struggling heart, where be they now ?—
Full soon the Aspirant of the plough,
    The prompt, the brave,
Slept, with the obscurest, in the low
    And silent grave.

I mourned with thousands, but as one
More deeply grieved, for He was gone
Whose light I hailed when first it shone,
    And showed my youth
How Verse may build a princely throne
    On humble truth.

Alas ! where'er the current tends,
Regret pursues and with it blends,—
Huge Criffel's hoary top ascends
    By Skiddaw seen,—
Neighbours we were, and loving friends
    We might have been ;

True friends though diversely inclined ;
But heart with heart and mind with mind,
Where the main fibres are entwined,
    Through Nature's skill,
May even by contraries be joined
    More closely still.

The tear will start, and let it flow ;
Thou " poor Inhabitant below,"
At this dread moment—even so—
    Might we together
Have sate and talked where gowans blow,
    Or on wild heather.

What treasures would have then been placed
Within my reach ; of knowledge graced
By fancy what a rich repast !
    But why go on ?—
Oh ! spare to sweep, thou mournful blast,
    His grave grass-grown.

There, too, a Son, his joy and pride,
(Not three weeks past the Stripling died,)
Lies gathered to his Father's side,

Soul-moving sight !
Yet one to which is not denied
Some sad delight :

For *he* is safe, a quiet bed
Hath early found among the dead,
Harboured where none can be misled,
        Wronged, or distrest ;
And surely here it may be said
        That such are blest.

And oh for Thee, by pitying grace
Checked oft-times in a devious race,
May He who halloweth the place
        Where Man is laid
Receive thy Spirit in the embrace
        For which it prayed !

Sighing I turned away ; but ere
Night fell I heard, or seemed to hear,
Music that sorrow comes not near,
        A ritual hymn,
Chaunted in love that casts out fear
        By Seraphim.

TO A HIGHLAND GIRL *

AT INVERSNEYDE, UPON LOCH LOMOND

SWEET Highland Girl, a very shower
Of beauty is thy earthly dower !
Twice seven consenting years have shed
Their utmost bounty on thy head :

---

* This delightful creature and her demeanour are particularly described in my Sister's Journal. The sort of prophecy with which the
verses conclude has, through God's goodness, been realised ; and now,
approaching the close of my 73rd year, I have a most vivid remembrance
of her and the beautiful objects with which she was surrounded.

And these grey rocks ; that household lawn ;
Those trees, a veil just half withdrawn ;
This fall of water that doth make
A murmur near the silent lake ;
This little bay ; a quiet road
That holds in shelter thy Abode—
In truth together do ye seem
Like something fashioned in a dream ;
Such Forms as from their covert peep
When earthly cares are laid asleep !
But, O fair Creature ! in the light
Of common day, so heavenly bright,
I bless Thee, Vision as thou art,
I bless thee with a human heart ;
God shield thee to thy latest years !
Thee, neither know I, nor thy peers ;
And yet my eyes are filled with tears.

    With earnest feeling I shall pray
For thee when I am far away :
For never saw I mien, or face,
In which more plainly I could trace
Benignity and home-bred sense
Ripening in perfect innocence.
Here scattered, like a random seed,
Remote from men, Thou dost not need
The embarrassed look of shy distress,
And maidenly shamefacedness :
Thou wear'st upon thy forehead clear
The freedom of a Mountaineer :
A face with gladness overspread !
Soft smiles, by human kindness bred !
And seemliness complete, that sways
Thy courtesies, about thee plays ;
With no restraint, but such as springs
From quick and eager visitings
Of thoughts that lie beyond the reach
Of thy few words of English speech :
A bondage sweetly brooked, a strife

That gives thy gestures grace and life !
So have I, not unmoved in mind,
Seen birds of tempest-loving kind—
Thus beating up against the wind.
    What hand but would a garland cull
For thee who art so beautiful ?
O happy pleasure ! here to dwell
Beside thee in some heathy dell ;
Adopt your homely ways, and dress,
A Shepherd, thou a Shepherdess !
But I could frame a wish for thee
More like a grave reality :
Thou art to me but as a wave
Of the wild sea ; and I would have
Some claim upon thee, if I could,
Though but of common neighbourhood.
What joy to hear thee, and to see !
Thy elder Brother I would be,
Thy Father—anything to thee !
    Now thanks to Heaven ! that of its grace
Hath led me to this lonely place.
Joy have I had ; and going hence
I bear away my recompense.
In spots like these it is we prize
Our Memory, feel that she hath eyes :
Then, why should I be loth to stir ?
I feel this place was made for her ;
To give new pleasure like the past,
Continued long as life shall last.
Nor am I loth, though pleased at heart,
Sweet Highland Girl ! from thee to part :
For I, methinks, till I grow old,
As fair before me shall behold,
As I do now, the cabin small,
The lake, the bay, the waterfall ;
And thee, the Spirit of them all !

STEPPING WESTWARD *

" What, you are stepping westward ? "—" *Yea.*"
—'Twould be a *wildish* destiny,
If we, who thus together roam
In a strange Land, and far from home,
Were in this place the guests of Chance :
Yet who would stop, or fear to advance,
Though home or shelter he had none,
With such a sky to lead him on ?

The dewy ground was dark and cold ;
Behind, all gloomy to behold ;
And stepping westward seemed to be
A kind of *heavenly* destiny :
I liked the greeting ; 'twas a sound
Of something without place or bound ;
And seemed to give me spiritual right
To travel through that region bright.

The voice was soft, and she who spake
Was walking by her native lake :
The salutation had to me
The very sound of courtesy :
Its power was felt ; and while my eye
Was fixed upon the glowing Sky,
The echo of the voice enwrought
A human sweetness with the thought
Of travelling through the world that lay
Before me in my endless way.

* While my Fellow-traveller and I were walking by the side of Loch Ketterine, one fine evening after sunset, in our road to a Hut where, in the course of our Tour, we had been hospitably entertained some weeks before, we met, in one of the loneliest parts of that solitary region, two well-dressed Women, one of whom said to us, by way of greeting, " What, you are stepping westward ? "—*The Author.*

THE SOLITARY REAPER

BEHOLD her, single in the field,
Yon solitary Highland Lass !
Reaping and singing by herself ;
Stop here, or gently pass !
Alone she cuts and binds the grain,
And sings a melancholy strain ;
O listen ! for the Vale profound
Is overflowing with the sound.

No Nightingale did ever chaunt
More welcome notes to weary bands
Of travellers in some shady haunt,
Among Arabian sands :
A voice so thrilling ne'er was heard
In spring-time from the Cuckoo-bird,
Breaking the silence of the seas
Among the farthest Hebrides.

Will no one tell me what she sings ?—
Perhaps the plaintive numbers flow
For old, unhappy, far-off things,
And battles long ago :
Or is it some more humble lay,
Familiar matter of to-day ?
Some natural sorrow, loss, or pain,
That has been, and may be again ?

Whate'er the theme, the Maiden sang
As if her song could have no ending ;
I saw her singing at her work,
And o'er the sickle bending ;—
I listened, motionless and still ;
And, as I mounted up the hill,
The music in my heart I bore,
Long after it was heard no more.

YARROW UNVISITED *

FROM Stirling castle we had seen
The mazy Forth unravelled ;
Had trod the banks of Clyde, and Tay,
And with the Tweed had travelled ;
And when we came to Clovenford,
Then said my " *winsome Marrow*,"
" Whate'er betide, we'll turn aside,
And see the Braes of Yarrow."

" Let Yarrow folk, *frae* Selkirk town,
Who have been buying, selling,
Go back to Yarrow, 'tis their own ;
Each maiden to her dwelling !
On Yarrow's banks let herons feed,
Hares couch, and rabbits burrow !
But we will downward with the Tweed,
Nor turn aside to Yarrow.

" There's Galla Water, Leader Haughs,
Both lying right before us ;
And Dryborough, where with chiming Tweed
The lintwhites sing in chorus ;
There's pleasant Tiviot-dale, a land
Made blithe with plough and harrow :
Why throw away a needful day
To go in search of Yarrow ?

" What's Yarrow but a river bare,
That glides the dark hills under ?
There are a thousand such elsewhere
As worthy of your wonder."

* See the various poems the scene of which is laid upon the banks of
the Yarrow ; in particular, the exquisite Ballad of Hamilton beginning
    " Busk ye, busk ye, my bonny, bonny Bride,
        Busk ye, busk ye, my winsome Marrow !—"

—Strange words they seemed of slight and scorn :
My True-love sighed for sorrow ;
And looked me in the face, to think
I thus could speak of Yarrow !

" Oh ! green," said I, " are Yarrow's holms,
And sweet is Yarrow flowing !
Fair hangs the apple frae the rock,
But we will leave it growing.
O'er hilly path, and open Strath,
We'll wander Scotland thorough ;
But, though so near, we will not turn
Into the dale of Yarrow.

" Let beeves and home-bred kine partake
The sweets of Burn-mill meadow ;
The swan on still St. Mary's Lake
Float double, swan and shadow !
We will not see them ; will not go,
To-day, nor yet to-morrow,
Enough if in our hearts we know
There's such a place as Yarrow.

" Be Yarrow stream unseen, unknown !
It must, or we shall rue it :
We have a vision of our own ;
Ah ! why should we undo it ?
The treasured dreams of times long past,
We'll keep them, winsome Marrow !
For when we're there, although 'tis fair,
'Twill be another Yarrow !

" If Care with freezing years should come,
And wandering seem but folly,—
Should we be loth to stir from home,
And yet be melancholy ;

Should life be dull, and spirits low,
'Twill soothe us in our sorrow,
That earth has something yet to show,
The bonny holms of Yarrow ! "

YARROW VISITED *

SEPTEMBER 1814

AND is this—Yarrow ?—*This* the Stream
Of which my fancy cherished,
So faithfully, a waking dream ?
An image that hath perished !
O that some Minstrel's harp were near,
To utter notes of gladness,
And chase this silence from the air,
That fills my heart with sadness !

---

* As mentioned in my verses on the death of the Ettrick Shepherd, my first visit to Yarrow was in his company. We had lodged the night before at Traquhair, where Hogg had joined us, and also Dr. Anderson, the Editor of the British Poets, who was on a visit at the Manse. Dr. A. walked with us till we came in view of the Vale of Yarrow, and, being advanced in life, he then turned back. The old Man was passionately fond of poetry, though with not much of a discriminating judgment, as the Volumes he edited sufficiently show. But I was much pleased to meet with him, and to acknowledge my obligation to his collection, which had been my brother John's companion in more than one voyage to India, and which he gave me before his departure from Grasmere, never to return. Through these Volumes I became first familiar with Chaucer, and so little money had I then to spare for books, that, in all probability, but for this same work, I should have known little of Drayton, Daniel, and other distinguished poets of the Elizabethan age, and their immediate successors, till a much later period of my life. I am glad to record this, not from any importance of its own, but as a tribute of gratitude to this simple-hearted old man, whom I never again had the pleasure of meeting. I seldom read or think of this poem without regretting that my dear Sister was not of the party, as she would have had so much delight in recalling the time when, travelling together in Scotland, we declined going in search of this celebrated stream, not altogether, I will frankly confess, for the reasons assigned in the poem on the occasion.

Yet why ?—a silvery current flows
With uncontrolled meanderings ;
Nor have these eyes by greener hills
Been soothed, in all my wanderings.
And, through her depths, Saint Mary's Lake
Is visibly delighted ;
For not a feature of those hills
Is in the mirror slighted.

A blue sky bends o'er Yarrow vale,
Save where that pearly whiteness
Is round the rising sun diffused,
A tender hazy brightness ;
Mild dawn of promise ! that excludes
All profitless dejection ;
Though not unwilling here to admit
A pensive recollection.

Where was it that the famous Flower
Of Yarrow Vale lay bleeding ?
His bed perchance was yon smooth mound
On which the herd is feeding :
And haply from this crystal pool,
Now peaceful as the morning,
The Water-wraith ascended thrice—
And gave his doleful warning.

Delicious is the Lay that sings
The haunts of happy Lovers,
The path that leads them to the grove,
The leafy grove that covers :
And Pity sanctifies the Verse
That paints, by strength of sorrow,
The unconquerable strength of love
Bear witness, rueful Yarrow !

But thou, that didst appear so fair
To fond imagination,

Dost rival in the light of day
Her delicate creation :
Meek loveliness is round thee spread,
A softness still and holy ;
The grace of forest charms decayed,
And pastoral melancholy.

That region left, the vale unfolds
Rich groves of lofty stature,
With Yarrow winding through the pomp
Of cultivated nature ;
And, rising from those lofty groves,
Behold a Ruin hoary !
The shattered front of Newark's Towers,
Renowned in Border story.

Fair scenes for childhood's opening bloom,
For sportive youth to stray in ;
For manhood to enjoy his strength ;
And age to wear away in !
Yon cottage seems a bower of bliss,
A covert for protection
Of tender thoughts, that nestle there—
The brood of chaste affection.

How sweet, on this autumnal day,
The wild-wood fruits to gather,
And on my True-love's forehead plant
A crest of blooming heather !
And what if I enwreathed my own !
'Twere no offence to reason ;
The sober Hills thus deck their brows
To meet the wintry season.

I see—but not by sight alone,
Loved Yarrow, have I won thee ;
A ray of fancy still survives—
Her sunshine plays upon thee !

Thy ever-youthful waters keep
A course of lively pleasure ;
And gladsome notes my lips can breathe,
Accordant to the measure.

The vapours linger round the Heights,
They melt, and soon must vanish ;
One hour is theirs, nor more is mine—
Sad thought, which I would banish,
But that I know, where'er I go,
Thy genuine image, Yarrow !
Will dwell with me—to heighten joy,
And cheer my mind in sorrow.

YARROW REVISITED

[The following stanzas are a memorial of a day passed with Sir Walter Scott and other Friends visiting the Banks of the Yarrow under his guidance, immediately before his departure from Abbotsford, for Naples.]

THE gallant Youth, who may have gained,
    Or seeks, a " winsome Marrow,"
Was but an Infant in the lap
    When first I looked on Yarrow ;
Once more, by Newark's Castle-gate
    Long left without a warder,
I stood, looked, listened, and with Thee,
    Great Minstrel of the Border !

Grave thoughts ruled wide on that sweet day,
    Their dignity installing
In gentle bosoms, while sere leaves
    Were on the bough, or falling ;
But breezes played, and sunshine gleamed—
    The forest to embolden ;
Reddened the fiery hues, and shot
    Transparence through the golden.

For busy thoughts the Stream flowed on
　In foamy agitation ;
And slept in many a crystal pool
　For quiet contemplation :
No public and no private care
　The freeborn mind enthralling,
We made a day of happy hours,
　Our happy days recalling.

Brisk Youth appeared, the Morn of youth,
　With freaks of graceful folly,—
Life's temperate Noon, her sober Eve,
　Her Night not melancholy ;
Past, present, future, all appeared
　In harmony united,
Like guests that meet, and some from far,
　By cordial love invited.

And if, as Yarrow, through the woods
　And down the meadow ranging,
Did meet us with unaltered face,
　Though we were changed and changing ;
If, *then*, some natural shadows spread
　Our inward prospect over,
The soul's deep valley was not slow
　Its brightness to recover.

Eternal blessings on the Muse,
　And her divine employment !
The blameless Muse, who trains her Sons
　For hope and calm enjoyment ;
Albeit sickness, lingering yet,
　Has o'er their pillow brooded ;
And Care waylays their steps—a Sprite
　Not easily eluded.

For thee, O Scott ! compelled to change
　Green Eildon-hill and Cheviot

For warm Vesuvio's vine-clad slopes ;
  And leave thy Tweed and Tiviot
For mild Sorento's breezy waves ;
  May classic Fancy, linking
With native Fancy her fresh aid,
  Preserve thy heart from sinking !

Oh ! while they minister to thee,
  Each vying with the other,
May Health return to mellow Age
  With Strength, her venturous brother ;
And Tiber, and each brook and rill
  Renowned in song and story,
With unimagined beauty shine,
  Nor lose one ray of glory !

For Thou, upon a hundred streams,
  By tales of love and sorrow,
Of faithful love, undaunted truth,
  Hast shed the power of Yarrow ;
And streams unknown, hills yet unseen,
  Wherever they invite Thee,
At parent Nature's grateful call,
  With gladness must requite Thee.

A gracious welcome shall be thine,
  Such looks of love and honour
As thy own Yarrow gave to me
  When first I gazed upon her ;
Beheld what I had feared to see,
  Unwilling to surrender
Dreams treasured up from early days,
  The holy and the tender.

And what, for this frail world, were all
  That mortals do or suffer,
Did no responsive harp, no pen,
  Memorial tribute offer ?

Yea, what were mighty Nature's self?
  Her features, could they win us,
Unhelped by the poetic voice
  That hourly speaks within us?

Nor deem that localised Romance
  Plays false with our affections;
Unsanctifies our tears—made sport
  For fanciful dejections:
Ah, no! the visions of the past
  Sustain the heart in feeling
Life as she is—our changeful Life,
  With friends and kindred dealing.

Bear witness, Ye, whose thoughts that day
  In Yarrow's groves were centred;
Who through the silent portal arch
  Of mouldering Newark entered;
And clomb the winding stair that once
  Too timidly was mounted
By the " last Minstrel," (not the last!)
  Ere he his Tale recounted.

Flow on for ever, Yarrow Stream!
  Fulfil thy pensive duty,
Well pleased that future Bards should chant
  For simple hearts thy beauty;
To dream-light dear while yet unseen,
  Dear to the common sunshine,
And dearer still, as now I feel,
  To memory's shadowy moonshine!

EXPOSTULATION AND REPLY

" WHY, William, on that old grey stone,
Thus for the length of half a day,
Why, William, sit you thus alone,
And dream your time away?

" Where are your books ?—that light bequeathed
To Beings else forlorn and blind !
Up ! up ! and drink the spirit breathed
From dead men to their kind.

" You look round on your Mother Earth,
As if she for no purpose bore you ;
As if you were her first-born birth,
And none had lived before you ! "

One morning thus, by Esthwaite lake,
When life was sweet, I knew not why,
To me my good friend Matthew spake,
And thus I made reply :

" The eye—it cannot choose but see ;
We cannot bid the ear be still ;
Our bodies feel, where'er they be,
Against or with our will.

" Nor less I deem that there are Powers
Which of themselves our minds impress ;
That we can feed this mind of ours
In a wise passiveness.

" Think you, 'mid all this mighty sum
Of things for ever speaking,
That nothing of itself will come,
But we must still be seeking ?

" —Then ask not wherefore, here, alone,
Conversing as I may,
I sit upon this old grey stone,
And dream my time away."

THE TABLES TURNED

AN EVENING SCENE ON THE SAME SUBJECT

Up ! up ! my Friend, and quit your books ;
Or surely you'll grow double :
Up ! up ! my Friend, and clear your looks ;
Why all this toil and trouble ?

The sun, above the mountain's head,
A freshening lustre mellow
Through all the long green fields has spread,
His first sweet evening yellow.

Books ! 'tis a dull and endless strife :
Come, hear the woodland linnet,
How sweet his music ! on my life,
There's more of wisdom in it.

And hark ! how blithe the throstle sings !
He, too, is no mean preacher :
Come forth into the light of things,
Let Nature be your teacher.

She has a world of ready wealth,
Our minds and hearts to bless—
Spontaneous wisdom breathed by health,
Truth breathed by cheerfulness.

One impulse from a vernal wood
May teach you more of man,
Of moral evil and of good,
Than all the sages can.

Sweet is the lore which Nature brings ;
Our meddling intellect
Mis-shapes the beauteous forms of things :—
We murder to dissect.

Enough of Science and of Art ;
Close up those barren leaves ;
Come forth, and bring with you a heart
That watches and receives.

A POET'S EPITAPH

ART thou a Statist in the van
Of public conflicts trained and bred ?
—First learn to love one living man ;
Then may'st thou think upon the dead.

A Lawyer art thou ?—draw not nigh !
Go, carry to some fitter place
The keenness of that practised eye,
The hardness of that sallow face.

Art thou a Man of purple cheer ?
A rosy Man, right plump to see ?
Approach ; yet, Doctor, not too near,
This grave no cushion is for thee.

Or art thou one of gallant pride,
A Soldier and no man of chaff ?
Welcome !—but lay thy sword aside,
And lean upon a peasant's staff.

Physician art thou ? one, all eyes,
Philosopher ! a fingering slave,
One that would peep and botanise
Upon his mother's grave ?

Wrapt closely in thy sensual fleece,
O turn aside,—and take, I pray,
That he below may rest in peace,
Thy ever-dwindling soul, away !

A Moralist perchance appears ;
Led, Heaven knows how ! to this poor sod :
And he has neither eyes nor ears ;
Himself his world, and his own God ;

One to whose smooth-rubbed soul can cling
Nor form, nor feeling, great or small ;
A reasoning, self-sufficing thing,
An intellectual All-in-all !

Shut close the door ; press down the latch ;
Sleep in thy intellectual crust ;
Nor lose ten tickings of thy watch
Near this unprofitable dust.

But who is He, with modest looks,
And clad in homely russet brown ?
He murmurs near the running brooks
A music sweeter than their own.

He is retired as noontide dew,
Or fountain in a noon-day grove ;
And you must love him, ere to you
He will seem worthy of your love.

The outward shows of sky and earth,
Of hill and valley, he has viewed ;
And impulses of deeper birth
Have come to him in solitude.

In common things that round us lie
Some random truths he can impart,—
The harvest of a quiet eye
That broods and sleeps on his own heart.

But he is weak ; both Man and Boy,
Hath been an idler in the land ;
Contented if he might enjoy
The things which others understand.

—Come hither in thy hour of strength ;
Come, weak as is a breaking wave !
Here stretch thy body at full length ;
Or build thy house upon this grave.

TO MY SISTER

It is the first mild day of March :
Each minute sweeter than before
The redbreast sings from the tall larch
That stands beside our door.

There is a blessing in the air,
Which seems a sense of joy to yield
To the bare trees, and mountains bare,
And grass in the green field.

My sister ! ('tis a wish of mine)
Now that our morning meal is done,
Make haste, your morning task resign ;
Come forth and feel the sun.

Edward will come with you ;—and, pray,
Put on with speed your woodland dress ;
And bring no book : for this one day
We'll give to idleness.

No joyless forms shall regulate
Our living calendar :
We from to-day, my Friend, will date
The opening of the year.

Love, now a universal birth,
From heart to heart is stealing,
From earth to man, from man to earth :
—It is the hour of feeling.

One moment now may give us more
Than years of toiling reason :
Our minds shall drink at every pore
The spirit of the season.

Some silent laws our hearts will make,
Which they shall long obey :
We for the year to come may take
Our temper from to-day.

And from the blessed power that rolls
About, below, above,
We'll frame the measure of our souls :
They shall be tuned to love.

Then come, my Sister ! come, I pray,
With speed put on your woodland dress ;
And bring no book : for this one day
We'll give to idleness.

TO A YOUNG LADY

WHO HAD BEEN REPROACHED FOR TAKING LONG WALKS IN THE COUNTRY

DEAR Child of Nature, let them rail !
—There is a nest in a green dale,
A harbour and a hold ;
Where thou, a Wife and Friend, shalt see
Thy own heart-stirring days, and be
A light to young and old.

There, healthy as a shepherd boy,
And treading among flowers of joy
Which at no season fade,
Thou, while thy babes around thee cling,
Shalt show us how divine a thing
A Woman may be made.

Thy thoughts and feelings shall not die,
Nor leave thee, when grey hairs are nigh,
A melancholy slave ;
But an old age serene and bright,
And lovely as a Lapland night,
Shall lead thee to thy grave.

LINES WRITTEN IN EARLY SPRING

I HEARD a thousand blended notes,
While in a grove I sate reclined,
In that sweet mood when pleasant thoughts
Bring sad thoughts to the mind.

To her fair works did Nature link
The human soul that through me ran ;
And much it grieved my heart to think
What man has made of man.

Through primrose tufts, in that green bower,
The periwinkle trailed its wreaths ;
And 'tis my faith that every flower
Enjoys the air it breathes.

The birds around me hopped and played,
Their thoughts I cannot measure :—
But the least motion which they made
It seemed a thrill of pleasure.

The budding twigs spread out their fan,
To catch the breezy air ;
And I must think, do all I can,
That there was pleasure there.

If this belief from heaven be sent,
If such be Nature's holy plan,
Have I not reason to lament
What man has made of man ?

THE FOUNTAIN

A CONVERSATION

WE talked with open heart, and tongue
Affectionate and true,
A pair of friends, though I was young,
And Matthew seventy-two.

We lay beneath a spreading oak,
Beside a mossy seat ;
And from the turf a fountain broke,
And gurgled at our feet.

" Now, Matthew ! " said I, " let us match
This water's pleasant tune
With some old border-song, or catch
That suits a summer's noon ;

" Or of the church-clock and the chimes
Sing here beneath the shade,
That half-mad thing of witty rhymes
Which you last April made ! "

In silence Matthew lay, and eyed
The spring beneath the tree ;
And thus the dear old Man replied,
The grey-haired man of glee :

" No check, no stay, this Streamlet fears ;
How merrily it goes !
'Twill murmur on a thousand years,
And flow as now it flows.

" And here, on this delightful day,
I cannot choose but think
How oft, a vigorous man, I lay
Beside this fountain's brink.

" My eyes are dim with childish tears,
My heart is idly stirred,
For the same sound is in my ears
Which in those days I heard.

" Thus fares it still in our decay :
And yet the wiser mind
Mourns less for what age takes away
Than what it leaves behind.

" The blackbird amid leafy trees,
The lark above the hill,
Let loose their carols when they please,
Are quiet when they will.

" With Nature never do *they* wage
A foolish strife ; they see
A happy youth, and their old age
Is beautiful and free :

" But we are pressed by heavy laws ;
And often, glad no more,
We wear a face of joy, because
We have been glad of yore.

" If there be one who need bemoan
His kindred laid in earth,
The household hearts that were his own ;
It is the man of mirth.

" My days, my Friend, are almost gone,
My life has been approved,
And many love me ; but by none
Am I enough beloved."

" Now both himself and me he wrongs,
The man who thus complains ;
I live and sing my idle songs
Upon these happy plains ;

" And, Matthew, for thy children dead
I'll be a son to thee ! "
At this he grasped my hand, and said,
" Alas ! that cannot be."

We rose up from the fountain-side ;
And down the smooth descent
Of the green sheep-track did we glide ;
And through the wood we went ;

And, ere we came to Leonard's rock,
He sang those witty rhymes
About the crazy old church-clock,
And the bewildered chimes.

SEPTEMBER 1819

THE sylvan slopes with corn-clad fields
Are hung, as if with golden shields,
Bright trophies of the sun !
Like a fair sister of the sky,
Unruffled doth the blue lake lie,
The mountains looking on.

And, sooth to say, yon vocal grove,
Albeit uninspired by love,
By love untaught to ring,
May well afford to mortal ear
An impulse more profoundly dear
Than music of the Spring.

For *that* from turbulence and heat
Proceeds, from some uneasy seat
In nature's struggling frame,
Some region of impatient life :
And jealousy, and quivering strife,
Therein a portion claim.

This, this is holy ;—while I hear
These vespers of another year,
This hymn of thanks and praise,
My spirit seems to mount above
The anxieties of human love,
And earth's precarious days.

But list !—though winter storms be nigh,
Unchecked is that soft harmony :
There lives Who can provide
For all his creatures ; and in Him,
Even like the radiant Seraphim,
These choristers confide.

UPON THE SAME OCCASION

DEPARTING summer hath assumed
An aspect tenderly illumed,
The gentlest look of spring ;
That calls from yonder leafy shade
Unfaded, yet prepared to fade,
A timely carolling.

No faint and hesitating trill,
Such tribute as to winter chill
The lonely redbreast pays !
Clear, loud, and lively is the din,
From social warblers gathering in
Their harvest of sweet lays.

Nor doth the example fail to cheer
Me, conscious that my leaf is sere,
And yellow on the bough :—
Fall, rosy garlands, from my head !
Ye myrtle wreaths, your fragrance shed
Around a younger brow !

Yet will I temperately rejoice ;
Wide is the range, and free the choice
Of undiscordant themes ;
Which, haply, kindred souls may prize
Not less than vernal ecstasies,
And passion's feverish dreams.

For deathless powers to verse belong,
And they like Demi-gods are strong
On whom the Muses smile ;
But some their function have disclaimed,
Best pleased with what is aptliest framed
To enervate and defile.

Not such the initiatory strains
Committed to the silent plains
In Britain's earliest dawn :
Trembled the groves, the stars grew pale,
While all-too-daringly the veil
Of nature was withdrawn !

Nor such the spirit-stirring note
When the live chords Alcæus smote,
Inflamed by sense of wrong ;
Woe ! woe to Tyrants ! from the lyre
Broke threateningly, in sparkles dire
Of fierce vindictive song.

And not unhallowed was the page
By wingèd Love inscribed, to assuage
The pangs of vain pursuit ;
Love listening while the Lesbian Maid
With finest touch of passion swayed
Her own Æolian lute.

O ye, who patiently explore
The wreck of Herculanean lore,
What rapture ! could ye seize

Some Theban fragment, or unroll
One precious, tender-hearted, scroll
Of pure Simonides.

That were, indeed, a genuine birth
Of poesy ; a bursting forth
Of genius from the dust :
What Horace gloried to behold,
What Maro loved, shall we enfold ?
Can haughty Time be just !

THE SMALL CELANDINE

THERE is a Flower, the lesser Celandine,
That shrinks, like many more, from cold and rain ;
And, the first moment that the sun may shine,
Bright as the sun himself, 'tis out again !

When hailstones have been falling, swarm on swarm,
Or blasts the green field and the trees distrest,
Oft have I seen it muffled up from harm,
In close self-shelter, like a Thing at rest.

But lately, one rough day, this Flower I passed
And recognised it, though an altered form,
Now standing forth an offering to the blast,
And buffeted at will by rain and storm.

I stopped, and said with inly-muttered voice,
" It doth not love the shower, nor seek the cold :
This neither is its courage nor its choice,
But its necessity in being old.

" The sunshine may not cheer it, nor the dew ;
It cannot help itself in its decay ;
Stiff in its members, withered, changed of hue."
And, in my spleen, I smiled that it was grey.

To be a Prodigal's Favourite—then, worse truth,
A Miser's Pensioner—behold our lot !
O Man, that from thy fair and shining youth
Age might but take the things Youth needed not !

ANIMAL TRANQUILLITY AND DECAY

THE little hedgerow birds,
That peck along the roads, regard him not.
He travels on, and in his face, his step,
His gait, is one expression : every limb,
His look and bending figure, all bespeak
A man who does not move with pain, but moves
With thought.—He is insensibly subdued
To settled quiet : he is one by whom
All effort seems forgotten ; one to whom
Long patience hath such mild composure given,
That patience now doth seem a thing of which
He hath no need.   He is by nature led
To peace so perfect that the young behold
With envy, what the Old Man hardly feels.

LINES

[Composed at Grasmere, during a walk one Evening, after a stormy day, the Author having just read in a Newspaper that the dissolution of Mr. Fox was hourly expected.]

LOUD is the Vale ! the Voice is up
With which she speaks when storms are gone,
A mighty unison of streams !
Of all her Voices, One !

Loud is the Vale ;—this inland Depth
In peace is roaring like the Sea ;
Yon star upon the mountain-top
Is listening quietly.

Sad was I, even to pain deprest,
Importunate and heavy load ! *
The Comforter hath found me here,
Upon this lonely road ;

And many thousands now are sad—
Wait the fulfilment of their fear ;
For he must die who is their stay,
Their glory disappear.

A Power is passing from the earth
To breathless Nature's dark abyss ;
But when the great and good depart
What is it more than this—

That Man, who is from God sent forth,
Doth yet again to God return ?—
Such ebb and flow must ever be,
Then wherefore should we mourn ?

ELEGIAC STANZAS

SUGGESTED BY A PICTURE OF PEELE CASTLE, IN A STORM,
PAINTED BY SIR GEORGE BEAUMONT

I WAS thy neighbour once, thou rugged Pile !
Four summer weeks I dwelt in sight of thee :
I saw thee every day ; and all the while
Thy Form was sleeping on a glassy sea.

So pure the sky, so quiet was the air !
So like, so very like, was day to day !
Whene'er I looked, thy Image still was there ;
It trembled, but it never passed away.

* Importuna e grave salma.—MICHAEL ANGELO.

How perfect was the calm ! it seemed no sleep ;
No mood, which season takes away, or brings :
I could have fancied that the mighty Deep
Was even the gentlest of all gentle Things.

Ah ! THEN, if mine had been the Painter's hand,
To express what then I saw ; and add the gleam,
The light that never was, on sea or land,
The consecration, and the Poet's dream ;

I would have planted thee, thou hoary Pile,
Amid a world how different from this !
Beside a sea that could not cease to smile ;
On tranquil land, beneath a sky of bliss.

Thou shouldst have seemed a treasure-house divine
Of peaceful years ; a chronicle of heaven ;—
Of all the sunbeams that did ever shine
The very sweetest had to thee been given.

A Picture had it been of lasting ease,
Elysian quiet, without toil or strife ;
No motion but the moving tide, a breeze,
Or merely silent Nature's breathing life.

Such, in the fond illusion of my heart,
Such Picture would I at that time have made :
And seen the soul of truth in every part,
A stedfast peace that might not be betrayed.

So once it would have been,—'tis so no more ;
I have submitted to a new control :
A power is gone, which nothing can restore ;
A deep distress hath humanised my Soul.

Not for a moment could I now behold
A smiling sea, and be what I have been :
The feeling of my loss will ne'er be old ;
This, which I know, I speak with mind serene.

Then, Beaumont, Friend! who would have been the
    Friend,
If he had lived, of Him whom I deplore,
This work of thine I blame not, but commend;
This sea in anger, and that dismal shore.

O 'tis a passionate Work!—yet wise and well,
Well chosen is the spirit that is here;
That Hulk which labours in the deadly swell,
This rueful sky, this pageantry of fear!

And this huge Castle, standing here sublime,
I love to see the look with which it braves,
Cased in the unfeeling armour of old time,
The lightning, the fierce wind, and trampling waves.

Farewell, farewell the heart that lives alone,
Housed in a dream, at distance from the Kind!
Such happiness, wherever it be known,
Is to be pitied; for 'tis surely blind.

But welcome fortitude, and patient cheer,
And frequent sights of what is to be borne!
Such sights, or worse, as are before me here,—
Not without hope we suffer and we mourn.

TO THE DAISY

Sweet Flower! belike one day to have
A place upon thy Poet's grave,
I welcome thee once more:
But He, who was on land, at sea,
My Brother, too, in loving thee,
Although he loved more silently,
Sleeps by his native shore.

Ah ! hopeful, hopeful was the day
When to that Ship he bent his way,
To govern and to guide :
His wish was gained : a little time
Would bring him back in manhood's prime
And free for life, these hills to climb ;
With all his wants supplied.

And full of hope day followed day
While that stout Ship at anchor lay
Beside the shores of Wight ;
The May had then made all things green ;
And, floating there, in pomp serene,
That Ship was goodly to be seen,
His pride and his delight !

Yet then, when called ashore, he sought
The tender peace of rural thought :
In more than happy mood
To your abodes, bright daisy Flowers !
He then would steal at leisure hours,
And loved you glittering in your bowers
A starry multitude.

But hark the word !—the ship is gone ;—
Returns from her long course :—anon
Sets sail :—in season due,
Once more on English earth they stand ;
But, when a third time from the land
They parted, sorrow was at hand
For Him and for his crew.

Ill-fated Vessel !—ghastly shock !
—At length delivered from the rock,
The deep she hath regained ;
And through the stormy night they steer ;
Labouring for life, in hope and fear,
To reach a safer shore—how near,
Yet not to be attained !

" Silence ! " the brave Commander cried :
To that calm word a shriek replied,
It was the last death-shriek.
—A few (my soul oft sees that sight)
Survive upon the tall mast's height ;
But one dear remnant of the night—
For Him in vain I seek.

Six weeks beneath the moving sea
He lay in slumber quietly ;
Unforced by wind or wave
To quit the Ship for which he died,
(All claims of duty satisfied ;)
And there they found him at her side ;
And bore him to the grave.

Vain service ! yet not vainly done
For this, if other end were none,
That He, who had been cast
Upon a way of life unmeet
For such a gentle Soul and sweet,
Should find an undisturbed retreat
Near what he loved, at last—

That neighbourhood of grove and field
To Him a resting-place should yield.
A meek man and a brave !
The birds shall sing and ocean make
A mournful murmur for *his* sake ;
And Thou, sweet Flower, shalt sleep and wake
Upon his senseless grave.

TO MAY

THOUGH many suns have risen and set
    Since thou, blithe May, wert born,
And Bards, who hailed thee, may forget
    Thy gifts, thy beauty scorn ;

There are who to a birthday strain
   Confine not harp and voice,
But evermore throughout thy reign
   Are grateful and rejoice !

Delicious odours ! music sweet,
   Too sweet to pass away !
Oh for a deathless song to meet
   The soul's desire—a lay
That, when a thousand years are told,
   Should praise thee, genial Power !
Through summer heat, autumnal cold,
   And winter's dreariest hour.

Earth, sea, thy presence feel—nor less,
   If yon ethereal blue
With its soft smile the truth express,
   The heavens have felt it too.
The inmost heart of man if glad
   Partakes a livelier cheer ;
And eyes that cannot but be sad
   Let fall a brightened tear.

Since thy return, through days and weeks
   Of hope that grew by stealth,
How many wan and faded cheeks
   Have kindled into health !
The Old, by thee revived, have said,
   " Another year is ours ; "
And wayworn Wanderers, poorly fed,
   Have smiled upon thy flowers.

Who tripping lisps a merry song
   Amid his playful peers ?
The tender Infant who was long
   A prisoner of fond fears ;

But now, when every sharp-edged blast
   Is quiet in its sheath,
His Mother leaves him free to taste
   Earth's sweetness in thy breath.

Thy help is with the weed that creeps
   Along the humblest ground ;
No cliff so bare but on its steeps
   Thy favours may be found ;
But most on some peculiar nook
   That our own hands have drest,
Thou and thy train are proud to look,
   And seem to love it best.

And yet how pleased we wander forth
   When May is whispering, " Come !
Choose from the bowers of virgin earth
   The happiest for your home ;
Heaven's bounteous love through me is spread
   From sunshine, clouds, winds, waves,
Drops on the mouldering turret's head,
   And on your turf-clad graves ! "

Such greeting heard, away with sighs
   For lilies that must fade,
Or " the rathe primrose as it dies
   Forsaken " in the shade !
Vernal fruitions and desires
   Are linked in endless chase ;
While, as one kindly growth retires,
   Another takes its place.

And what if thou, sweet May, hast known
   Mishap by worm and blight ;
If expectations newly blown
   Have perished in thy sight ;

If loves and joys, while up they sprung,
    Were caught as in a snare ;
Such is the lot of all the young,
    However bright and fair.

Lo ! Streams that April could not check
    Are patient of thy rule ;
Gurgling in foamy water-break,
    Loitering in glassy pool :
By thee, thee only, could be sent
    Such gentle mists as glide,
Curling with unconfirmed intent,
    On that green mountain's side.

How delicate the leafy veil
    Through which yon house of God
Gleams, mid the peace of this deep dale
    By few but shepherds trod !
And lowly huts, near beaten ways,
    No sooner stand attired
In thy fresh wreaths, than they for praise
    Peep forth, and are admired.

Season of fancy and of hope,
    Permit not for one hour,
A blossom from thy crown to drop
    Nor add to it a flower !
Keep, lovely May, as if by touch
    Of self-restraining art,
This modest charm of not too much,
    Part seen, imagined part !

TO A CHILD

WRITTEN IN HER ALBUM

SMALL service is true service while it lasts :
Of humblest Friends, bright Creature ! scorn not one :
The Daisy, by the shadow that it casts,
Protects the lingering dew-drop from the Sun.

THE PRIMROSE OF THE ROCK

[Written at Rydal Mount. The Rock stands on the right hand a little way leading up the middle road from Rydal to Grasmere. We have been in the habit of calling it the glow-worm rock from the number of glow-worms we have often seen hanging on it as described. The tuft of primrose has, I fear, been washed away by the heavy rains.]

A ROCK there is whose homely front
   The passing traveller slights ;
Yet there the glow-worms hang their lamps,
   Like stars, at various heights ;
And one coy Primrose to that Rock
   The vernal breeze invites.

What hideous warfare hath been waged,
   What kingdoms overthrown,
Since first I spied that Primrose-tuft
   And marked it for my own ;
A lasting link in Nature's chain
   From highest heaven let down !

The flowers, still faithful to the stems,
   Their fellowship renew ;
The stems are faithful to the root,
   That worketh out of view ;
And to the rock the root adheres
   In every fibre true.

Close clings to earth the living rock,
   Though threatening still to fall ;
The earth is constant to her sphere ;
   And God upholds them all :
So blooms this lonely Plant, nor dreads
   Her annual funeral.

    *   *   *   *   *   *

Here closed the meditative strain ;
　But air breathed soft that day,
The hoary mountain-heights were cheered,
　The sunny vale looked gay ;
And to the Primrose of the Rock
　I gave this after-lay.

I sang—Let myriads of bright flowers,
　Like Thee, in field and grove
Revive unenvied ;—mightier far,
　Than tremblings that reprove
Our vernal tendencies to hope,
　Is God's redeeming love ;

That love which changed—for wan disease,
　For sorrow that had bent
O'er hopeless dust, for withered age—
　Their moral element,
And turned the thistles of a curse
　To types beneficent.

Sin-blighted though we are, we too,
　The reasoning Sons of Men,
From one oblivious winter called
　Shall rise, and breathe again ;
And in eternal summer lose
　Our threescore years and ten.

To humbleness of heart descends
　This prescience from on high,
The faith that elevates the just,
　Before and when they die ;
And makes each soul a separate heaven,
　A court for Deity.

LOVING AND LIKING

IRREGULAR VERSES ADDRESSED TO A CHILD

By my Sister

THERE'S more in words than I can teach :
Yet listen, Child !—I would not preach ;
But only give some plain directions
To guide your speech and your affections.
Say not you *love* a roasted fowl,
But you may love a screaming owl,
And, if you can, the unwieldy toad
That crawls from his secure abode
Within the mossy garden wall
When evening dews begin to fall.
Oh mark the beauty of his eye :
What wonders in that circle lie !
So clear, so bright, our fathers said
He wears a jewel in his head !
And when, upon some showery day
Into a path or public way
A frog leaps out from bordering grass,
Startling the timid as they pass,
Do you observe him, and endeavour
To take the intruder into favour ;
Learning from him to find a reason
For a light heart in a dull season.
And you may love him in the pool,
That is for him a happy school,
In which he swims as taught by nature
Fit pattern for a human creature,
Glancing amid the water bright,
And sending upward sparkling light.
    Nor blush if o'er your heart be stealing
A love for things that have no feeling :

The spring's first rose by you espied,
May fill your breast with joyful pride ;
And you may love the strawberry-flower,
And love the strawberry in its bower ;
But when the fruit, so often praised
For beauty, to your lip is raised,
Say not you *love* the delicate treat,
But *like* it, enjoy it, and thankfully eat.

   Long may you love your pensioner mouse,
Though one of a tribe that torment the house :
Nor dislike for her cruel sport the cat,
Deadly foe both of mouse and rat ;
Remember she follows the law of her kind,
And Instinct is neither wayward nor blind.
Then think of her beautiful gliding form,
Her tread that would scarcely crush a worm,
And her soothing song by the winter fire,
Soft as the dying throb of the lyre.

   I would not circumscribe your love :
It may soar with the eagle and brood with the dove
May pierce the earth with the patient mole,
Or track the hedgehog to his hole.
Loving and liking are the solace of life,
Rock the cradle of joy, smooth the death-bed of strife.
You love your father and your mother,
Your grown-up and your baby brother ;
You love your sister, and your friends,
And countless blessings which God sends :
And while these right affections play,
You *live* each moment of your day ;
They lead you on to full content,
And likings fresh and innocent,
That store the mind, the memory feed,
And prompt to many a gentle deed :
But *likings* come, and pass away ;
'Tis *love* that remains till our latest day :
Our heavenward guide is holy love,
And will be our bliss with saints above.

THE REDBREAST

SUGGESTED IN A WESTMORELAND COTTAGE

DRIVEN in by Autumn's sharpening air
From half-stripped woods and pastures bare,
Brisk Robin seeks a kindlier home :
Not like a beggar is he come,
But enters as a looked-for guest,
Confiding in his ruddy breast,
As if it were a natural shield
Charged with a blazon on the field,
Due to that good and pious deed
Of which we in the Ballad read.
But pensive fancies putting by,
And wild-wood sorrows, speedily
He plays the expert ventriloquist ;
And, caught by glimpses now—now missed,
Puzzles the listener with a doubt
If the soft voice he throws about
Comes from within doors or without !
Was ever such a sweet confusion,
Sustained by delicate illusion ?
He's at your elbow—to your feeling
The notes are from the floor or ceiling ;
And there's a riddle to be guessed,
'Till you have marked his heaving chest,
And busy throat whose sink and swell,
Betray the Elf that loves to dwell
In Robin's bosom, as a chosen cell.

   Heart-pleased we smile upon the Bird
If seen, and with like pleasure stirred
Commend him, when he's only heard.
But small and fugitive our gain
Compared with *hers* who long hath lain,
With languid limbs and patient head
Reposing on a lone sick-bed ;

Where now, she daily hears a strain
That cheats her of too busy cares,
Eases her pain, and helps her prayers.
And who but this dear Bird beguiled
The fever of that pale-faced Child ;
Now cooling, with his passing wing,
Her forehead, like a breeze of Spring :
Recalling now, with descant soft
Shed round her pillow from aloft,
Sweet thoughts of angels hovering nigh,
And the invisible sympathy
Of " Matthew, Mark, and Luke, and John,
Blessing the bed she lies upon " ? *
And sometimes, just as listening ends
In slumber, with the cadence blends
A dream of that low-warbled hymn
Which old folk, fondly pleased to trim
Lamps of faith, now burning dim,
Say that the Cherubs carved in stone,
When clouds gave way at dead of night
And the ancient church was filled with light,
Used to sing in heavenly tone,
Above and round the sacred places
They guard, with wingèd baby-faces.
      Thrice happy Creature ! in all lands
Nurtured by hospitable hands :
Free entrance to this cot has he,
Entrance and exit both *yet* free ;
And, when the keen unruffled weather
That thus brings man and bird together,
Shall with its pleasantness be past,
And casement closed and door made fast,
To keep at bay the howling blast,

* The words—
            " Matthew, Mark, and Luke, and John,
                Bless the bed that I lie on,"
are part of a child's prayer, still in general use through the northern
counties.

He needs not fear the season's rage,
For the whole house is Robin's cage.
Whether the bird flit here or there,
O'er table *lilt*, or perch on chair,
Though some may frown and make a stir,
To scare him as a trespasser,
And he belike will flinch or start,
Good friends he has to take his part ;
One chiefly, who with voice and look
Pleads for him from the chimney-nook,
Where sits the Dame, and wears away
Her long and vacant holiday ;
With images about her heart,
Reflected from the years gone by,
On human nature's second infancy.

CHARACTER OF THE HAPPY WARRIOR

Who is the happy Warrior ?   Who is he
That every man in arms should wish to be ?
—It is the generous Spirit, who, when brought
Among the tasks of real life, hath wrought
Upon the plan that pleased his boyish thought :
Whose high endeavours are an inward light
That makes the path before him always bright :
Who, with a natural instinct to discern
What knowledge can perform, is diligent to learn ;
Abides by this resolve, and stops not there,
But makes his moral being his prime care ;
Who, doomed to go in company with Pain,
And Fear, and Bloodshed, miserable train !
Turns his necessity to glorious gain ;
In face of these doth exercise a power
Which is our human nature's highest dower ;
Controls them and subdues, transmutes, bereaves
Of their bad influence, and their good receives :

By objects, which might force the soul to abate
Her feeling, rendered more compassionate ;
Is placable—because occasions rise
So often that demand such sacrifice ;
More skilful in self-knowledge, even more pure,
As tempted more ; more able to endure,
As more exposed to suffering and distress ;
Thence, also, more alive to tenderness.
—'Tis he whose law is reason ; who depends
Upon that law as on the best of friends ;
Whence, in a state where men are tempted still
To evil for a guard against worse ill,
And what in quality or act is best
Doth seldom on a right foundation rest,
He labours good on good to fix, and owes
To virtue every triumph that he knows :
—Who, if he rise to station of command,
Rises by open means ; and there will stand
On honourable terms, or else retire,
And in himself possess his own desire :
Who comprehends his trust, and to the same
Keeps faithful with a singleness of aim ;
And therefore does not stoop, nor lie in wait
For wealth, or honours, or for worldly state ;
Whom they must follow ; on whose head must fall,
Like showers of manna, if they come at all :
Whose powers shed round him in the common strife,
Or mild concerns of ordinary life,
A constant influence, a peculiar grace ;
But who, if he be called upon to face
Some awful moment to which Heaven has joined
Great issues, good or bad for human kind,
Is happy as a Lover ; and attired
With sudden brightness, like a Man inspired ;
And, through the heat of conflict, keeps the law
In calmness made, and sees what he foresaw ;
Or if an unexpected call succeed,
Come when it will, is equal to the need :

—He who, though thus endued as with a sense
And faculty for storm and turbulence,
Is yet a Soul whose master-bias leans
To homefelt pleasures and to gentle scenes ;
Sweet images ! which, wheresoe'er he be,
Are at his heart ; and such fidelity
It is his darling passion to approve ;
More brave for this, that he hath much to love :—
'Tis, finally, the Man, who, lifted high,
Conspicuous object in a Nation's eye,
Or left unthought-of in obscurity,—
Who, with a toward or untoward lot,
Prosperous or adverse, to his wish or not—
Plays, in the many games of life, that one
Where what he most doth value must be won :
Whom neither shape of danger can dismay,
Nor thought of tender happiness betray ;
Who, not content that former worth stand fast,
Looks forward, persevering to the last,
From well to better, daily self-surpast :
Who, whether praise of him must walk the earth
For ever, and to noble deeds give birth,
Or he must fall, to sleep without his fame,
And leave a dead unprofitable name—
Finds comfort in himself and in his cause ;
And, while the mortal mist is gathering, draws
His breath in confidence of Heaven's applause :
This is the happy Warrior ; this is He
That every Man in arms should wish to be.

PART II

NARRATIVE POEMS

NARRATIVE POEMS

LUCY GRAY

OR, SOLITUDE

Oft I had heard of Lucy Gray :
And, when I crossed the wild,
I chanced to see at break of day
The solitary child.

No mate, no comrade Lucy knew ;
She dwelt on a wide moor,
—The sweetest thing that ever grew
Beside a human door !

You yet may spy the fawn at play,
The hare upon the green ;
But the sweet face of Lucy Gray
Will never more be seen.

" To-night will be a stormy night—
You to the town must go ;
And take a lantern, Child, to light
Your mother through the snow."

" That, Father ! will I gladly do :
'Tis scarcely afternoon—
The minster-clock has just struck two,
And yonder is the moon ! "

At this the Father raised his hook,
And snapped a faggot-band ;
He plied his work ;—and Lucy took
The lantern in her hand.

Not blither is the mountain roe :
With many a wanton stroke
Her feet disperse the powdery snow,
That rises up like smoke.

The storm came on before its time :
She wandered up and down ;
And many a hill did Lucy climb :
But never reached the town.

The wretched parents all that night
Went shouting far and wide ;
But there was neither sound nor sight
To serve them for a guide.

At day-break on a hill they stood
That overlooked the moor ;
And thence they saw the bridge of wood,
A furlong from their door.

They wept—and, turning homeward, cried,
" In heaven we all shall meet ; "
—When in the snow the mother spied
The print of Lucy's feet.

Then downwards from the steep hill's edge
They tracked the footmarks small ;
And through the broken hawthorn hedge,
And by the long stone-wall ;

And then an open field they crossed :
The marks were still the same ;
They tracked them on, nor ever lost ;
And to the bridge they came.

They followed from the snowy bank
Those footmarks, one by one,
Into the middle of the plank ;
And further there were none !

—Yet some maintain that to this day
She is a living child ;
That you may see sweet Lucy Gray
Upon the lonesome wild.

O'er rough and smooth she trips along,
And never looks behind ;
And sings a solitary song
That whistles in the wind.

ALICE FELL ;

OR, POVERTY

THE post-boy drove with fierce career,
For threatening clouds the moon had drowned ;
When, as we hurried on, my ear
Was smitten with a startling sound.

As if the wind blew many ways,
I heard the sound,—and more and more,
It seemed to follow with the chaise,
And still I heard it as before.

At length I to the boy called out ;
He stopped his horses at the word,
But neither cry, nor voice, nor shout,
Nor aught else like it, could be heard.

The boy then smacked his whip, and fast
The horses scampered through the rain ;
But, hearing soon upon the blast
The cry, I bade him halt again.

Forthwith alighting on the ground,
" Whence comes," said I, " this piteous moan ? "
And there a little Girl I found,
Sitting behind the chaise, alone.

" My cloak ! " no other word she spake,
But loud and bitterly she wept,
As if her innocent heart would break ;
And down from off her seat she leapt.

" What ails you, child ? "—she sobbed, " Look here ! "
I saw it in the wheel entangled,
A weather-beaten rag as e'er
From any garden scare-crow dangled.

There, twisted between nave and spoke,
It hung, nor could at once be freed ;
But our joint pains unloosed the cloak,
A miserable rag indeed !

" And whither are you going, child,
To-night along these lonesome ways ? "
" To Durham," answered she, half wild—
" Then come with me into the chaise."

Insensible to all relief
Sat the poor girl, and forth did send
Sob after sob, as if her grief
Could never, never have an end.

" My child, in Durham do you dwell ? "
She checked herself in her distress,
And said, " My name is Alice Fell ;
I'm fatherless and motherless.

" And I to Durham, Sir, belong."
Again, as if the thought would choke
Her very heart, her grief grew strong ;
And all was for her tattered cloak !

The chaise drove on ; our journey's end
Was nigh ; and, sitting by my side,
As if she had lost her only friend
She wept, nor would be pacified.

Up to the tavern-door we post ;
Of Alice and her grief I told ;
And I gave money to the host,
To buy a new cloak for the old.

" And let it be of duffil grey,
As warm a cloak as man can sell ! "
Proud creature was she the next day,
The little orphan, Alice Fell !

WE ARE SEVEN

———A SIMPLE Child,
That lightly draws its breath,
And feels its life in every limb,
What should it know of death ?

I met a little cottage Girl :
She was eight years old, she said :
Her hair was thick with many a curl
That clustered round her head.

She had a rustic, woodland air,
And she was wildly clad :
Her eyes were fair, and very fair :
—Her beauty made me glad.

" Sisters and brothers, little Maid,
How many may you be ? "
" How many ?   Seven in all," she said,
And wondering looked at me.

" And where are they ? I pray you tell."
She answered, " Seven are we ;
And two of us at Conway dwell,
And two are gone to sea.

" Two of us in the church-yard lie,
My sister and my brother ;
And, in the church-yard cottage, I
Dwell near them with my mother."

" You say that two at Conway dwell,
And two are gone to sea,
Yet ye are seven !—I pray you tell,
Sweet Maid, how this may be."

Then did the little Maid reply,
" Seven boys and girls are we ;
Two of us in the church-yard lie,
Beneath the church-yard tree."

" You run about, my little Maid,
Your limbs they are alive ;
If two are in the church-yard laid,
Then ye are only five."

" Their graves are green, they may be seen,"
The little Maid replied,
" Twelve steps or more from my mother's door,
And they are side by side.

" My stockings there I often knit,
My kerchief there I hem ;
And there upon the ground I sit,
And sing a song to them.

" And often after sunset, Sir,
When it is light and fair,
I take my little porringer,
And eat my supper there.

" The first that died was sister Jane ;
In bed she moaning lay,
Till God released her of her pain ;
And then she went away.

" So in the church-yard she was laid ;
And, when the grass was dry,
Together round her grave we played,
My brother John and I.

" And when the ground was white with snow,
And I could run and slide,
My brother John was forced to go,
And he lies by her side."

" How many are you, then," said I,
" If they two are in heaven ? "
Quick was the little Maid's reply,
" O Master ! we are seven."

" But they are dead ; those two are dead !
Their spirits are in heaven ! "
'Twas throwing words away ; for still
The little Maid would have her will,
And said, " Nay, we are seven ! "

ANECDOTE FOR FATHERS

I HAVE a boy of five years old ;
His face is fair and fresh to see ;
His limbs are cast in beauty's mould,
And dearly he loves me.

One morn we strolled on our dry walk,
Our quiet home all full in view,
And held such intermitted talk
As we are wont to do.

My thoughts on former pleasures ran ;
I thought of Kilve's delightful shore,
Our pleasant home when spring began,
A long, long year before.

A day it was when I could bear
Some fond regrets to entertain ;
With so much happiness to spare,
I could not feel a pain.

The green earth echoed to the feet
Of lambs that bounded through the glade,
From shade to sunshine, and as fleet
From sunshine back to shade.

Birds warbled round me—and each trace
Of inward sadness had its charm ;
Kilve, thought I, was a favoured place,
And so is Liswyn farm.

My boy beside me tripped, so slim
And graceful in his rustic dress !
And, as we talked, I questioned him,
In very idleness.

" Now tell me, had you rather be,"
I said, and took him by the arm,
" On Kilve's smooth shore, by the green sea,
Or here at Liswyn farm ? "

In careless mood he looked at me,
While still I held him by the arm,
And said, " At Kilve I'd rather be
Than here at Liswyn farm."

" Now, little Edward, say why so :
My little Edward, tell me why."—
" I cannot tell, I do not know."—
" Why, this is strange," said I ;

" For here are woods, hills smooth and warm :
There surely must some reason be
Why you would change sweet Liswyn farm
For Kilve by the green sea."

At this, my boy hung down his head,
He blushed with shame, nor made reply ;
And three times to the child I said,
" Why, Edward, tell me why ? "

His head he raised—there was in sight,
It caught his eye, he saw it plain—
Upon the house-top, glittering bright,
A broad and gilded vane.

Then did the boy his tongue unlock,
And eased his mind with this reply :
" At Kilve there was no weather-cock ;
And that's the reason why."

O dearest, dearest boy ! my heart
For better lore would seldom yearn,
Could I but teach the hundredth part
Of what from thee I learn.

THE PET-LAMB

A PASTORAL

THE dew was falling fast, the stars began to blink ;
I heard a voice ; it said, " Drink, pretty creature, drink ! "
And, looking o'er the hedge, before me I espied
A snow-white mountain-lamb with a Maiden at its side.

Nor sheep nor kine were near ; the lamb was all alone,
And by a slender cord was tethered to a stone ;
With one knee on the grass did the little Maiden kneel,
While to that mountain-lamb she gave its evening meal.

The lamb, while from her hand he thus his supper took,
Seemed to feast with head and ears ; and his tail with
    pleasure shook.

" Drink, pretty creature, drink," she said in such a tone
That I almost received her heart into my own.

'Twas little Barbara Lewthwaite, a child of beauty rare !
I watched them with delight, they were a lovely pair.
Now with her empty can the Maiden turned away :
But ere ten yards were gone her footsteps did she stay.

Right towards the lamb she looked ; and from a shady
    place
I unobserved could see the workings of her face :
If Nature to her tongue could measured numbers bring,
Thus, thought I, to her lamb that little Maid might sing :

" What ails thee, young One ? what ?   Why pull so at
    thy cord ?
Is it not well with thee ? well both for bed and board ?
Thy plot of grass is soft, and green as grass can be ;
Rest, little young One, rest ; what is't that aileth thee ?

" What is it thou wouldst seek ?   What is wanting to
    thy heart ?
Thy limbs are they not strong ?   And beautiful thou art :
This grass is tender grass ; these flowers they have no
    peers ;
And that green corn all day is rustling in thy ears !

" If the sun be shining hot, do but stretch thy woollen
    chain,
This beech is standing by, its covert thou canst gain ;
For rain and mountain-storms ! the like thou need'st not
    fear,
The rain and storm are things that scarcely can come
    here.

" Rest, little young One, rest ; thou hast forgot the day
When my father found thee first in places far away ;

Many flocks were on the hills, but thou wert owned by
    none,
And thy mother from thy side for evermore was gone.

" He took thee in his arms, and in pity brought thee
    home :
A blessèd day for thee ! then whither wouldst thou
    roam ?
A faithful nurse thou hast ; the dam that did thee yean
Upon the mountain-tops no kinder could have been.

" Thou know'st that twice a day I have brought thee in
    this can
Fresh water from the brook, as clear as ever ran ;
And twice in the day, when the ground is wet with dew,
I bring thee draughts of milk, warm milk it is and new.

" Thy limbs will shortly be twice as stout as they are
    now,
Then I'll yoke thee to my cart like a pony in the plough ;
My playmate thou shalt be ; and when the wind is cold
Our hearth shall be thy bed, our house shall be thy fold.

" It will not, will not rest !—Poor creature, can it be
That 'tis thy mother's heart which is working so in thee ?
Things that I know not of belike to thee are dear,
And dreams of things which thou canst neither see nor
    hear.

" Alas ! the mountain-tops that look so green and fair !
I've heard of fearful winds and darkness that come there ;
The little brooks that seem all pastime and all play,
When they are angry, roar like lions for their prey.

" Here thou need'st not dread the raven in the sky ;
Night and day thou art safe,—our cottage is hard by.
Why bleat so after me ?   Why pull so at thy chain ?
Sleep—and at break of day I will come to thee again ! "

—As homeward through the lane I went with lazy feet,
This song to myself did I oftentimes repeat ;
And it seemed, as I retraced the ballad line by line,
That but half of it was hers, and one half of it was *mine.*

Again, and once again, did I repeat the song ;
" Nay," said I, " more than half to the damsel must
    belong,
For she looked with such a look and she spake with such
    a tone,
That I almost received her heart into my own."

THE COMPLAINT

OF A FORSAKEN INDIAN WOMAN

[When a Northern Indian, from sickness, is unable to continue his
journey with his companions, he is left behind, covered over with
deer-skins, and is supplied with water, food, and fuel, if the situation
of the place will afford it. He is informed of the track which his companions intend to pursue, and if he be unable to follow, or overtake
them, he perishes alone in the desert ; unless he should have the good
fortune to fall in with some other tribes of Indians. The females are
equally, or still more, exposed to the same fate. See that very interesting work Hearne's *Journey from Hudson's Bay to the Northern
Ocean.* In the high northern latitudes, as the same writer informs us,
when the northern lights vary their position in the air, they make a
rustling and a crackling noise, as alluded to in the following poem.]

    Before I see another day,
    Oh let my body die away !
    In sleep I heard the northern gleams ;
    The stars, they were among my dreams ;
    In rustling conflict through the skies,
    I heard, I saw the flashes drive,
    And yet they are upon my eyes,
    And yet I am alive ;
    Before I see another day,
    Oh let my body die away !

My fire is dead : it knew no pain ;
Yet is it dead, and I remain :
All stiff with ice the ashes lie ;
And they are dead, and I will die.
When I was well, I wished to live,
For clothes, for warmth, for food, and fire
But they to me no joy can give,
No pleasure now, and no desire.
Then here contented will I lie !
Alone, I cannot fear to die.

Alas ! ye might have dragged me on
Another day, a single one !
Too soon I yielded to despair ;
Why did ye listen to my prayer ?
When ye were gone my limbs were stronger ;
And oh, how grievously I rue,
That, afterwards, a little longer,
My friends, I did not follow you !
For strong and without pain I lay,
Dear friends, when ye were gone away.

My Child ! they gave thee to another,
A woman who was not thy mother.
When from my arms my Babe they took,
On me how strangely did he look !
Through his whole body something ran,
A most strange working did I see ;
—As if he strove to be a man,
That he might pull the sledge for me :
And then he stretched his arms, how wild !
Oh mercy ! like a helpless child.

My little joy ! my little pride !
In two days more I must have died.
Then do not weep and grieve for me ;
I feel I must have died with thee.
O wind, that o'er my head art flying

The way my friends their course did bend,
I should not feel the pain of dying,
Could I with thee a message send ;
Too soon, my friends, ye went away ;
For I had many things to say.

I'll follow you across the snow ;
Ye travel heavily and slow ;
In spite of all my weary pain
I'll look upon your tents again.
—My fire is dead, and snowy white
The water which beside it stood :
The wolf has come to me to-night,
And he has stolen away my food.
For ever left alone am I ;
Then wherefore should I fear to die ?

Young as I am, my course is run,
I shall not see another sun ;
I cannot lift my limbs to know
If they have any life or no.
My poor forsaken Child, if I
For once could have thee close to me,
With happy heart I then would die,
And my last thought would happy be ;
But thou, dear Babe, art far away,
Nor shall I see another day.

THE LAST OF THE FLOCK

IN distant countries have I been,
And yet I have not often seen
A healthy man, a man full grown,
Weep in the public roads, alone.
But such a one, on English ground,

And in the broad highway, I met ;
Along the broad highway he came,
His cheeks with tears were wet :
Sturdy he seemed, though he was sad ;
And in his arms a Lamb he had.

He saw me, and he turned aside,
As if he wished himself to hide :
And with his coat did then essay
To wipe those briny tears away.
I followed him, and said, " My friend,
What ails you ? wherefore weep you so ? "
—" Shame on me, Sir ! this lusty Lamb,
He makes my tears to flow.
To-day I fetched him from the rock ;
He is the last of all my flock.

" When I was young, a single man,
And after youthful follies ran,
Though little given to care and thought,
Yet, so it was, an ewe I bought ;
And other sheep from her I raised,
As healthy sheep as you might see ;
And then I married, and was rich
As I could wish to be ;
Of sheep I numbered a full score,
And every year increased my store.

" Year after year my stock it grew ;
And from this one, this single ewe,
Full fifty comely sheep I raised,
As fine a flock as ever grazed !
Upon the Quantock hills they fed ;
They throve, and we at home did thrive :
—This lusty Lamb of all my store
Is all that is alive ;
And now I care not if we die,
And perish all of poverty.

" Six Children, Sir ! had I to feed ;
Hard labour in a time of need !
My pride was tamed, and in our grief
I of the Parish asked relief.
They said, I was a wealthy man ;
My sheep upon the uplands fed,
And it was fit that thence I took
Whereof to buy us bread.
' Do this : how can we give to you,'
They cried, ' what to the poor is due ? '

" I sold a sheep, as they had said,
And bought my little children bread,
And they were healthy with their food ;
For me—it never did me good.
A woeful time it was for me,
To see the end of all my gains,
The pretty flock which I had reared
With all my care and pains,
To see it melt like snow away—
For me it was a woeful day.

" Another still ! and still another !
A little lamb, and then its mother !
It was a vein that never stopped—
Like blood-drops from my heart they dropped.
'Till thirty were not left alive
They dwindled, dwindled, one by one ;
And I may say, that many a time
I wished they all were gone—
Reckless of what might come at last
Were but the bitter struggle past.

" To wicked deeds I was inclined,
And wicked fancies crossed my mind ;
And every man I chanced to see,
I thought he knew some ill of me :
No peace, no comfort could I find,

No ease, within doors or without ;
And, crazily and wearily
I went my work about ;
And oft was moved to flee from home,
And hide my head where wild beasts roam.

" Sir ! 'twas a precious flock to me,
As dear as my own children be ;
For daily with my growing store
I loved my children more and more.
Alas ! it was an evil time ;
God cursed me in my sore distress ;
I prayed, yet every day I thought
I loved my children less ;
And every week, and every day,
My flock it seemed to melt away.

" They dwindled, Sir, sad sight to see !
From ten to five, from five to three,
A lamb, a wether, and a ewe ;—
And then at last from three to two ;
And, of my fifty, yesterday
I had but only one :
And here it lies upon my arm,
Alas ! and I have none ;—
To-day I fetched it from the rock ;
It is the last of all my flock."

THE AFFLICTION OF MARGARET ——

WHERE art thou, my beloved Son,
Where art thou, worse to me than dead ?
Oh find me, prosperous or undone !
Or, if the grave be now thy bed,
Why am I ignorant of the same
That I may rest ; and neither blame
Nor sorrow may attend thy name ?

Seven years, alas ! to have received
No tidings of an only child ;
To have despaired, have hoped, believed,
And been for evermore beguiled ;
Sometimes with thoughts of very bliss !
I catch at them, and then I miss ;
Was ever darkness like to this ?

He was among the prime in worth,
An object beauteous to behold ;
Well born, well bred ; I sent him forth
Ingenuous, innocent, and bold :
If things ensued that wanted grace,
As hath been said, they were not base ;
And never blush was on my face.

Ah ! little doth the young one dream,
When full of play and childish cares,
What power is in his wildest scream,
Heard by his mother unawares !
He knows it not, he cannot guess :
Years to a mother bring distress ;
But do not make her love the less.

Neglect me ! no, I suffered long
From that ill thought ; and, being blind,
Said, " Pride shall help me in my wrong ;
Kind mother have I been, as kind
As ever breathed : " and that is true ;
I've wet my path with tears like dew,
Weeping for him when no one knew.

My Son, if thou be humbled, poor,
Hopeless of honour and of gain,
Oh ! do not dread thy mother's door ;
Think not of me with grief and pain :
I now can see with better eyes ;
And worldly grandeur I despise,
And fortune with her gifts and lies.

Alas! the fowls of heaven have wings,
And blasts of heaven will aid their flight;
They mount—how short a voyage brings
The wanderers back to their delight!
Chains tie us down by land and sea;
And wishes, vain as mine, may be
All that is left to comfort thee.

Perhaps some dungeon hears thee groan,
Maimed, mangled by inhuman men;
Or thou upon a desert thrown
Inheritest the lion's den;
Or hast been summoned to the deep,
Thou, thou and all thy mates, to keep
An incommunicable sleep.

I look for ghosts; but none will force
Their way to me: 'tis falsely said
That there was ever intercourse
Between the living and the dead;
For, surely, then I should have sight
Of him I wait for day and night,
With love and longings infinite.

My apprehensions come in crowds;
I dread the rustling of the grass;
The very shadows of the clouds
Have power to shake me as they pass:
I question things and do not find
One that will answer to my mind;
And all the world appears unkind.

Beyond participation lie
My troubles, and beyond relief:
If any chance to heave a sigh,
They pity me, and not my grief.
Then come to me, my Son, or send
Some tidings that my woes may end;
I have no other earthly friend!

THE SAILOR'S MOTHER

[Written at Town-end, Grasmere. I met this woman near the
Wishing-gate, on the high-road that then led from Grasmere to Amble-
side. Her appearance was exactly as here described, and such was
her account, nearly to the letter.]

ONE morning (raw it was and wet—
A foggy day in winter time)
A Woman on the road I met,
Not old, though something past her prime :
Majestic in her person, tall and straight ;
And like a Roman matron's was her mien and gait.

The ancient spirit is not dead ;
Old times, thought I, are breathing there ;
Proud was I that my country bred
Such strength, a dignity so fair :
She begged an alms, like one in poor estate ;
I looked at her again, nor did my pride abate.

When from these lofty thoughts I woke,
" What is it," said I, " that you bear,
Beneath the covert of your Cloak,
Protected from this cold damp air ? "
She answered, soon as she the question heard,
" A simple burthen, Sir, a little Singing-bird."

And, thus continuing, she said,
" I had a Son, who many a day
Sailed on the seas, but he is dead ;
In Denmark he was cast away :
And I have travelled weary miles to see
If aught which he had owned might still remain for me.

" The bird and cage they both were his :
'Twas my Son's bird ; and neat and trim
He kept it : many voyages
The singing-bird had gone with him ;

When last he sailed, he left the bird behind ;
From bodings, as might be, that hung upon his mind.

" He to a fellow-lodger's care
Had left it, to be watched and fed,
And pipe its song in safety ;—there
I found it when my Son was dead ;
And now, God help me for my little wit !
I bear it with me, Sir ;—he took so much delight in it."

MICHAEL

A PASTORAL POEM

IF from the public way you turn your steps
Up the tumultuous brook of Greenhead Ghyll,
You will suppose that with an upright path
Your feet must struggle ; in such bold ascent
The pastoral mountains front you, face to face.
But, courage ! for around that boisterous brook
The mountains have all opened out themselves,
And made a hidden valley of their own.
No habitation can be seen ; but they
Who journey thither find themselves alone
With a few sheep, with rocks and stones, and kites
That overhead are sailing in the sky.
It is in truth an utter solitude ;
Nor should I have made mention of this Dell
But for one object which you might pass by,
Might see and notice not. Beside the brook
Appears a straggling heap of unhewn stones !
And to that simple object appertains
A story—unenriched with strange events,
Yet not unfit, I deem, for the fireside,
Or for the summer shade. It was the first
Of those domestic tales that spake to me

Of shepherds, dwellers in the valleys, men
Whom I already loved ; not verily
For their own sakes, but for the fields and hills
Where was their occupation and abode.
And hence this Tale, while I was yet a Boy
Careless of books, yet having felt the power
Of Nature, by the gentle agency
Of natural objects, led me on to feel
For passions that were not my own, and think
(At random and imperfectly indeed)
On man, the heart of man, and human life.
Therefore, although it be a history
Homely and rude, I will relate the same
For the delight of a few natural hearts ;
And, with yet fonder feeling, for the sake
Of youthful Poets, who among these hills
Will be my second self when I am gone.

    UPON the forest-side in Grasmere Vale
There dwelt a Shepherd, Michael was his name ;
An old man, stout of heart, and strong of limb.
His bodily frame had been from youth to age
Of an unusual strength : his mind was keen,
Intense, and frugal, apt for all affairs,
And in his shepherd's calling he was prompt
And watchful more than ordinary men.
Hence had he learned the meaning of all winds,
Of blasts of every tone ; and, oftentimes,
When others heeded not, He heard the South
Make subterraneous music, like the noise
Of bagpipers on distant Highland hills.
The Shepherd, at such warning, of his flock
Bethought him, and he to himself would say,
" The winds are now devising work for me ! "
And, truly, at all times, the storm, that drives
The traveller to a shelter, summoned him
Up to the mountains : he had been alone
Amid the heart of many thousand mists,
That came to him, and left him, on the heights.

So lived he till his eightieth year was past.
And grossly that man errs, who should suppose
That the green valleys, and the streams and rocks,
Were things indifferent to the Shepherd's thoughts.
Fields, where with cheerful spirits he had breathed
The common air ; hills, which with vigorous step
He had so often climbed ; which had impressed
So many incidents upon his mind
Of hardship, skill or courage, joy or fear ;
Which, like a book, preserved the memory
Of the dumb animals, whom he had saved,
Had fed or sheltered, linking to such acts
The certainty of honourable gain ;
Those fields, those hills—what could they less ? had laid
Strong hold on his affections, were to him
A pleasurable feeling of blind love,
The pleasure which there is in life itself.
  His days had not been passed in singleness.
His Helpmate was a comely matron, old—
Though younger than himself full twenty years.
She was a woman of a stirring life,
Whose heart was in her house : two wheels she had
Of antique form ; this large, for spinning wool ;
That small, for flax ; and if one wheel had rest
It was because the other was at work.
The Pair had but one inmate in their house,
An only Child, who had been born to them
When Michael, telling o'er his years, began
To deem that he was old,—in shepherd's phrase,
With one foot in the grave.   This only Son,
With two brave sheep-dogs tried in many a storm,
The one of an inestimable worth,
Made all their household.   I may truly say,
That they were as a proverb in the vale
For endless industry.   When day was gone,
And from their occupations out of doors
The Son and Father were come home, even then,
Their labour did not cease ; unless when all

Turned to the cleanly supper-board, and there,
Each with a mess of pottage and skimmed milk,
Sat round the basket piled with oaten cakes,
And their plain home-made cheese.   Yet when the meal
Was ended, Luke (for so the Son was named)
And his old Father both betook themselves
To such convenient work as might employ
Their hands by the fireside ; perhaps to card
Wool for the Housewife's spindle, or repair
Some injury done to sickle, flail, or scythe,
Or other implement of house or field.
    Down from the ceiling, by the chimney's edge,
That in our ancient uncouth country style
With huge and black projection overbrowed
Large space beneath, as duly as the light
Of day grew dim the Housewife hung a lamp ;
An aged utensil, which had performed
Service beyond all others of its kind.
Early at evening did it burn—and late,
Surviving comrade of uncounted hours,
Which, going by from year to year, had found,
And left, the couple neither gay perhaps
Nor cheerful, yet with objects and with hopes,
Living a life of eager industry.
And now, when Luke had reached his eighteenth year,
There by the light of this old lamp they sate,
Father and Son, while far into the night
The Housewife plied her own peculiar work,
Making the cottage through the silent hours
Murmur as with the sound of summer flies.
This light was famous in its neighbourhood,
And was a public symbol of the life
That thrifty Pair had lived.   For, as it chanced,
Their cottage on a plot of rising ground
Stood single, with large prospect, north and south,
High into Easedale, up to Dunmail-Raise,
And westward to the village near the lake ;
And from this constant light, so regular

And so far seen, the House itself, by all
Who dwelt within the limits of the vale,
Both old and young, was named THE EVENING STAR
  Thus living on through such a length of years,
The Shepherd, if he loved himself, must needs
Have loved his Helpmate ; but to Michael's heart
This son of his old age was yet more dear—
Less from instinctive tenderness, the same
Fond spirit that blindly works in the blood of all—
Than that a child, more than all other gifts
That earth can offer to declining man,
Brings hope with it, and forward-looking thoughts,
And stirrings of inquietude, when they
By tendency of nature needs must fail.
Exceeding was the love he bare to him,
His heart and his heart's joy ! For oftentimes
Old Michael, while he was a babe in arms,
Had done him female service, not alone
For pastime and delight, as is the use
Of fathers, but with patient mind enforced
To acts of tenderness ; and he had rocked
His cradle, as with a woman's gentle hand.

  And, in a later time, ere yet the Boy
Had put on boy's attire, did Michael love,
Albeit of a stern unbending mind,
To have the Young-one in his sight, when he
Wrought in the field, or on his shepherd's stool
Sate with a fettered sheep before him stretched
Under the large old oak, that near his door
Stood single, and, from matchless depth of shade,
Chosen for the Shearer's covert from the sun,
Thence in our rustic dialect was called
The CLIPPING TREE,* a name which yet it bears.
There, while they two were sitting in the shade,
With others round them, earnest all and blithe,
Would Michael exercise his heart with looks

---

* Clipping is the word used in the North of England for shearing.

Of fond correction and reproof bestowed
Upon the Child, if he disturbed the sheep
By catching at their legs, or with his shouts
Scared them, while they lay still beneath the shears.

And when by Heaven's good grace the boy grew up
A healthy Lad, and carried in his cheek
Two steady roses that were five years old ;
Then Michael from a winter coppice cut
With his own hand a sapling, which he hooped
With iron, making it throughout in all
Due requisites a perfect shepherd's staff,
And gave it to the Boy ; wherewith equipt
He as a watchman oftentimes was placed
At gate or gap, to stem or turn the flock ;
And, to his office prematurely called,
There stood the urchin, as you will divine,
Something between a hindrance and a help ;
And for this cause not always, I believe,
Receiving from his Father hire of praise ;
Though nought was left undone which staff, or voice,
Or looks, or threatening gestures, could perform.

But soon as Luke, full ten years old, could stand
Against the mountain blasts ; and to the heights,
Not fearing toil, nor length of weary ways,
He with his Father daily went, and they
Were as companions, why should I relate
That objects which the Shepherd loved before
Were dearer now ? that from the Boy there came
Feelings and emanations—things which were
Light to the sun and music to the wind ;
And that the old Man's heart seemed born again ?

Thus in his Father's sight the boy grew up :
And now, when he had reached his eighteenth year,
He was his comfort and his daily hope.

While in this sort the simple household lived
From day to day, to Michael's ear there came
Distressful tidings.   Long before the time
Of which I speak, the Shepherd had been bound

In surety for his brother's son, a man
Of an industrious life, and ample means ;
But unforeseen misfortunes suddenly
Had prest upon him ; and old Michael now
Was summoned to discharge the forfeiture,
A grievous penalty, but little less
Than half his substance. This unlooked-for claim,
At the first hearing, for a moment took
More hope out of his life than he supposed
That any old man ever could have lost.
As soon as he had armed himself with strength
To look his trouble in the face, it seemed
The Shepherd's sole resource to sell at once
A portion of his patrimonial fields.
Such was his first resolve ; he thought again,
And his heart failed him. " Isabel," said he,
Two evenings after he had heard the news,
" I have been toiling more than seventy years,
And in the open sunshine of God's love
Have we all lived ; yet if these fields of ours
Should pass into a stranger's hand, I think
That I could not lie quiet in my grave.
Our lot is a hard lot ; the sun himself
Has scarcely been more diligent than I ;
And I have lived to be a fool at last
To my own family. An evil man
That was, and made an evil choice, if he
Were false to us ; and if he were not false,
There are ten thousand to whom loss like this
Had been no sorrow. I forgive him ;—but
'Twere better to be dumb than to talk thus.

    When I began, my purpose was to speak
Of remedies and of a cheerful hope.
Our Luke shall leave us, Isabel ; the land
Shall not go from us, and it shall be free ;
He shall possess it, free as is the wind
That passes over it. We have, thou know'st,
Another kinsman—he will be our friend

In this distress.   He is a prosperous man,
Thriving in trade—and Luke to him shall go,
And with his kinsman's help and his own thrift
He quickly will repair this loss, and then
He may return to us.   If here he stay,
What can be done ?   Where every one is poor,
What can be gained ? "

                              At this the old Man paused,
And Isabel sat silent, for her mind
Was busy, looking back into past times.
There's Richard Bateman, thought she to herself,
He was a parish-boy—at the church-door
They made a gathering for him, shillings, pence
And halfpennies, wherewith the neighbours bought
A basket, which they filled with pedlar's wares ;
And, with this basket on his arm, the lad
Went up to London, found a master there,
Who, out of many, chose the trusty boy
To go and overlook his merchandise
Beyond the seas ; where he grew wondrous rich,
And left estates and monies to the poor,
And, at his birth-place, built a chapel, floored
With marble which he sent from foreign lands.
These thoughts, and many others of like sort,
Passed quickly through the mind of Isabel,
And her face brightened.   The old Man was glad,
And thus resumed :—" Well, Isabel ! this scheme,
These two days, has been meat and drink to me.
Far more than we have lost is left us yet.
—We have enough—I wish indeed that I
Were younger ;—but this hope is a good hope.
—Make ready Luke's best garments, of the best
Buy for him more, and let us send him forth
To-morrow, or the next day, or to-night :
—If he *could* go, the Boy should go to-night."
     Here Michael ceased, and to the fields went forth
With a light heart.   The Housewife for five days
Was restless morn and night, and all day long

Wrought on with her best fingers to prepare
Things needful for the journey of her son.
But Isabel was glad when Sunday came
To stop her in her work : for, when she lay
By Michael's side, she through the last two nights
Heard him, how he was troubled in his sleep ;
And when they rose at morning she could see
That all his hopes were gone.   That day at noon
She said to Luke, while they two by themselves
Were sitting at the door, " Thou must not go :
We have no other Child but thee to lose,
None to remember—do not go away,
For if thou leave thy Father he will die."
The Youth made answer with a jocund voice ;
And Isabel, when she had told her fears,
Recovered heart.   That evening her best fare
Did she bring forth, and all together sat
Like happy people round a Christmas fire.

   With daylight Isabel resumed her work ;
And all the ensuing week the house appeared
As cheerful as a grove in Spring : at length
The expected letter from their kinsman came,
With kind assurances that he would do
His utmost for the welfare of the Boy ;
To which, requests were added, that forthwith
He might be sent to him.   Ten times or more
The letter was read over ; Isabel
Went forth to show it to the neighbours round ;
Nor was there at that time on English land
A prouder heart than Luke's.   When Isabel
Had to her house returned, the old Man said,
" He shall depart to-morrow."   To this word
The Housewife answered, talking much of things
Which, if at such short notice he should go,
Would surely be forgotten.   But at length
She gave consent, and Michael was at ease.

   Near the tumultuous brook of Greenhead Ghyll,
In that deep valley, Michael had designed

To build a Sheepfold; and, before he heard
The tidings of his melancholy loss,
For this same purpose he had gathered up
A heap of stones, which by the streamlet's edge
Lay thrown together, ready for the work.
With Luke that evening thitherward he walked:
And soon as they had reached the place he stopped,
And thus the old Man spake to him:—" My Son,
To-morrow thou wilt leave me: with full heart
I look upon thee, for thou art the same
That wert a promise to me ere thy birth,
And all thy life hast been my daily joy.
I will relate to thee some little part
Of our two histories; 'twill do thee good
When thou art from me, even if I should touch
On things thou canst not know of.——After thou
First cam'st into the world—as oft befalls
To new-born infants—thou didst sleep away
Two days, and blessings from thy Father's tongue
Then fell upon thee.   Day by day passed on,
And still I loved thee with increasing love.
Never to living ear came sweeter sounds
Than when I heard thee by our own fireside
First uttering, without words, a natural tune;
While thou, a feeding babe, didst in thy joy
Sing at thy Mother's breast.   Month followed month,
And in the open fields my life was passed
And on the mountains; else I think that thou
Hadst been brought up upon thy Father's knees.
But we were playmates, Luke: among these hills,
As well thou knowest, in us the old and young
Have played together, nor with me didst thou
Lack any pleasure which a boy can know."
Luke had a manly heart; but at these words
He sobbed aloud.   The old Man grasped his hand,
And said, " Nay, do not take it so—I see
That these are things of which I need not speak.
—Even to the utmost I have been to thee

A kind and a good Father : and herein
I but repay a gift which I myself
Received at others' hands ; for, though now old
Beyond the common life of man, I still
Remember them who loved me in my youth.
Both of them sleep together : here they lived,
As all their Forefathers had done ; and when
At length their time was come, they were not loth
To give their bodies to the family mould.
I wished that thou should'st live the life they lived :
But, 'tis a long time to look back, my Son,
And see so little gain from threescore years.
These fields were burthened when they came to me ;
Till I was forty years of age, not more
Than half of my inheritance was mine.
I toiled and toiled ; God blessed me in my work,
And till these three weeks past the land was free.
—It looks as if it never could endure
Another Master.   Heaven forgive me, Luke,
If I judge ill for thee, but it seems good
That thou should'st go."
                                        At this the old Man paused ;
Then, pointing to the stones near which they stood,
Thus, after a short silence, he resumed :
" This was a work for us ; and now, my Son,
It is a work for me.   But, lay one stone—
Here, lay it for me, Luke, with thine own hands.
Nay, Boy, be of good hope ;—we both may live
To see a better day.   At eighty-four
I still am strong and hale ;—do thou thy part ;
I will do mine.—I will begin again
With many tasks that were resigned to thee :
Up to the heights, and in among the storms,
Will I without thee go again, and do
All works which I was wont to do alone,
Before I knew thy face.—Heaven bless thee, Boy !
Thy heart these two weeks has been beating fast
With many hopes ; it should be so—yes—yes—

(2,508)   5

I knew that thou could'st never have a wish
To leave me, Luke : thou hast been bound to me
Only by links of love : when thou art gone,
What will be left to us !—But, I forget
My purposes. Lay now the corner-stone,
As I requested ; and hereafter, Luke,
When thou art gone away, should evil men
Be thy companions, think of me, my Son,
And of this moment ; hither turn thy thoughts,
And God will strengthen thee : amid all fear
And all temptation, Luke, I pray that thou
May'st bear in mind the life thy Fathers lived,
Who, being innocent, did for that cause
Bestir them in good deeds. Now, fare thee well—
When thou return'st, thou in this place wilt see
A work which is not here : a covenant
'Twill be between us ; but, whatever fate
Befall thee, I shall love thee to the last,
And bear thy memory with me to the grave."
    The Shepherd ended here ; and Luke stooped down,
And, as his Father had requested, laid
The first stone of the Sheepfold. At the sight
The old Man's grief broke from him ; to his heart
He pressed his Son, he kissèd him and wept ;
And to the house together they returned.
—Hushed was that House in peace, or seeming peace,
Ere the night fell :—with morrow's dawn the Boy
Began his journey, and when he had reached
The public way, he put on a bold face ;
And all the neighbours, as he passed their doors,
Came forth with wishes and with farewell prayers,
That followed him till he was out of sight.
    A good report did from their Kinsman come,
Of Luke and his well-doing : and the Boy
Wrote loving letters, full of wondrous news,
Which, as the Housewife phrased it, were throughout
" The prettiest letters that were ever seen."
Both parents read them with rejoicing hearts.

So, many months passed on : and once again
The Shepherd went about his daily work
With confident and cheerful thoughts ; and now
Sometimes when he could find a leisure hour
He to that valley took his way, and there
Wrought at the Sheepfold.   Meantime Luke began
To slacken in his duty ; and, at length,
He in the dissolute city gave himself
To evil courses : ignominy and shame
Fell on him, so that he was driven at last
To seek a hiding-place beyond the seas.

   There is a comfort in the strength of love ;
'Twill make a thing endurable, which else
Would overset the brain, or break the heart :
I have conversed with more than one who well
Remember the old Man, and what he was
Years after he had heard this heavy news.
His bodily frame had been from youth to age
Of an unusual strength.   Among the rocks
He went, and still looked up to sun and cloud
And listened to the wind ; and, as before,
Performed all kinds of labour for his sheep,
And for the land, his small inheritance.
And to that hollow dell from time to time
Did he repair, to build the Fold of which
His flock had need.   'Tis not forgotten yet
The pity which was then in every heart
For the old Man—and 'tis believed by all
That many and many a day he thither went,
And never lifted up a single stone.

   There, by the Sheepfold, sometimes was he seen
Sitting alone, or with his faithful Dog,
Then old, beside him, lying at his feet.
The length of full seven years, from time to time,
He at the building of this Sheepfold wrought,
And left the work unfinished when he died.
Three years, or little more, did Isabel
Survive her Husband : at her death the estate

Was sold, and went into a stranger's hand.
The Cottage which was named the EVENING STAR
Is gone—the ploughshare has been through the ground
On which it stood ; great changes have been wrought
In all the neighbourhood :—yet the oak is left
That grew beside their door ; and the remains
Of the unfinished Sheepfold may be seen
Beside the boisterous brook of Greenhead Ghyll.

THE SEVEN SISTERS;

OR, THE SOLITUDE OF BINNORIE

SEVEN Daughters had Lord Archibald,
All children of one mother :
You could not say in one short day
What love they bore each other.
A garland, of seven lilies, wrought !
Seven Sisters that together dwell ;
But he, bold Knight as ever fought,
Their Father, took of them no thought,
He loved the wars so well.
Sing, mournfully, oh ! mournfully,
The solitude of Binnorie !

Fresh blows the wind, a western wind,
And from the shores of Erin,
Across the wave, a Rover brave
To Binnorie is steering :
Right onward to the Scottish strand
The gallant ship is borne ;
The warriors leap upon the land,
And hark ! the Leader of the band
Hath blown his bugle horn.
Sing, mournfully, oh ! mournfully,
The solitude of Binnorie.

Beside a grotto of their own,
With boughs above them closing,
The Seven are laid, and in the shade
They lie like fawns reposing.
But now, upstarting with affright
At noise of man and steed,
Away they fly to left, to right—
Of your fair household, Father-knight,
Methinks you take small heed !
Sing, mournfully, oh ! mournfully,
The solitude of Binnorie.

Away the seven fair Campbells fly,
And, over hill and hollow,
With menace proud, and insult loud,
The youthful Rovers follow.
Cried they, " Your Father loves to roam :
Enough for him to find
The empty house when he comes home ;
For us your yellow ringlets comb,
For us be fair and kind ! "
Sing, mournfully, oh ! mournfully,
The solitude of Binnorie.

Some close behind, some side to side,
Like clouds in stormy weather ;
They run, and cry, " Nay, let us die,
And let us die together."
A lake was near ; the shore was steep ;
There never foot had been ;
They ran, and with a desperate leap
Together plunged into the deep,
Nor ever more were seen.
Sing, mournfully, oh ! mournfully,
The solitude of Binnorie.

The stream that flows out of the lake,
As through the glen it rambles,

Repeats a moan o'er moss and stone,
For those seven lovely Campbells.
Seven little Islands, green and bare,
Have risen from out the deep :
The fishers say, those sisters fair,
By faeries all are buried there,
And there together sleep.
Sing, mournfully, oh ! mournfully,
The solitude of Binnorie.

THE HORN OF EGREMONT CASTLE

[A tradition transferred from the ancient mansion of Hutton John,
the seat of the Hudlestons, to Egremont Castle.]

ERE the Brothers through the gateway
Issued forth with old and young,
To the Horn Sir Eustace pointed
Which for ages there had hung.
Horn it was which none could sound,
No one upon living ground,
Save He who came as rightful Heir
To Egremont's Domains and Castle fair.

Heirs from times of earliest record
Had the House of Lucie born,
Who of right had held the Lordship
Claimed by proof upon the Horn :
Each at the appointed hour
Tried the Horn,—it owned his power ;
He was acknowledged : and the blast,
Which good Sir Eustace sounded, was the last.

With his lance Sir Eustace pointed,
And to Hubert thus said he,
" What I speak this Horn shall witness
For thy better memory.

Hear, then, and neglect me not !
At this time, and on this spot,
The words are uttered from my heart,
As my last earnest prayer ere we depart.

" On good service we are going
Life to risk by sea and land,
In which course if Christ our Saviour
Do my sinful soul demand,
Hither come thou back straightway,
Hubert, if alive that day ;
Return, and sound the Horn, that we
May have a living House still left in thee ! "

" Fear not," quickly answered Hubert ;
" As I am thy Father's son,
What thou askest, noble Brother,
With God's favour shall be done."
So were both right well content :
Forth they from the Castle went,
And at the head of their Array
To Palestine the Brothers took their way.

Side by side they fought (the Lucies
Were a line for valour famed),
And where'er their strokes alighted,
There the Saracens were tamed.
Whence, then, could it come—the thought—
By what evil spirit brought ?
Oh ! can a brave Man wish to take
His Brother's life, for Lands' and Castle's sake ?

" Sir ! " the Ruffians said to Hubert,
" Deep he lies in Jordan flood."
Stricken by this ill assurance,
Pale and trembling Hubert stood.
" Take your earnings."—Oh ! that I
Could have *seen* my Brother die !

It was a pang that vexed him then ;
And oft returned, again, and yet again.

Months passed on, and no Sir Eustace !
Nor of him were tidings heard ;
Wherefore, bold as day, the Murderer
Back again to England steered.
To his Castle Hubert sped ;
Nothing has he now to dread.
But silent and by stealth he came,
And at an hour which nobody could name.

None could tell if it were night-time
Night or day, at even or morn ;
No one's eye had seen him enter,
No one's ear had heard the Horn.
But bold Hubert lives in glee :
Months and years went smilingly ;
With plenty was his table spread ;
And bright the Lady is who shares his bed.

Likewise he had sons and daughters ;
And, as good men do, he sate
At his board by these surrounded,
Flourishing in fair estate.
And while thus in open day
Once he sate, as old books say,
A blast was uttered from the Horn,
Where by the Castle-gate it hung forlorn.

'Tis the breath of good Sir Eustace !
He is come to claim his right :
Ancient castle, woods, and mountains
Hear the challenge with delight.
Hubert ! though the blast be blown
He is helpless and alone :
Thou hast a dungeon, speak the word !
And there he may be lodged, and thou be Lord.

Speak !—astounded Hubert cannot ;
And, if power to speak he had,
All are daunted, all the household
Smitten to the heart, and sad.
'Tis Sir Eustace ; if it be
Living man, it must be he !
Thus Hubert thought in his dismay,
And by a postern-gate he slunk away.

Long, and long was he unheard of :
To his Brother then he came,
Made confession, asked forgiveness,
Asked it by a brother's name,
And by all the saints in heaven ;
And of Eustace was forgiven :
Then in a convent went to hide
His melancholy head, and there he died.

But Sir Eustace, whom good angels
Had preserved from murderers' hands,
And from Pagan chains had rescued,
Lived with honour on his lands.
Sons he had, saw sons of theirs :
And through ages, heirs of heirs,
A long posterity renowned,
Sounded the Horn which they alone could sound.

GOODY BLAKE AND HARRY GILL

A TRUE STORY

Oh ! what's the matter ? what's the matter ?
What is't that ails young Harry Gill ?
That evermore his teeth they chatter,
Chatter, chatter, chatter still !

Of waistcoats Harry has no lack,
Good duffle grey, and flannel fine ;
He has a blanket on his back,
And coats enough to smother nine.

In March, December, and in July,
'Tis all the same with Harry Gill ;
The neighbours tell, and tell you truly,
His teeth they chatter, chatter still.
At night, at morning, and at noon,
'Tis all the same with Harry Gill ;
Beneath the sun, beneath the moon,
His teeth they chatter, chatter still.

Young Harry was a lusty drover,
And who so stout of limb as he ?
His cheeks were red as ruddy clover ;
His voice was like the voice of three.
Old Goody Blake was old and poor ;
Ill fed she was, and thinly clad ;
And any man who passed her door
Might see how poor a hut she had.

All day she spun in her poor dwelling :
And then her three hours' work at night,
Alas ! 'twas hardly worth the telling,
It would not pay for candle-light.
Remote from sheltered village-green,
On a hill's northern side she dwelt,
Where from sea-blasts the hawthorns lean,
And hoary dews are slow to melt.

By the same fire to boil their pottage,
Two poor old Dames, as I have known,
Will often live in one small cottage ;
But she, poor Woman ! housed alone.

'Twas well enough when summer came,
The long, warm, lightsome summer-day,
Then at her door the *canty* Dame
Would sit, as any linnet, gay.

But when the ice our streams did fetter,
Oh then how her old bones would shake !
You would have said, if you had met her,
'Twas a hard time for Goody Blake.
Her evenings then were dull and dead :
Sad case it was, as you may think,
For very cold to go to bed ;
And then for cold not sleep a wink.

O joy for her ! whene'er in winter
The winds at night had made a rout ;
And scattered many a lusty splinter
And many a rotten bough about.
Yet never had she, well or sick,
As every man who knew her says,
A pile beforehand, turf or stick,
Enough to warm her for three days.

Now, when the frost was past enduring,
And made her poor old bones to ache,
Could any thing be more alluring
Than an old hedge to Goody Blake ?
And, now and then, it must be said,
When her old bones were cold and chill,
She left her fire, or left her bed,
To seek the hedge of Harry Gill.

Now Harry he had long suspected
This trespass of old Goody Blake ;
And vowed that she should be detected—
That he on her would vengeance take.

And oft from his warm fire he'd go,
And to the fields his road would take ;
And there, at night, in frost and snow,
He watched to seize old Goody Blake.

And once, behind a rick of barley,
Thus looking out did Harry stand :
The moon was full and shining clearly,
And crisp with frost the stubble land.
—He hears a noise—he's all awake—
Again ?—on tip-toe down the hill
He softly creeps—'tis Goody Blake ;
She's at the hedge of Harry Gill !

Right glad was he when he beheld her :
Stick after stick did Goody pull :
He stood behind a bush of elder,
Till she had filled her apron full.
When with her load she turned about,
The by-way back again to take ;
He started forward, with a shout,
And sprang upon poor Goody Blake.

And fiercely by the arm he took her,
And by the arm he held her fast,
And fiercely by the arm he shook her,
And cried, " I've caught you then at last ! "—
Then Goody, who had nothing said,
Her bundle from her lap let fall ;
And, kneeling on the sticks, she prayed
To God that is the judge of all.

She prayed, her withered hand uprearing,
While Harry held her by the arm—
" God ! who art never out of hearing,
O may he never more be warm ! "

The cold, cold moon above her head,
Thus on her knees did Goody pray ;
Young Harry heard what she had said :
And icy cold he turned away.

He went complaining all the morrow
That he was cold and very chill :
His face was gloom, his heart was sorrow ;
Alas ! that day for Harry Gill !
That day he wore a riding-coat,
But not a whit the warmer he :
Another was on Thursday brought,
And ere the Sabbath he had three.

'Twas all in vain, a useless matter,
And blankets were about him pinned ;
Yet still his jaws and teeth they clatter ;
Like a loose casement in the wind.
And Harry's flesh it fell away ;
And all who see him say, 'tis plain,
That, live as long as live he may,
He never will be warm again.

No word to any man he utters,
A-bed or up, to young or old ;
But ever to himself he mutters,
" Poor Harry Gill is very cold."
A-bed or up, by night or day ;
His teeth they chatter, chatter still.
Now think, ye farmers all, I pray,
Of Goody Blake and Harry Gill !

THE REVERIE OF POOR SUSAN

At the corner of Wood Street, when daylight appears,
Hangs a Thrush that sings loud, it has sung for three
    years :

Poor Susan has passed by the spot, and has heard
In the silence of morning the song of the Bird.

'Tis a note of enchantment ; what ails her ?   She sees
A mountain ascending, a vision of trees ;
Bright volumes of vapour through Lothbury glide,
And a river flows on through the vale of Cheapside.

Green pastures she views in the midst of the dale,
Down which she so often has tripped with her pail ;
And a single small cottage, a nest like a dove's,
The one only dwelling on earth that she loves.

She looks, and her heart is in heaven : but they fade,
The mist and the river, the hill and the shade :
The stream will not flow, and the hill will not rise,
And the colours have all passed away from her eyes !

POWER OF MUSIC

An Orpheus ! an Orpheus ! yes, Faith may grow bold,
And take to herself all the wonders of old ;—
Near the stately Pantheon you'll meet with the same
In the street that from Oxford hath borrowed its name.

His station is there ; and he works on the crowd,
He sways them with harmony merry and loud ;
He fills with his power all their hearts to the brim—
Was aught ever heard like his fiddle and him ?

What an eager assembly ! what an empire is this !
The weary have life, and the hungry have bliss ;
The mourner is cheered, and the anxious have rest ;
And the guilt-burthened soul is no longer opprest.

As the Moon brightens round her the clouds of the night,
So He, where he stands, is a centre of light ;
It gleams on the face, there, of dusky-browed Jack,
And the pale-visaged Baker's, with basket on back.

That errand-bound 'Prentice was passing in haste—
What matter ! he's caught—and his time runs to waste ;
The Newsman is stopped, though he stops on the fret ;
And the half-breathless Lamplighter—he's in the net !

The Porter sits down on the weight which he bore ;
The Lass with her barrow wheels hither her store ;—
If a thief could be here he might pilfer at ease ;
She sees the Musician, 'tis all that she sees !

He stands, backed by the wall ;—he abates not his din ;
His hat gives him vigour, with boons dropping in,
From the old and the young, from the poorest ; and there !
The one-pennied Boy has his penny to spare.

O blest are the hearers, and proud be the hand
Of the pleasure it spreads through so thankful a band ;
I am glad for him, blind as he is !—all the while
If they speak 'tis to praise, and they praise with a smile.

That tall Man, a giant in bulk and in height,
Not an inch of his body is free from delight ;
Can he keep himself still, if he would ? oh, not he !
The music stirs in him like wind through a tree.

Mark that Cripple who leans on his crutch ; like a tower
That long has leaned forward, leans hour after hour !—
That Mother, whose spirit in fetters is bound,
While she dandles the Babe in her arms to the sound.

Now, coaches and chariots ! roar on like a stream ;
Here are twenty souls happy as souls in a dream :
They are deaf to your murmurs—they care not for you,
Nor what ye are flying, nor what ye pursue !

STAR-GAZERS

WHAT crowd is this ? what have we here ! we must not
    pass it by ;
A Telescope upon its frame, and pointed to the sky ;
Long is it as a barber's pole, or mast of little boat,
Some little pleasure-skiff, that doth on Thames's waters
    float.

The Showman chooses well his place, 'tis Leicester's busy
    Square ;
And is as happy in his night, for the heavens are blue and
    fair ;
Calm, though impatient, is the crowd ; each stands ready
    with the fee,
And envies him that's looking ;—what an insight must
    it be !

Yet, Showman, where can lie the cause ? Shall thy
    Implement have blame,
A boaster, that when he is tried, fails, and is put to
    shame ?
Or is it good as others are, and be their eyes in fault ?
Their eyes, or minds ? or, finally, is yon resplendent
    vault ?

Is nothing of that radiant pomp so good as we have here ?
Or gives a thing but small delight that never can be
    dear ?
The silver moon with all her vales, and hills of mightiest
    fame,
Doth she betray us when they're seen ? or are they but
    a name ?

Or is it rather that Conceit rapacious is and strong,
And bounty never yields so much but it seems to do her
    wrong ?

Or is it, that when human Souls a journey long have had
And are returned into themselves, they cannot but be
      sad ?

Or must we be constrained to think that these Spectators
      rude,
Poor in estate, of manners base, men of the multitude,
Have souls which never yet have risen, and therefore
      prostrate lie ?
No, no, this cannot be ;—men thirst for power and
      majesty !

Does, then, a deep and earnest thought the blissful mind
      employ
Of him who gazes, or has gazed ? a grave and steady
      joy,
That doth reject all show of pride, admits no outward
      sign,
Because not of this noisy world, but silent and divine !

Whatever be the cause, 'tis sure that they who pry and
      pore
Seem to meet with little gain, seem less happy than
      before :
One after One they take their turn, nor have I one espied
That doth not slackly go away, as if dissatisfied.

BEGGARS

She had a tall man's height or more ;
Her face from summer's noontide heat
No bonnet shaded, but she wore
A mantle, to her very feet
Descending with a graceful flow,
And on her head a cap as white as new-fallen snow.

Her skin was of Egyptian brown :
Haughty, as if her eye had seen
Its own light to a distance thrown,
She towered, fit person for a Queen
To lead those ancient Amazonian files ;
Or ruling Bandit's wife among the Grecian isles.

Advancing, forth she stretched her hand
And begged an alms with doleful plea
That ceased not ; on our English land
Such woes, I knew, could never be ;
And yet a boon I gave her, for the creature
Was beautiful to see—a weed of glorious feature.

I left her, and pursued my way ;
And soon before me did espy
A pair of little Boys at play,
Chasing a crimson butterfly ;
The taller followed with his hat in hand,
Wreathed round with yellow flowers the gayest of the land.

The other wore a rimless crown
With leaves of laurel stuck about ;
And, while both followed up and down,
Each whooping with a merry shout,
In their fraternal features I could trace
Unquestionable lines of that wild Suppliant's face.

Yet *they*, so blithe of heart, seemed fit
For finest tasks of earth or air :
Wings let them have, and they might flit
Precursors to Aurora's car,
Scattering fresh flowers ; though happier far, I ween,
To hunt their fluttering game o'er rock and level green.

They dart across my path—but lo,
Each ready with a plaintive whine !
Said I, " not half an hour ago
Your Mother has had alms of mine."

" That cannot be," one answered—" she is dead : "—
I looked reproof—they saw—but neither hung his head.

" She has been dead, Sir, many a day."—
" Hush, boys ! you're telling me a lie ;
It was your Mother, as I say ! "
And, in the twinkling of an eye,
" Come ! Come ! " cried one, and without more ado,
Off to some other play the joyous Vagrants flew !

SEQUEL TO THE " BEGGARS "

COMPOSED MANY YEARS AFTER

WHERE are they now, those wanton Boys ?
For whose free range the dædal earth
Was filled with animated toys,
And implements of frolic mirth ;
With tools for ready wit to guide ;
And ornaments of seemlier pride,
More fresh, more bright, than princes wear ;
For what one moment flung aside,
Another could repair ;
What good or evil have they seen
Since I their pastime witnessed here,
Their daring wiles, their sportive cheer ?
I ask—but all is dark between !
    They met me in a genial hour,
When universal nature breathed
As with the breath of one sweet flower,—
A time to overrule the power
Of discontent, and check the birth
Of thoughts with better thoughts at strife,
The most familiar bane of life
Since parting Innocence bequeathed
Mortality to Earth !

Soft clouds, the whitest of the year,
Sailed through the sky—the brooks ran clear ;
The lambs from rock to rock were bounding ;
With songs the budded groves resounding ;
And to my heart are still endeared
The thoughts with which it then was cheered :
The faith which saw that gladsome pair
Walk through the fire with unsinged hair.
Or, if such faith must needs deceive—
Then, Spirits of beauty and of grace,
Associates in that eager chase ;
Ye, who within the blameless mind
Your favourite seat of empire find—
Kind Spirits ! may we not believe
That they, so happy and so fair
Through your sweet influence, and the care
Of pitying Heaven, at least were free
From touch of *deadly* injury ?
Destined whate'er their earthly doom,
For mercy and immortal bloom !

RUTH

WHEN Ruth was left half desolate,
Her Father took another Mate ;
And Ruth, not seven years old,
A slighted child, at her own will
Went wandering over dale and hill,
In thoughtless freedom, bold.

And she had made a pipe of straw,
And music from that pipe could draw
Like sounds of winds and floods ;
Had built a bower upon the green,
As if she from her birth had been
An infant of the woods.

Beneath her father's roof, alone
She seemed to live ; her thoughts her own,
Herself her own delight ;
Pleased with herself, nor sad, nor gay ;
And, passing thus the live-long day,
She grew to woman's height.

There came a Youth from Georgia's shore—
A military casque he wore,
With splendid feathers drest ;
He brought them from the Cherokees ;
The feathers nodded in the breeze,
And made a gallant crest.

From Indian blood you deem him sprung :
But no ! he spake the English tongue,
And bore a soldier's name ;
And, when America was free
From battle and from jeopardy,
He 'cross the ocean came.

With hues of genius on his cheek
In finest tones the Youth could speak :
—While he was yet a boy,
The moon, the glory of the sun,
And streams that murmur as they run,
Had been his dearest joy.

He was a lovely Youth ! I guess
The panther in the wilderness
Was not so fair as he ;
And, when he chose to sport and play,
No dolphin ever was so gay
Upon the tropic sea.

Among the Indians he had fought,
And with him many tales he brought
Of pleasure and of fear ;

Such tales as told to any maid
By such a Youth, in the green shade
Were perilous to hear.

He told of girls—a happy rout !
Who quit their fold with dance and shout,
Their pleasant Indian town,
To gather strawberries all day long :
Returning with a choral song
When daylight is gone down.

He spake of plants that hourly change
Their blossoms, through a boundless range
Of intermingling hues ;
With budding, fading, faded flowers
They stand the wonder of the bowers
From morn to evening dews.

He told of the magnolia, spread
High as a cloud, high over head !
The cypress and her spire ;
—Of flowers that with one scarlet gleam
Cover a hundred leagues, and seem
To set the hills on fire.

The Youth of green savannahs spake,
And many an endless, endless lake,
With all its fairy crowds
Of islands, that together lie
As quietly as spots of sky
Among the evening clouds.

" How pleasant," then he said, " it were
A fisher or a hunter there,
In sunshine or in shade
To wander with an easy mind ;
And build a household fire, and find
A home in every glade !

" What days and what bright years ! Ah me !
Our life were life indeed, with thee
So passed in quiet bliss,
And all the while," said he, " to know
That we were in a world of woe,
On such an earth as this ! "

And then he sometimes interwove
Fond thoughts about a father's love ;
" For there," said he, " are spun
Around the heart such tender ties,
That our own children to our eyes
Are dearer than the sun.

" Sweet Ruth ! and could you go with me
My helpmate in the woods to be,
Our shed at night to rear ;
Or run, my own adopted bride,
A sylvan huntress at my side,
And drive the flying deer !

" Belovèd Ruth ! "—No more he said,
The wakeful Ruth at midnight shed
A solitary tear :
She thought again—and did agree
With him to sail across the sea,
And drive the flying deer.

" And now, as fitting is and right,
We in the church our faith will plight,
A husband and a wife."
Even so they did ; and I may say
That to sweet Ruth that happy day
Was more than human life.

Through dream and vision did she sink,
Delighted all the while to think
That on those lonesome floods,

And green savannahs, she should share
His board with lawful joy, and bear
His name in the wild woods.

But, as you have before been told,
This Stripling, sportive, gay, and bold,
And, with his dancing crest,
So beautiful, through savage lands
Had roamed about, with vagrant bands
Of Indians in the West.

The wind, the tempest roaring high,
The tumult of a tropic sky,
Might well be dangerous food
For him, a Youth to whom was given
So much of earth—so much of heaven,
And such impetuous blood.

Whatever in those climes he found
Irregular in sight or sound
Did to his mind impart
A kindred impulse, seemed allied
To his own powers, and justified
The workings of his heart.

Nor less, to feed voluptuous thought,
The beauteous forms of nature wrought,
Fair trees and gorgeous flowers ;
The breezes their own languor lent ;
The stars had feelings, which they sent
Into those favoured bowers.

Yet, in his worst pursuits, I ween
That sometimes there did intervene
Pure hopes of high intent :
For passions linked to forms so fair
And stately, needs must have their share
Of noble sentiment.

But ill he lived, much evil saw,
With men to whom no better law
Nor better life was known ;
Deliberately, and undeceived,
Those wild men's vices he received,
And gave them back his own.

His genius and his moral frame
Were thus impaired, and he became
The slave of low desires :
A Man who without self-control
Would seek what the degraded soul
Unworthily admires.

And yet he with no feigned delight
Had wooed the Maiden, day and night
Had loved her, night and morn :
What could he less than love a Maid
Whose heart with so much nature played ?
So kind and so forlorn !

Sometimes, most earnestly, he said,
" O Ruth ! I have been worse than dead ;
False thoughts, thoughts bold and vain,
Encompassed me on every side
When I, in confidence and pride,
Had crossed the Atlantic main.

" Before me shone a glorious world—
Fresh as a banner bright, unfurled
To music suddenly :
I looked upon those hills and plains,
And seemed as if let loose from chains,
To live at liberty.

" No more of this ; for now, by thee
Dear Ruth ! more happily set free
With nobler zeal I burn ;

My soul from darkness is released,
Like the whole sky when to the east
The morning doth return."

Full soon that better mind was gone ;
No hope, no wish remained, not one,—
They stirred him now no more ;
New objects did new pleasure give,
And once again he wished to live
As lawless as before.

Meanwhile, as thus with him it fared,
They for the voyage were prepared,
And went to the sea-shore,
But, when they thither came, the Youth
Deserted his poor Bride, and Ruth
Could never find him more.

God help thee, Ruth !—Such pains she had,
That she in half a year was mad,
And in a prison housed ;
And there, with many a doleful song
Made of wild words, her cup of wrong
She fearfully caroused.

Yet sometimes milder hours she knew
Nor wanted sun, nor rain, nor dew,
Nor pastimes of the May ;
—They all were with her in her cell ;
And a clear brook with cheerful knell
Did o'er the pebbles play.

When Ruth three seasons thus had lain,
There came a respite to her pain ;
She from her prison fled ;
But of the Vagrant none took thought ;
And where it liked her best she sought
Her shelter and her bread.

Among the fields she breathed again :
The master-current of her brain
Ran permanent and free ;
And, coming to the Banks of Tone,
There did she rest ; and dwell alone
Under the greenwood tree.

The engines of her pain, the tools
That shaped her sorrow, rocks and pools
And airs that gently stir
The vernal leaves—she loved them still ;
Nor ever taxed them with the ill
Which had been done to her.

A Barn her *winter* bed supplies ;
But, till the warmth of summer skies
And summer days is gone,
(And all do in this tale agree)
She sleeps beneath the greenwood tree,
And other home hath none.

An innocent life, yet far astray !
And Ruth will, long before her day,
Be broken down and old :
Sore aches she needs must have ! but less
Of mind, than body's wretchedness,
From damp, and rain, and cold.

If she is prest by want of food,
She from her dwelling in the wood
Repairs to a road-side ;
And there she begs at one steep place
Where up and down with easy pace
The horseman-travellers ride.

That oaten pipe of hers is mute,
Or thrown away ; but with a flute
Her loneliness she cheers :

This flute, made of a hemlock stalk.
At evening in his homeward walk
The Quantock woodman hears.

I, too, have passed her on the hills
Setting her little water-mills
By spouts and fountains wild—
Such small machinery as she turned
Ere she had wept, ere she had mourned,
A young and happy Child !

Farewell ! and when thy days are told,
Ill-fated Ruth, in hallowed mould
Thy corpse shall buried be,
For thee a funeral bell shall ring,
And all the congregation sing
A Christian psalm for thee.

LAODAMIA

" WITH sacrifice before the rising morn
Vows have I made by fruitless hope inspired ;
And from the infernal Gods, 'mid shades forlorn
Of night, my slaughtered Lord have I required :
Celestial pity I again implore ;—
Restore him to my sight—great Jove, restore ! "

So speaking, and by fervent love endowed
With faith, the Suppliant heavenward lifts her hands ;
While, like the sun emerging from a cloud,
Her countenance brightens—and her eye expands ;
Her bosom heaves and spreads, her stature grows ;
And she expects the issue in repose.

O terror ! what hath she perceived ?—O joy !
What doth she look on ?—whom doth she behold ?
Her Hero slain upon the beach of Troy ?

His vital presence ? his corporeal mould ?
It is—if sense deceive her not—'tis He !
And a God leads him, wingèd Mercury !

Mild Hermes spake—and touched her with his wand
That calms all fear ; " Such grace hath crowned thy
    prayer,
Laodamía ! that at Jove's command
Thy Husband walks the paths of upper air :
He comes to tarry with thee three hours' space ;
Accept the gift, behold him face to face ! "

Forth sprang the impassioned Queen her Lord to clasp ;
Again that consummation she essayed ;
But unsubstantial Form eludes her grasp
As often as that eager grasp was made.
The Phantom parts—but parts to re-unite,
And re-assume his place before her sight.

" Protesiláus, lo ! thy guide is gone !
Confirm, I pray, the vision with thy voice :
This is our palace,—yonder is thy throne ;
Speak, and the floor thou tread'st on will rejoice.
Not to appal me have the gods bestowed
This precious boon ; and blest a sad abode."

" Great Jove, Laodamía ! doth not leave
His gifts imperfect :—Spectre though I be,
I am not sent to scare thee or deceive ;
But in reward of thy fidelity.
And something also did my worth obtain ;
For fearless virtue bringeth boundless gain.

" Thou knowest, the Delphic oracle foretold
That the first Greek who touched the Trojan strand
Should die ; but me the threat could not withhold :
A generous cause a victim did demand ;
And forth I leapt upon the sandy plain ;
A self-devoted chief—by Hector slain."

" Supreme of Heroes—bravest, noblest, best !
Thy matchless courage I bewail no more,
Which then, when tens of thousands were deprest
By doubt, propelled thee to the fatal shore ;
Thou found'st—and I forgive thee—here thou art—
A nobler counsellor than my poor heart.

" But thou, though capable of sternest deed,
Wert kind as resolute, and good as brave ;
And he, whose power restores thee, hath decreed
Thou should'st elude the malice of the grave :
Redundant are thy locks, thy lips as fair
As when their breath enriched Thessalian air.

" No Spectre greets me,—no vain Shadow this ;
Come, blooming Hero, place thee by my side !
Give, on this well-known couch, one nuptial kiss
To me, this day, a second time thy bride ! "
Jove frowned in heaven : the conscious Parcæ threw
Upon those roseate lips a Stygian hue.

" This visage tells thee that my doom is past :
Nor should the change be mourned, even if the joys
Of sense were able to return as fast
And surely as they vanish.   Earth destroys
Those raptures duly—Erebus disdains :
Calm pleasures there abide—majestic pains.

" Be taught, O faithful Consort, to control
Rebellious passion : for the Gods approve
The depth, and not the tumult, of the soul ;
A fervent, not ungovernable, love.
Thy transports moderate ; and meekly mourn
When I depart, for brief is my sojourn—"

" Ah, wherefore ?—Did not Hercules by force
Wrest from the guardian Monster of the tomb
Alcestis, a reanimated corse,

Given back to dwell on earth in vernal bloom ?
Medea's spells dispersed the weight of years,
And Æson stood a youth 'mid youthful peers.

" The Gods to us are merciful—and they
Yet further may relent : for mightier far
Than strength of nerve and sinew, or the sway
Of magic potent over sun and star,
Is love, though oft to agony distrest,
And though his favourite seat be feeble woman's breast.

" But if thou goest, I follow—" " Peace ! " he said,—
She looked upon him and was calmed and cheered ;
The ghastly colour from his lips had fled ;
In his deportment, shape, and mien, appeared
Elysian beauty, melancholy grace,
Brought from a pensive though a happy place.

He spake of love, such love as Spirits feel
In worlds whose course is equable and pure ;
No fears to beat away—no strife to heal—
The past unsighed for, and the future sure ;
Spake of heroic arts in graver mood
Revived, with finer harmony pursued ;

Of all that is most beauteous—imaged there
In happier beauty ; more pellucid streams,
An ampler ether, a diviner air,
And fields invested with purpureal gleams ;
Climes which the sun, who sheds the brightest day
Earth knows, is all unworthy to survey.

Yet there the Soul shall enter which hath earned
That privilege by virtue.—" Ill," said he,
" The end of man's existence I discerned,
Who from ignoble games and revelry
Could draw, when we had parted, vain delight,
While tears were thy best pastime, day and night ;

" And while my youthful peers before my eyes
(Each hero following his peculiar bent)
Prepared themselves for glorious enterprise
By martial sports,—or, seated in the tent,
Chieftains and kings in council were detained ;
What time the fleet at Aulis lay enchained.

" The wished-for wind was given :—I then revolved
The oracle, upon the silent sea ;
And, if no worthier led the way, resolved
That, of a thousand vessels, mine should be
The foremost prow in pressing to the strand,—
Mine the first blood that tinged the Trojan sand.

" Yet bitter, oft-times bitter, was the pang
When of thy loss I thought, belovèd Wife !
On thee too fondly did my memory hang,
And on the joys we shared in mortal life,—
The paths which we had trod—these fountains, flowers,
My new-planned cities, and unfinished towers.

" But should suspense permit the Foe to cry,
' Behold they tremble !—haughty their array,
Yet of their number no one dares to die ? '
In soul I swept the indignity away :
Old frailties then recurred :—but lofty thought,
In act embodied, my deliverance wrought.

" And Thou, though strong in love, art all too weak
In reason, in self-government too slow ;
I counsel thee by fortitude to seek
Our blest re-union in the shades below.
The invisible world with thee hath sympathised ;
Be thy affections raised and solemnised.

" Learn, by a mortal yearning, to ascend—
Seeking a higher object. Love was given,
Encouraged, sanctioned, chiefly for that end ;

For this the passion to excess was driven—
That self might be annulled : her bondage prove
The fetters of a dream, opposed to love."——

Aloud she shrieked ! for Hermes reappears !
Round the dear Shade she would have clung—'tis vain :
The hours are past—too brief had they been years ;
And him no mortal effort can detain :
Swift, toward the realms that know not earthly day,
He through the portal takes his silent way,
And on the palace-floor a lifeless corse She lay.

Thus, all in vain exhorted and reproved,
She perished ; and, as for a wilful crime,
By the just Gods whom no weak pity moved,
Was doomed to wear out her appointed time,
Apart from happy Ghosts, that gather flowers
Of blissful quiet 'mid unfading bowers.

—Yet tears to human suffering are due ;
And mortal hopes defeated and o'erthrown
Are mourned by man, and not by man alone,
As fondly he believes.—Upon the side
Of Hellespont (such faith was entertained)
A knot of spiry trees for ages grew
From out the tomb of him for whom she died ;
And ever, when such stature they had gained
That Ilium's walls were subject to their view,
The tree's tall summits withered at the sight ;
A constant interchange of growth and blight !

RESOLUTION AND INDEPENDENCE

THERE was a roaring in the wind all night ;
The rain came heavily and fell in floods ;
But now the sun is rising calm and bright ;
(2,508)

6

The birds are singing in the distant woods ;
Over his own sweet voice the Stock-dove broods ;
The Jay makes answer as the Magpie chatters ;
And all the air is filled with pleasant noise of waters.

All things that love the sun are out of doors ;
The sky rejoices in the morning's birth ;
The grass is bright with rain-drops ;—on the moors
The hare is running races in her mirth ;
And with her feet she from the plashy earth
Raises a mist, that, glittering in the sun,
Runs with her all the way, wherever she doth run.

I was a Traveller then upon the moor,
I saw the hare that raced about with joy ;
I heard the woods and distant waters roar ;
Or heard them not, as happy as a boy :
The pleasant season did my heart employ :
My old remembrances went from me wholly ;
And all the ways of men, so vain and melancholy.

But, as it sometimes chanceth, from the might
Of joy in minds that can no further go,
As high as we have mounted in delight
In our dejection do we sink as low ;
To me that morning did it happen so ;
And fears and fancies thick upon me came ;
Dim sadness—and blind thoughts, I knew not, nor
     could name.

I heard the sky-lark warbling in the sky ;
And I bethought me of the playful hare :
Even such a happy Child of earth am I ;
Even as these blissful creatures do I fare ;
Far from the world I walk, and from all care ;
But there may come another day to me—
Solitude, pain of heart, distress, and poverty.

My whole life I have lived in pleasant thought,
As if life's business were a summer mood ;
As if all needful things would come unsought
To genial faith, still rich in genial good ;
But how can He expect that others should
Build for him, sow for him, and at his call
Love him, who for himself will take no heed at all ?

I thought of Chatterton, the marvellous Boy,
The sleepless Soul that perished in his pride ;
Of Him who walked in glory and in joy
Following his plough, along the mountain-side :
By our own spirits are we deified :
We Poets in our youth begin in gladness ;
But thereof come in the end despondency and madness.

Now, whether it were by peculiar grace,
A leading from above, a something given,
Yet it befell, that, in this lonely place,
When I with these untoward thoughts had striven,
Beside a pool bare to the eye of heaven
I saw a Man before me unawares :
The oldest man he seemed that ever wore grey hairs.

As a huge stone is sometimes seen to lie
Couched on the bald top of an eminence ;
Wonder to all who do the same espy,
By what means it could thither come, and whence ;
So that it seems a thing endued with sense :
Like a sea-beast crawled forth, that on a shelf
Of rock or sand reposeth, there to sun itself ;

Such seemed this Man, not all alive nor dead,
Nor all asleep—in his extreme old age :
His body was bent double, feet and head
Coming together in life's pilgrimage ;
As if some dire constraint of pain, or rage
Of sickness felt by him in times long past,
A more than human weight upon his frame had cast.

Himself he propped, limbs, body, and pale face,
Upon a long grey staff of shaven wood :
And, still as I drew near with gentle pace,
Upon the margin of that moorish flood
Motionless as a cloud the old Man stood,
That heareth not the loud winds when they call
And moveth all together, if it move at all.

At length, himself unsettling, he the pond
Stirred with his staff, and fixedly did look
Upon the muddy water, which he conned,
As if he had been reading in a book :
And now a stranger's privilege I took ;
And, drawing to his side, to him did say,
" This morning gives us promise of a glorious day."

A gentle answer did the old Man make,
In courteous speech which forth he slowly drew :
And him with further words I thus bespake,
" What occupation do you there pursue ?
This is a lonesome place for one like you."
Ere he replied, a flash of mild surprise
Broke from the sable orbs of his yet-vivid eyes.

His words came feebly, from a feeble chest,
But each in solemn order followed each,
With something of a lofty utterance drest—
Choice word and measured phrase, above the reach
Of ordinary men ; a stately speech ;
Such as grave Livers do in Scotland use,
Religious men, who give to God and man their dues.

He told, that to these waters he had come
To gather leeches, being old and poor :
Employment hazardous and wearisome !
And he had many hardships to endure :
From pond to pond he roamed, from moor to moor ;
Housing, with God's good help, by choice or chance,
And in this way he gained an honest maintenance.

The old Man still stood talking by my side ;
But now his voice to me was like a stream
Scarce heard ; nor word from word could I divide ;
And the whole body of the Man did seem
Like one whom I had met with in a dream ;
Or like a man from some far region sent,
To give me human strength, by apt admonishment.

My former thoughts returned : the fear that kills ;
And hope that is unwilling to be fed ;
Cold, pain, and labour, and all fleshly ills ;
And mighty Poets in their misery dead.
—Perplexed, and longing to be comforted,
My question eagerly did I renew,
" How is it that you live, and what is it you do ? "

He with a smile did then his words repeat ;
And said, that, gathering leeches, far and wide
He travelled ; stirring thus about his feet
The waters of the pools where they abide.
" Once I could meet with them on every side ;
But they have dwindled long by slow decay ;
Yet still I persevere, and find them where I may."

While he was talking thus, the lonely place,
The old Man's shape, and speech—all troubled me :
In my mind's eye I seemed to see him pace
About the weary moors continually,
Wandering about alone and silently.
While I these thoughts within myself pursued,
He, having made a pause, the same discourse renewed.

And soon with this he other matter blended,
Cheerfully uttered, with demeanour kind,
But stately in the main ; and when he ended,
I could have laughed myself to scorn to find
In that decrepit Man so firm a mind.
" God," said I, " be my help and stay secure ;
I'll think of the Leech-gatherer on the lonely moor ! "

THE THORN

" There is a Thorn—it looks so old,
In truth, you'd find it hard to say
How it could ever have been young,
It looks so old and grey.
Not higher than a two years' child
It stands erect, this aged Thorn ;
No leaves it has, no prickly points ;
It is a mass of knotted joints,
A wretched thing forlorn.
It stands erect, and like a stone
With lichens is it overgrown.

" Like rock or stone, it is o'ergrown,
With lichens to the very top,
And hung with heavy tufts of moss,
A melancholy crop :
Up from the earth these mosses creep,
And this poor Thorn they clasp it round
So close, you'd say that they are bent
With plain and manifest intent
To drag it to the ground ;
And all have joined in one endeavour
To bury this poor Thorn for ever.

" High on a mountain's highest ridge,
Where oft the stormy winter gale
Cuts like a scythe, while through the clouds
It sweeps from vale to vale ;
Not five yards from the mountain path,
This Thorn you on your left espy ;
And to the left, three yards beyond,
You see a little muddy pond
Of water—never dry
Though but of compass small, and bare
To thirsty suns and parching air.

" And, close beside this aged Thorn,
There is a fresh and lovely sight,
A beauteous heap, a hill of moss,
Just half a foot in height.
All lovely colours there you see,
All colours that were ever seen ;
And mossy network too is there,
As if by hand of lady fair
The work had woven been ;
And cups, the darlings of the eye,
So deep is their vermilion dye.

" Ah me ! what lovely tints are there
Of olive green and scarlet bright.
In spikes, in branches, and in stars,
Green, red, and pearly white !
This heap of earth o'ergrown with moss,
Which close beside the Thorn you see,
So fresh in all its beauteous dyes,
Is like an infant's grave in size,
As like as like can be ;
But never, never any where,
An infant's grave was half so fair.

" Now would you see this aged Thorn,
This pond, and beauteous hill of moss,
You must take care and choose your time
The mountain when to cross.
For oft there sits between the heap
So like an infant's grave in size,
And that same pond of which I spoke,
A Woman in a scarlet cloak,
And to herself she cries,
' Oh misery ! oh misery !
Oh woe is me ! oh misery ! '

" At all times of the day and night
This wretched Woman thither goes ;

And she is known to every star,
And every wind that blows ;
And there, beside the Thorn, she sits
When the blue daylight's in the skies,
And when the whirlwind's on the hill,
Or frosty air is keen and still,
And to herself she cries,
' Oh misery ! oh misery !
Oh woe is me ! oh misery ! ' "

" Now wherefore, thus, by day and night,
In rain, in tempest, and in snow,
Thus to the dreary mountain-top
Does this poor Woman go ?
And why sits she beside the Thorn
When the blue daylight's in the sky,
Or when the whirlwind's on the hill,
Or frosty air is keen and still,
And wherefore does she cry ?—
O wherefore ? wherefore ? tell me why
Does she repeat that doleful cry ? "

" I cannot tell ; I wish I could ;
For the true reason no one knows ;
But would you gladly view the spot,
The spot to which she goes ;
The hillock like an infant's grave,
The pond—and Thorn, so old and grey ;
Pass by her door—'tis seldom shut—
And, if you see her in her hut—
Then to the spot away !
I never heard of such as dare
Approach the spot when she is there."

" But wherefore to the mountain-top
Can this unhappy Woman go ?
Whatever star is in the skies,
Whatever wind may blow ? "

" Full twenty years are past and gone
Since she (her name is Martha Ray)
Gave with a maiden's true good-will
Her company to Stephen Hill ;
And she was blithe and gay,
While friends and kindred all approved
Of him whom tenderly she loved.

" And they had fixed the wedding day,
The morning that must wed them both ;
But Stephen to another Maid
Had sworn another oath ;
And, with this other Maid, to church
Unthinking Stephen went—
Poor Martha ! on that woeful day
A pang of pitiless dismay
Into her soul was sent ;
A fire was kindled in her breast,
Which might not burn itself to rest.

" They say, full six months after this,
While yet the summer leaves were green,
She to the mountain-top would go,
And there was often seen.
What could she seek ? or wish to hide ?
Her state to any eye was plain ;
She was with child, and she was mad ;
Yet often was she sober sad
From her exceeding pain.
O guilty Father—would that death
Had saved him from that breach of faith !

" Sad case for such a brain to hold
Communion with a stirring child !
Sad case, as you may think, for one
Who had a brain so wild !
Last Christmas-eve we talked of this,
And grey-haired Wilfred of the glen

Held that the unborn infant wrought
About its mother's heart, and brought
Her senses back again :
And, when at last her time drew near,
Her looks were calm, her senses clear.

" More know I not, I wish I did,
And it should all be told to you ;
For what became of this poor child
No mortal ever knew ;
Nay—if a child to her was born
No earthly tongue could ever tell ;
And if 'twas born alive or dead,
Far less could this with proof be said ;
But some remember well,
That Martha Ray about this time
Would up the mountain often climb.

" And all that winter, when at night
The wind blew from the mountain-peak,
'Twas worth your while, though in the dark,
The churchyard path to seek :
For many a time and oft were heard
Cries coming from the mountain head :
Some plainly living voices were ;
And others, I've heard many swear,
Were voices of the dead :
I cannot think, whate'er they say,
They had to do with Martha Ray.

" But that she goes to this old Thorn,
The Thorn which I described to you,
And there sits in a scarlet cloak
I will be sworn is true.
For one day with my telescope,
To view the ocean wide and bright,
When to this country first I came,
Ere I had heard of Martha's name,
I climbed the mountain's height :—

A storm came on, and I could see
No object higher than my knee.

" 'Twas mist and rain, and storm and rain :
No screen, no fence could I discover ;
And then the wind ! in sooth, it was
A wind full ten times over.
I looked around, I thought I saw
A jutting crag,—and off I ran,
Head-foremost, through the driving rain,
The shelter of the crag to gain ;
And, as I am a man,
Instead of jutting crag, I found
A Woman seated on the ground.

" I did not speak—I saw her face ;
Her face !—it was enough for me ;
I turned about and heard her cry,
' Oh misery ! oh misery ! '
And there she sits, until the moon
Through half the clear blue sky will go ;
And, when the little breezes make
The waters of the pond to shake,
As all the country know,
She shudders, and you hear her cry,
' Oh misery ! oh misery ! ' "

" But what's the Thorn ? and what's the pond ?
And what the hill of moss to her ?
And what the creeping breeze that comes
The little pond to stir ? "
" I cannot tell ; but some will say
She hanged her baby on the tree ;
Some say she drowned it in the pond,
Which is a little step beyond :
But all and each agree,
The little Babe was buried there,
Beneath that hill of moss so fair.

" I've heard, the moss is spotted red
With drops of that poor infant's blood ;
But kill a new-born infant thus,
I do not think she could !
Some say, if to the pond you go,
And fix on it a steady view,
The shadow of a babe you trace,
A baby and a baby's face,
And that it looks at you ;
Whene'er you look on it, 'tis plain
The baby looks at you again.

" And some had sworn an oath that she
Should be to public justice brought ;
And for the little infant's bones
With spades they would have sought.
But instantly the hill of moss
Before their eyes began to stir !
And, for full fifty yards around,
The grass—it shook upon the ground !
Yet all do still aver
The little Babe lies buried there,
Beneath that hill of moss so fair.

" I cannot tell how this may be,
But plain it is the Thorn is bound
With heavy tufts of moss that strive
To drag it to the ground ;
And this I know, full many a time,
When she was on the mountain high,
By day, and in the silent night,
When all the stars shone clear and bright,
That I have heard her cry,
' Oh misery ! oh misery !
Oh woe is me ! oh misery ! ' "

HART-LEAP WELL

[Hart-leap Well is a small spring of water, about five miles from Richmond in Yorkshire, and near the side of the road that leads from Richmond to Askrigg. Its name is derived from a remarkable Chase, the memory of which is preserved by the monuments spoken of in the second Part of the following Poem, which monuments do now exist as I have there described them.]

THE Knight had ridden down from Wensley Moor
With the slow motion of a summer's cloud,
And now, as he approached a vassal's door,
" Bring forth another horse ! " he cried aloud.

" Another horse ! "—That shout the vassal heard
And saddled his best Steed, a comely grey ;
Sir Walter mounted him ; he was the third
Which he had mounted on that glorious day.

Joy sparkled in the prancing courser's eyes ;
The horse and horseman are a happy pair ;
But, though Sir Walter like a falcon flies,
There is a doleful silence in the air.

A rout this morning left Sir Walter's Hall,
That as they galloped made the echoes roar ;
But horse and man are vanished, one and all ;
Such race, I think, was never seen before.

Sir Walter, restless as a veering wind,
Calls to the few tired dogs that yet remain :
Blanch, Swift, and Music, noblest of their kind,
Follow, and up the weary mountain strain.

The Knight hallooed, he cheered and chid them on
With suppliant gestures and upbraidings stern ;
But breath and eyesight fail ; and, one by one,
The dogs are stretched among the mountain fern.

Where is the throng, the tumult of the race?
The bugles that so joyfully were blown?
—This chase it looks not like an earthly chase;
Sir Walter and the Hart are left alone.

The poor Hart toils along the mountain-side;
I will not stop to tell how far he fled,
Nor will I mention by what death he died;
But now the Knight beholds him lying dead.

Dismounting, then, he leaned against a thorn;
He had no follower, dog, nor man, nor boy:
He neither cracked his whip, nor blew his horn,
But gazed upon the spoil with silent joy.

Close to the thorn on which Sir Walter leaned,
Stood his dumb partner in this glorious feat;
Weak as a lamb the hour that it is yeaned;
And white with foam as if with cleaving sleet.

Upon his side the Hart was lying stretched:
His nostril touched a spring beneath a hill,
And with the last deep groan his breath had fetched
The waters of the spring were trembling still.

And now, too happy for repose or rest,
(Never had living man such joyful lot!)
Sir Walter walked all round, north, south, and west,
And gazed and gazed upon that darling spot.

And climbing up the hill—(it was at least
Four roods of sheer ascent) Sir Walter found
Three several hoof-marks which the hunted Beast
Had left imprinted on the grassy ground.

Sir Walter wiped his face, and cried, " Till now
Such sight was never seen by human eyes:
Three leaps have borne him from this lofty brow,
Down to the very fountain where he lies.

" I'll build a pleasure-house upon this spot,
And a small arbour, made for rural joy ;
'Twill be the traveller's shed, the pilgrim's cot,
A place of love for damsels that are coy.

" A cunning artist will I have to frame
A basin for that fountain in the dell !
And they who do make mention of the same,
From this day forth, shall call it HART-LEAP WELL.

" And, gallant Stag ! to make thy praises known,
Another monument shall here be raised ;
Three several pillars, each a rough-hewn stone,
And planted where thy hoofs the turf have grazed.

" And, in the summer-time when days are long,
I will come hither with my Paramour ;
And with the dancers and the minstrel's song
We will make merry in that pleasant bower.

" Till the foundations of the mountains fail
My mansion with its arbour shall endure ;—
The joy of them who till the fields of Swale,
And them who dwell among the woods of Ure ! "

Then home he went, and left the Hart, stone-dead,
With breathless nostrils stretched above the spring.
—Soon did the Knight perform what he had said ;
And far and wide the fame thereof did ring.

Ere thrice the Moon into her port had steered,
A cup of stone received the living well ;
Three pillars of rude stone Sir Walter reared,
And built a house of pleasure in the dell.

And near the fountain, flowers of stature tall
With trailing plants and trees were intertwined,—
Which soon composed a little sylvan hall,
A leafy shelter from the sun and wind.

And thither, when the summer days were long,
Sir Walter led his wondering Paramour ;
And with the dancers and the minstrel's song
Made merriment within that pleasant bower.

The Knight, Sir Walter, died in course of time,
And his bones lie in his paternal vale.—
But there is matter for a second rhyme,
And I to this would add another tale.

PART SECOND

The moving accident is not my trade ;
To freeze the blood I have no ready arts :
'Tis my delight, alone in summer shade,
To pipe a simple song for thinking hearts.

As I from Hawes to Richmond did repair,
It chanced that I saw standing in a dell
Three aspens at three corners of a square ;
And one, not four yards distant, near a well.

What this imported I could ill divine :
And, pulling now the rein my horse to stop,
I saw three pillars standing in a line,—
The last stone-pillar on a dark hill-top.

The trees were grey, with neither arms nor head ;
Half wasted the square mound of tawny green ;
So that you just might say, as then I said,
" Here in old time the hand of man hath been."

I looked upon the hill both far and near,
More doleful place did never eye survey ;
It seemed as if the spring-time came not here,
And Nature here were willing to decay.

I stood in various thoughts and fancies lost,
When one, who was in shepherd's garb attired,
Came up the hollow :—him did I accost,
And what this place might be I then inquired.

The Shepherd stopped, and that same story told
Which in my former rhyme I have rehearsed.
" A jolly place," said he, " in times of old !
But something ails it now : the spot is curst.

" You see these lifeless stumps of aspen wood—
Some say that they are beeches, others elms—
These were the bower ; and here a mansion stood,
The finest palace of a hundred realms !

" The arbour does its own condition tell ;
You see the stones, the fountain, and the stream ;
But as to the great Lodge ! you might as well
Hunt half a day for a forgotten dream.

" There's neither dog nor heifer, horse nor sheep,
Will wet his lips within that cup of stone ;
And oftentimes, when all are fast asleep,
This water doth send forth a dolorous groan.

" Some say that here a murder has been done,
And blood cries out for blood : but, for my part,
I've guessed, when I've been sitting in the sun,
That it was all for that unhappy Hart.

" What thoughts must through the creature's brain have
        past !
Even from the topmost stone, upon the steep,
Are but three bounds—and look, Sir, at this last—
O Master ! it has been a cruel leap.

" For thirteen hours he ran a desperate race ;
And in my simple mind we cannot tell
What cause the Hart might have to love this place,
And come and make his death-bed near the well.

" Here on the grass perhaps asleep he sank,
Lulled by the fountain in the summer-tide ;
This water was perhaps the first he drank
When he had wandered from his mother's side.

" In April here beneath the flowering thorn
He heard the birds their morning carols sing ;
And he, perhaps, for aught we know, was born
Not half a furlong from that self-same spring.

" Now, here is neither grass nor pleasant shade ;
The sun on drearier hollow never shone ;
So will it be, as I have often said,
Till trees, and stones, and fountain, all are gone."

" Grey-headed Shepherd, thou hast spoken well ;
Small difference lies between thy creed and mine :
This Beast not unobserved by Nature fell ;
His death was mourned by sympathy divine.

" The Being, that is in the clouds and air,
That is in the green leaves among the groves,
Maintains a deep and reverential care
For the unoffending creatures whom he loves.

" The pleasure-house is dust :—behind, before,
This is no common waste, no common gloom ;
But Nature, in due course of time, once more
Shall here put on her beauty and her bloom.

" She leaves these objects to a slow decay,
That what we are, and have been, may be known ;
But at the coming of the milder day,
These monuments shall all be overgrown.

" One lesson, Shepherd, let us two divide,
Taught both by what she shows, and what conceals ;
Never to blend our pleasure or our pride
With sorrow of the meanest thing that feels."

SONG AT THE FEAST OF BROUGHAM CASTLE

UPON THE RESTORATION OF LORD CLIFFORD, THE SHEP-
HERD, TO THE ESTATES AND HONOURS OF HIS
ANCESTORS.*

HIGH in the breathless Hall the Minstrel sate,
And Emont's murmur mingled with the Song.—
The words of ancient time I thus translate,
A festal strain that hath been silent long :—

* Henry Lord Clifford, etc., who is the subject of this poem, was the
son of John Lord Clifford, who was slain at Towton Field, which John
Lord Clifford, as is known to the reader of English history, was the
person who after the Battle of Wakefield slew, in the pursuit, the
young Earl of Rutland, son of the Duke of York, who had fallen in
the battle, " in part of revenge " (say the authors of the *History of
Cumberland and Westmoreland*) ; " for the Earl's father had slain his,"
A deed which worthily blemished the author (saith Speed) ; but who,
as he adds, " dare promise any thing temperate of himself in the heat
of martial fury ? chiefly, when it was resolved not to leave any branch
of the York line standing ; for so one maketh this Lord to speak."
This, no doubt, I would observe by the bye, was an action sufficiently
in the vindictive spirit of the times, and yet not altogether so bad as
represented ; " for the Earl was no child, as some writers would have
him, but able to bear arms, being sixteen or seventeen years of age,
as is evident from this (say the Memoirs of the Countess of Pembroke,
who was laudably anxious to wipe away, as far as could be, this stigma
from the illustrious name to which she was born), that he was the next
child to King Edward the Fourth, which his mother had by Richard
Duke of York, and that King was then eighteen years of age : and for
the small distance betwixt her children, see Austin Vincent, in his *Book
of Nobility*, p. 622, where he writes of them all." It may further be
observed, that Lord Clifford, who was then himself only twenty-five
years of age, had been a leading man and commander two or three
years together in the army of Lancaster, before this time ; and, therefore, would be less likely to think that the Earl of Rutland might be
entitled to mercy from his youth.—But, independent of this act, at
best a cruel and savage one, the Family of Clifford had done enough
to draw upon them the vehement hatred of the House of York : so

" From town to town, from tower to tower,
    The red rose is a gladsome flower.
Her thirty years of winter past,
The red rose is revived at last ;
She lifts her head for endless spring,
For everlasting blossoming :
Both roses flourish, red and white :
In love and sisterly delight
    The two that were at strife are blended,
    And all old troubles now are ended.—

that after the Battle of Towton there was no hope for them but in
flight and concealment.   Henry, the subject of the poem, was deprived
of his estate and honours during the space of twenty-four years ; all
which time he lived as a shepherd in Yorkshire, or in Cumberland,
where the estate of his father-in-law (Sir Lancelot Threlkeld) lay.   He
was restored to his estate and honours in the first year of Henry the
Seventh.   It is recorded that, " when called to Parliament, he behaved
nobly and wisely ; but otherwise came seldom to London or the Court ;
and rather delighted to live in the country, where he repaired several
of his castles, which had gone to decay during the late troubles."
Thus far is chiefly collected from Nicholson and Burn ; and I can add,
from my own knowledge, that there is a tradition current in the village
of Threlkeld and its neighbourhood, his principal retreat, that in the
course of his shepherd-life he had acquired great astronomical knowledge.   I cannot conclude this note without adding a word upon the
subject of those numerous and noble feudal edifices, spoken of in the
poem, the ruins of some of which are, at this day, so great an ornament to that interesting country.   The Cliffords had always been distinguished for an honourable pride in these castles ; and we have seen
that, after the wars of York and Lancaster, they were rebuilt ; in the
civil wars of Charles the First they were again laid waste, and again
restored almost to their former magnificence by the celebrated Lady
Anne Clifford, Countess of Pembroke, etc.   Not more than twenty-
five years after this was done, when the estates of Clifford had passed
into the Family of Tufton, three of these castles, namely, Brough,
Brougham, and Pendragon, were demolished, and the timber and other
materials sold by Thomas Earl of Thanet.   We will hope that, when
this order was issued, the Earl had not consulted the text of Isaiah,
58th chap. 12th verse, to which the inscription placed over the gate
of Pendragon Castle by the Countess of Pembroke (I believe his grand-
mother), at the time she repaired that structure, refers the reader :—
" *And they that shall be of thee shall build the old waste places : thou
shalt raise up the foundations of many generations ; and thou shalt be
called, The repairer of the breach, The restorer of paths to dwell in.*"   The
Earl of Thanet, the present possessor of the estates, with a due respect
for the memory of his ancestors, and a proper sense of the value and
beauty of these remains of antiquity, has (I am told) given orders
that they shall be preserved from all depredations.

Joy ! joy to both ! but most to her
Who is the flower of Lancaster !
Behold her how She smiles to-day
On this great throng, this bright array !
Fair greeting doth she send to all
From every corner of the hall ;
But chiefly from above the board
Where sits in state our rightful Lord,
A Clifford to his own restored !
   They came with banner, spear, and shield,
And it was proved in Bosworth-field.
Not long the Avenger was withstood—
Earth helped him with the cry of blood :
St. George was for us, and the might
Of blessed Angels crowned the right.
Loud voice the Land has uttered forth,
We loudest in the faithful north :
Our fields rejoice, our mountains ring,
Our streams proclaim a welcoming ;
Our strong-abodes and castles see
The glory of their loyalty.
   How glad is Skipton at this hour—
Though lonely, a deserted Tower ;
Knight, squire, and yeoman, page and groom :
We have them at the feast of Brough'm.
How glad Pendragon—though the sleep
Of years be on her !—She shall reap
A taste of this great pleasure, viewing
As in a dream her own renewing.
Rejoiced is Brough, right glad I deem
Beside her little humble stream ;
And she that keepeth watch and ward
Her statelier Eden's course to guard ;
They both are happy at this hour,
Though each is but a lonely Tower :—
But here is perfect joy and pride
For one fair House by Emont's side,
This day, distinguished without peer

To see her Master and to cheer—
Him, and his Lady-mother dear !
  Oh ! it was a time forlorn
When the fatherless was born—
Give her wings that she may fly,
Or she sees her infant die !
Swords that are with slaughter wild
Hunt the Mother and the Child.
Who will take them from the light ?
—Yonder is a man in sight—
Yonder is a house—but where ?
No, they must not enter there.
To the caves, and to the brooks,
To the clouds of heaven she looks ;
She is speechless, but her eyes
Pray in ghostly agonies.
Blissful Mary, Mother mild,
Maid and Mother undefiled,
Save a Mother and her Child !

  Now Who is he that bounds with joy
On Carrock's side, a Shepherd-boy ?
No thoughts hath he but thoughts that pass
Light as the wind along the grass.
Can this be He who hither came
In secret, like a smothered flame ?
O'er whom such thankful tears were shed
For shelter, and a poor man's bread !
God loves the Child ; and God hath willed
That those dear words should be fulfilled,
The Lady's words, when forced away,
The last she to her Babe did say :
' My own, my own, thy Fellow-guest
I may not be ; but rest thee, rest,
For lowly shepherd's life is best ! '

  Alas ! when evil men are strong
No life is good, no pleasure long.
The Boy must part from Mosedale's groves,
And leave Blencathara's rugged coves,

And quit the flowers that summer brings
To Glenderamakin's lofty springs ;
Must vanish, and his careless cheer
Be turned to heaviness and fear.
—Give Sir Lancelot Threlkeld praise !
Hear it, good man, old in days !
Thou tree of covert and of rest
For this young Bird that is distrest ;
Among thy branches safe he lay,
And he was free to sport and play,
When falcons were abroad for prey.

  A recreant harp, that sings of fear
And heaviness in Clifford's ear !
I said, when evil men are strong,
No life is good, no pleasure long,
A weak and cowardly untruth !
Our Clifford was a happy Youth,
And thankful through a weary time,
That brought him up to manhood's prime.
—Again he wanders forth at will,
And tends a flock from hill to hill :
His garb is humble ; ne'er was seen
Such garb with such a noble mien ;
Among the shepherd grooms no mate
Hath he, a Child of strength and state !
Yet lacks not friends for simple glee,
Nor yet for higher sympathy.
To his side the fallow-deer
Came, and rested without fear ;
The eagle, lord of land and sea,
Stooped down to pay him fealty ;
And both the undying fish that swim
Through Bowscale-tarn did wait on him ;
The pair were servants of his eye
In their immortality ;
And glancing, gleaming, dark or bright,
Moved to and fro, for his delight.
He knew the rocks which Angels haunt

Upon the mountains visitant ;
He hath kenned them taking wing :
And into caves where Faeries sing
He hath entered ; and been told
By voices how men lived of old.
Among the heavens his eye can see
The face of thing that is to be ;
And, if that men report him right,
His tongue could whisper words of might.
—Now another day is come,
Fitter hope, and nobler doom ;
He hath thrown aside his crook,
And hath buried deep his book ;
Armour rusting in his halls
On the blood of Clifford calls ;—
' Quell the Scot,' exclaims the Lance—
Bear me to the heart of France,
Is the longing of the Shield—
Tell thy name, thou trembling Field ;
Field of death, where'er thou be,
Groan thou with our victory !
Happy day, and mighty hour,
When our Shepherd, in his power,
Mailed and horsed, with lance and sword,
To his ancestors restored
Like a reappearing Star,
Like a glory from afar,
First shall head the flock of war ! "

Alas ! the impassioned minstrel did not know
How, by Heaven's grace, this Clifford's heart was framed,
How he, long forced in humble walks to go,
Was softened into feeling, soothed, and tamed.

Love had he found in huts where poor men lie ;
His daily teachers had been woods and rills,
The silence that is in the starry sky,
The sleep that is among the lonely hills.

In him the savage virtue of the Race,
Revenge, and all ferocious thoughts were dead :
Nor did he change ; but kept in lofty place
The wisdom which adversity had bred.

Glad were the vales, and every cottage hearth ;
The Shepherd-lord was honoured more and more ;
And, ages after he was laid in earth,
" The good Lord Clifford " was the name he bore.

PETER BELL

A TALE

What's in a *Name ?*

. . . .

Brutus will start a Spirit as soon as Cæsar !

To ROBERT SOUTHEY, Esq., P.L., etc., etc.

MY DEAR FRIEND,
        The Tale of Peter Bell, which I now introduce
to your notice, and to that of the Public, has, in its Manuscript state, nearly survived its *minority ;*—for it first
saw the light in the summer of 1798.   During this long
interval, pains have been taken at different times to
make the production less unworthy of a favourable recep-
tion ; or, rather, to fit it for filling *permanently* a station,
however humble, in the Literature of our Country.   This
has, indeed, been the aim of all my endeavours in Poetry,
which, you know, have been sufficiently laborious to
prove that I deem the Art not lightly to be approached ;
and that the attainment of excellence in it may laudably
be made the principal object of intellectual pursuit by
any man, who, with reasonable consideration of circumstances, has faith in his own impulses.
The Poem of Peter Bell, as the Prologue will show, was

composed under a belief that the Imagination not only does not require for its exercise the intervention of super-natural agency, but that, though such agency be ex-cluded, the faculty may be called forth as imperiously and for kindred results of pleasure, by incidents, within the compass of poetic probability, in the humblest de-partments of daily life. Since that Prologue was written, *you* have exhibited most splendid effects of judicious dar-ing, in the opposite and usual course. Let this acknow-ledgment make my peace with the lovers of the super-natural ; and I am persuaded it will be admitted, that to you, as a Master in that province of the Art, the following Tale, whether from contrast or congruity, is not an unappropriate offering. Accept it, then, as a public testimony of affectionate admiration from one with whose name yours has been often coupled (to use your own words) for evil and for good ; and believe me to be, with earnest wishes that life and health may be granted you to complete the many important works in which you are engaged, and with high respect, most faithfully yours,

WILLIAM WORDSWORTH.

Rydal Mount, April 7, 1819.

PROLOGUE

THERE'S something in a flying horse,
There's something in a huge balloon ;
But through the clouds I'll never float
Until I have a little Boat,
Shaped like the crescent-moon.

And now I *have* a little Boat,
In shape a very crescent-moon.
Fast through the clouds my boat can sail ;
But if perchance your faith should fail,
Look up—and you shall see me soon !

The woods, my Friends, are round you roaring,
Rocking and roaring like a sea ;
The noise of danger's in your ears,
And ye have all a thousand fears
Both for my little Boat and me !

Meanwhile untroubled I admire
The pointed horns of my canoe ;
And, did not pity touch my breast,
To see how ye are all distrest,
Till my ribs ached, I'd laugh at you !

Away we go, my Boat and I—
Frail man ne'er sate in such another :
Whether among the winds we strive,
Or deep into the clouds we dive,
Each is contented with the other.

Away we go—and what care we
For treasons, tumults, and for wars ?
We are as calm in our delight
As is the crescent-moon so bright
Among the scattered stars.

Up goes my Boat among the stars
Through many a breathless field of light,
Through many a long blue field of ether,
Leaving ten thousand stars beneath her :
Up goes my little Boat so bright !

The Crab, the Scorpion, and the Bull—
We pry among them all ; have shot
High o'er the red-haired race of Mars,
Covered from top to toe with scars ;
Such company I like it not !

The towns in Saturn are decayed,
And melancholy Spectres throng them ;—

The Pleiads, that appear to kiss
Each other in the vast abyss,
With joy I sail among them.

Swift Mercury resounds with mirth,
Great Jove is full of stately bowers ;
But these, and all that they contain,
What are they to that tiny grain,
That little Earth of ours ?

Then back to Earth, the dear green Earth :—
Whole ages if I here should roam,
The world for my remarks and me
Would not a whit the better be ;
I've left my heart at home.

See ! there she is, the matchless Earth !
There spreads the famed Pacific Ocean !
Old Andes thrusts yon craggy spear
Through the grey clouds ; the Alps are here,
Like waters in commotion !

Yon tawny slip is Libya's sands ;
That silver thread the river Dnieper !
And look, where clothed in brightest green
Is a sweet Isle, of isles the Queen ;
Ye fairies, from all evil keep her !

And see the town where I was born !
Around those happy fields we span
In boyish gambols ;—I was lost
Where I have been, but on this coast
I feel I am a man.

Never did fifty things at once
Appear so lovely, never, never ;—
How tunefully the forests ring !
To hear the earth's soft murmuring
Thus could I hang for ever !

" Shame on you ! " cried my little Boat,
" Was ever such a homesick Loon,
Within a living Boat to sit,
And make no better use of it ;
A Boat twin-sister of the crescent-moon !

" Ne'er in the breast of full-grown Poet
Fluttered so faint a heart before ;—
Was it the music of the spheres
That overpowered your mortal ears ?
—Such din shall trouble them no more.

" These nether precincts do not lack
Charms of their own ;—then come with me ;
I want a comrade, and for you
There's nothing that I would not do ;
Nought is there that you shall not see.

" Haste ! and above Siberian snows
We'll sport amid the boreal morning ;
Will mingle with her lustres gliding
Among the stars, the stars now hiding,
And now the stars adorning.

" I know the secrets of a land
Where human foot did never stray ;
Fair is that land as evening skies,
And cool, though in the depth it lies
Of burning Africa.

" Or we'll into the realm of Faery,
Among the lovely shades of things ;
The shadowy forms of mountains bare,
And streams, and bowers, and ladies fair,
The shades of palaces and kings !

" Or, if you thirst with hardy zeal
Less quiet regions to explore,

Prompt voyage shall to you reveal
How earth and heaven are taught to feel
The might of magic lore ! "

" My little vagrant Form of light,
My gay and beautiful Canoe,
Well have you played your friendly part ;
As kindly take what from my heart
Experience forces—then adieu !

" Temptation lurks among your words ;
But, while these pleasures you're pursuing
Without impediment or let,
No wonder if you quite forget
What on the earth is doing.

" There was a time when all mankind
Did listen with a faith sincere
To tuneful tongues in mystery versed ;
Then Poets fearlessly rehearsed
The wonders of a wild career.

" Go—(but the world's a sleepy world,
And 'tis, I fear, an age too late)
Take with you some ambitious Youth !
For, restless Wanderer ! I, in truth,
Am all unfit to be your mate.

" Long have I loved what I behold,
The night that calms, the day that cheers ;
The common growth of mother-earth
Suffices me—her tears, her mirth,
Her humblest mirth and tears.

" The dragon's wing, the magic ring,
I shall not covet for my dower,
If I along that lowly way
With sympathetic heart may stray,
And with a soul of power.

" These given, what more need I desire
To stir, to soothe, or elevate ?
What nobler marvels than the mind
May in life's daily prospect find,
May find or there create ?

" A potent wand doth Sorrow wield ;
What spell so strong as guilty Fear !
Repentance is a tender Sprite ;
If aught on earth have heavenly might,
'Tis lodged within her silent tear.

" But grant my wishes,—let us now
Descend from this ethereal height ;
Then take thy way, adventurous Skiff,
More daring far than Hippogriff,
And be thy own delight !

" To the stone-table in my garden,
Loved haunt of many a summer hour,
The Squire is come : his daughter Bess
Beside him in the cool recess
Sits blooming like a flower.

" With these are many more convened ;
They know not I have been so far ;—
I see them there, in number nine,
Beneath the spreading Weymouth-pine !
I see them—there they are !

" There sits the Vicar and his Dame ;
And there my good friend, Stephen Otter ;
And, ere the light of evening fail,
To them I must relate the Tale
Of Peter Bell the Potter."

Off flew the Boat—away she flees,
Spurning her freight with indignation !

And I, as well as I was able,
On two poor legs, toward my stone-table
Limped on with sore vexation.

" O, here he is ! " cried little Bess—
She saw me at the garden door ;
" We've waited anxiously and long,"
They cried, and all around me throng,
Full nine of them or more !

" Reproach me not—your fears be still—
Be thankful we again have met ;—
Resume, my Friends ! within the shade
Your seats, and quickly shall be paid
The well-remembered debt."

I spake with faltering voice, like one
Not wholly rescued from the pale
Of a wild dream, or worse illusion ;
But, straight, to cover my confusion,
Began the promised Tale.

PART FIRST

ALL by the moonlight river side
Groaned the poor Beast—alas ! in vain ;
The staff was raised to loftier height,
And the blows fell with heavier weight
As Peter struck—and struck again.

" Hold ! " cried the Squire, " against the rules
Of common sense you're surely sinning ;
This leap is for us all too bold ;
Who Peter was, let that be told,
And start from the beginning."

——" A Potter,* Sir, he was by trade,"
Said I, becoming quite collected ;
" And wheresoever he appeared,
Full twenty times was Peter feared
For once that Peter was respected.

" He, two-and-thirty years or more,
Had been a wild and woodland rover ;
Had heard the Atlantic surges roar
On farthest Cornwall's rocky shore,
And trod the cliffs of Dover.

" And he had seen Caernarvon's towers,
And well he knew the spire of Sarum ;
And he had been where Lincoln bell
Flings o'er the fen that ponderous knell—
A far-renowned alarum !

" At Doncaster, at York, and Leeds,
And merry Carlisle had he been ;
And all along the Lowlands fair,
All through the bonny shire of Ayr
And far as Aberdeen.

" And he had been at Inverness ;
And Peter, by the mountain-rills,
Had danced his round with Highland lassies ;
And he had lain beside his asses
On lofty Cheviot Hills :

" And he had trudged through Yorkshire dales,
Among the rocks and winding *scars ;*
Where deep and low the hamlets lie
Beneath their little patch of sky
And little lot of stars :

---

* In the dialect of the North, a hawker of earthenware is thus designated.

(2,508)

7

" And all along the indented coast,
Bespattered with the salt-sea foam ;
Where'er a knot of houses lay
On headland, or in hollow bay ;—
Sure never man like him did roam !

" As well might Peter, in the Fleet,
Have been fast bound, a begging debtor ;—
He travelled here, he travelled there ;—
But not the value of a hair
Was heart or head the better.

" He roved among the vales and streams,
In the green wood and hollow dell ;
They were his dwellings night and day,—
But nature ne'er could find the way
Into the heart of Peter Bell.

" In vain, through every changeful year,
Did Nature lead him as before ;
A primrose by a river's brim
A yellow primrose was to him,
And it was nothing more.

" Small change it made on Peter's heart
To see his gentle panniered train
With more than vernal pleasure feeding,
Where'er the tender grass was leading
Its earliest green along the lane.

" In vain, through water, earth, and air,
The soul of happy sound was spread,
When Peter on some April morn,
Beneath the broom or budding thorn,
Made the warm earth his lazy bed.

" At noon, when, by the forest's edge,
He lay beneath the branches high,

The soft blue sky did never melt
Into his heart ; he never felt
The witchery of the soft blue sky !

" On a fair prospect some have looked
And felt, as I have heard them say,
As if the moving time had been
A thing as steadfast as the scene
On which they gazed themselves away.

" Within the breast of Peter Bell
The silent raptures found no place
He was a Carl as wild and rude
As ever hue-and-cry pursued,
As ever ran a felon's race.

" Of all that lead a lawless life,
Of all that love their lawless lives,
In city or in village small,
He was the wildest far of all ;—
He had a dozen wedded wives.

" Nay, start not !—wedded wives and twelve !
But how one wife could e'er come near him,
In simple truth I cannot tell ;
For, be it said of Peter Bell,
To see him was to fear him.

" Though Nature could not touch his heart
By lovely forms, and silent weather,
And tender sounds, yet you might see
At once, that Peter Bell and she
Had often been together.

" A savage wildness round him hung
As of a dweller out of doors ;
In his whole figure and his mien
A savage character was seen
Of mountains and of dreary moors.

" To all the unshaped half-human thoughts
Which solitary Nature feeds
'Mid summer storms or winter's ice,
Had Peter joined whatever vice
The cruel city breeds.

" His face was keen as is the wind
That cuts along the hawthorn-fence ;—
Of courage you saw little there,
But, in its stead, a medley air
Of cunning and of impudence.

" He had a dark and sidelong walk,
And long and slouching was his gait ;
Beneath his looks so bare and bold,
You might perceive, his spirit cold
Was playing with some inward bait.

" His forehead wrinkled was and furred ;
A work, one half of which was done
By thinking of his ' *whens* ' and ' *hows* ; '
And half, by knitting of his brows
Beneath the glaring sun.

" There was a hardness in his cheek,
There was a hardness in his eye,
As if the man had fixed his face,
In many a solitary place,
Against the wind and open sky ! "

ONE NIGHT, (and now my little Bess !
We've reached at last the promised Tale :)
One beautiful November night,
When the full moon was shining bright
Upon the rapid river Swale,

Along the river's winding banks
Peter was travelling all alone ;—
Whether to buy or sell, or led
By pleasure running in his head,
To me was never known.

He trudged along through copse and brake,
He trudged along o'er hill and dale ;
Nor for the moon cared he a tittle,
And for the stars he cared as little,
And for the murmuring river Swale.

But, chancing to espy a path
That promised to cut short the way
As many a wiser man hath done,
He left a trusty guide for one
That might his steps betray.

To a thick wood he soon is brought
Where cheerily his course he weaves,
And whistling loud may yet be heard,
Though often buried, like a bird
Darkling, among the boughs and leaves.

But quickly Peter's mood is changed,
And on he drives with cheeks that burn
In downright fury and in wrath ;—
There's little sign the treacherous path
Will to the road return !

The path grows dim, and dimmer still ;
Now up, now down, the Rover wends,
With all the sail that he can carry,
Till brought to a deserted quarry—
And there the pathway ends.

He paused—for shadows of strange shape,
Massy and black, before him lay ;

But through the dark, and through the cold,
And through the yawning fissures old,
Did Peter boldly press his way

Right through the quarry ;—and behold
A scene of soft and lovely hue !
Where blue and grey, and tender green,
Together make as sweet a scene
As ever human eye did view.

Beneath the clear blue sky he saw
A little field of meadow ground ;
But field or meadow name it not ;
Call it of earth a small green plot,
With rocks encompassed round.

The Swale flowed under the grey rocks,
But he flowed quiet and unseen ;—
You need a strong and stormy gale
To bring the noises of the Swale
To that green spot, so calm and green !

And is there no one dwelling here,
No hermit with his beads and glass ?
And does no little cottage look
Upon this soft and fertile nook ?
Does no one live near this green grass ?

Across the deep and quiet spot
Is Peter driving through the grass—
And now has reached the skirting trees ;
When, turning round his head, he sees
A solitary Ass.

" A Prize ! " cries Peter—but he first
Must spy about him far and near :
There's not a single house in sight,
No woodman's hut, no cottage light—
Peter, you need not fear !

There's nothing to be seen but woods,
And rocks that spread a hoary gleam,
And this one Beast, that from the bed
Of the green meadow hangs his head
Over the silent stream.

His head is with a halter bound ;
The halter seizing, Peter leapt
Upon the Creature's back, and plied
With ready heels his shaggy side ;
But still the Ass his station kept.

Then Peter gave a sudden jerk,
A jerk that from a dungeon-floor
Would have pulled up an iron ring ;
But still the heavy-headed Thing
Stood just as he had stood before !

Quoth Peter, leaping from his seat,
" There is some plot against me laid ; "
Once more the little meadow-ground
And all the hoary cliffs around
He cautiously surveyed.

All, all is silent—rocks and woods,
All still and silent—far and near !
Only the Ass, with motion dull,
Upon the pivot of his skull
Turns round his long left ear.

Thought Peter, What can mean all this ?
Some ugly witchcraft must be here !
—Once more the Ass, with motion dull,
Upon the pivot of his skull
Turned round his long left ear.

Suspicion ripened into dread ;
Yet with deliberate action slow,

His staff high-raising, in the pride
Of skill, upon the sounding hide,
He dealt a sturdy blow.

The poor Ass staggered with the shock ;
And then, as if to take his ease,
In quiet uncomplaining mood,
Upon the spot where he had stood,
Dropped gently down upon his knees :

As gently on his side he fell ;
And by the river's brink did lie ;
And, while he lay like one that mourned,
The patient Beast on Peter turned
His shining hazel eye.

'Twas but one mild, reproachful look,
A look more tender than severe ;
And straight in sorrow, not in dread,
He turned the eye-ball in his head
Towards the smooth river deep and clear.

Upon the Beast the sapling rings ;
His lank sides heaved, his limbs they stirred ;
He gave a groan, and then another,
Of that which went before the brother,
And then he gave a third.

All by the moonlight river side
He gave three miserable groans ;
And not till now hath Peter seen
How gaunt the Creature is,—how lean
And sharp his staring bones !

With legs stretched out and stiff he lay :—
No word of kind commiseration
Fell at the sight from Peter's tongue ;
With hard contempt his heart was wrung,
With hatred and vexation.

The meagre beast lay still as death ;
And Peter's lips with fury quiver ;
Quoth he, " You little mulish dog,
I'll fling your carcase like a log
Head-foremost down the river ! "

An impious oath confirmed the threat—
Whereat from the earth on which he lay
To all the echoes, south and north,
And east and west, the Ass sent forth
A long and clamorous bray !

This outcry, on the heart of Peter,
Seems like a note of joy to strike,—
Joy at the heart of Peter knocks ;
But in the echo of the rocks
Was something Peter did not like.

Whether to cheer his coward breast,
Or that he could not break the chain,
In this serene and solemn hour,
Twined round him by demoniac power,
To the blind work he turned again.

Among the rocks and winding crags ;
Among the mountains far away ;
Once more the ass did lengthen out
More ruefully a deep-drawn shout,
The hard dry see-saw of his horrible bray !

What is there now in Peter's heart !
Or whence the might of this strange sound ?
The moon uneasy looked and dimmer,
The broad blue heavens appeared to glimmer,
And the rocks staggered all around—

From Peter's hand the sapling dropped !
Threat has he none to execute ;

" If any one should come and see
That I am here, they'll think," quoth he,
" I'm helping this poor dying brute."

He scans the Ass from limb to limb,
And ventures now to uplift his eyes ;
More steady looks the moon, and clear,
More like themselves the rocks appear
And touch more quiet skies.

His scorn returns—his hate revives ;
He stoops the Ass's neck to seize
With malice—that again takes flight ;
For in the pool a startling sight
Meets him, among the inverted trees.

Is it the moon's distorted face ?
The ghost-like image of a cloud ?
Is it a gallows there portrayed ?
Is Peter of himself afraid ?
Is it a coffin,—or a shroud ?

A grisly idol hewn in stone ?
Or imp from witch's lap let fall ?
Perhaps a ring of shining fairies ?
Such as pursue their feared vagaries
In sylvan bower, or haunted hall ?

Is it a fiend that to a stake
Of fire his desperate self is tethering ?
Or stubborn spirit doomed to yell
In solitary ward or cell,
Ten thousand miles from all his brethren ?

Never did pulse so quickly throb,
And never heart so loudly panted ;
He looks, he cannot choose but look ;
Like some one reading in a book—
A book that is enchanted.

Ah, well-a-day for Peter Bell !
He will be turned to iron soon,
Meet Statue for the court of Fear !
His hat is up—and every hair
Bristles, and whitens in the moon !

He looks, he ponders, looks again ;
He sees a motion—hears a groan ;
His eyes will burst—his heart will break—
He gives a loud and frightful shriek,
And back he falls, as if his life were flown !

PART SECOND

WE left our Hero in a trance,
Beneath the alders, near the river ;
The Ass is by the river-side,
And, where the feeble breezes glide,
Upon the stream the moonbeams quiver.

A happy respite ! but at length
He feels the glimmering of the moon ;
Wakes with glazed eye, and feebly sighing—
To sink, perhaps, where he is lying,
Into a second swoon !

He lifts his head, he sees his staff ;
He touches—'tis to him a treasure !
Faint recollection seems to tell
That he is yet where mortals dwell—
A thought received with languid pleasure.

His head upon his elbow propped,
Becoming less and less perplexed,
Sky-ward he looks—to rock and wood—
And then—upon the glassy flood
His wandering eye is fixed.

Thought he, that is the face of one
In his last sleep securely bound !
So toward the stream his head he bent,
And downward thrust his staff, intent
    The river's depth to sound.

Now—like a tempest-shattered bark,
That overwhelmed and prostrate lies,
And in a moment to the verge
Is lifted of a foaming surge—
    Full suddenly the Ass doth rise !

His staring bones all shake with joy,
And close by Peter's side he stands :
While Peter o'er the river bends,
The little Ass his neck extends,
    And fondly licks his hands.

Such life is in the Ass's eyes,
Such life is in his limbs and ears ;
That Peter Bell, if he had been
The veriest coward ever seen,
    Must now have thrown aside his fears.

The Ass looks on—and to his work
Is Peter quietly resigned ;
He touches here—he touches there—
And now among the dead man's hair
    His sapling Peter has entwined.

He pulls—and looks—and pulls again ;
And he whom the poor Ass had lost,
The man who had been four days dead,
Head-foremost from the river's bed
    Uprises like a ghost !

And Peter draws him to dry land ;
And through the brain of Peter pass

Some poignant twitches, fast and faster ;
" No doubt," quoth he, " he is the Master
Of this poor miserable Ass ! "

The meagre Shadow that looks on—
What would he now ? what is he doing ?
His sudden fit of joy is flown,—
He on his knees hath laid him down,
As if he were his grief renewing :

But no—that Peter on his back
Must mount, he shows well as he can :
Thought Peter then, come weal or woe,
I'll do what he would have me do,
In pity to this poor drowned man.

With that resolve he boldly mounts
Upon the pleased and thankful Ass ;
And then, without a moment's stay,
That earnest Creature turned away
Leaving the body on the grass.

Intent upon his faithful watch,
The Beast four days and nights had past
A sweeter meadow ne'er was seen,
And there the Ass four days had been,
Nor ever once did break his fast :

Yet firm his step, and stout his heart ;
The mead is crossed—the quarry's mouth
Is reached ; but there the trusty guide
Into a thicket turns aside,
And deftly ambles towards the south.

When hark a burst of doleful sound !
And Peter honestly might say,
The like came never to his ears,
Though he has been, full thirty years,
A rover—night and day !

'Tis not a plover of the moors,
'Tis not a bittern of the fen;
Nor can it be a barking fox,
Nor night-bird chambered in the rocks,
Nor wild-cat in a woody glen!

The Ass is startled—and stops short
Right in the middle of the thicket;
And Peter, wont to whistle loud
Whether alone or in a crowd,
Is silent as a silent cricket.

What ails you now, my little Bess?
Well may you tremble and look grave!
This cry—that rings along the wood,
This cry—that floats adown the flood,
Comes from the entrance of a cave:

I see a blooming Wood-boy there,
And if I had the power to say
How sorrowful the wanderer is,
Your heart would be as sad as his
Till you had kissed his tears away!

Grasping a hawthorn branch in hand,
All bright with berries ripe and red,
Into the cavern's mouth he peeps;
Thence back into the moonlight creeps;
Whom seeks he—whom?—the silent dead.

His father!—Him doth he require—
Him hath he sought with fruitless pains,
Among the rocks, behind the trees;
Now creeping on his hands and knees,
Now running o'er the open plains.

And hither is he come at last,
When he through such a day has gone,

By this dark cave to be distrest
Like a poor bird—her plundered nest
Hovering around with dolorous moan !

Of that intense and piercing cry
The listening Ass conjectures well ;
Wild as it is, he there can read
Some intermingled notes that plead
With touches irresistible.

But Peter—when he saw the Ass
Not only stop but turn, and change
The cherished tenor of his pace
That lamentable cry to chase—
It wrought in him conviction strange ;

A faith that, for the dead man's sake
And this poor slave who loved him well,
Vengeance upon his head will fall,
Some visitation worse than all
Which ever till this night befell.

Meanwhile the Ass to reach his home,
Is striving stoutly as he may ;
But, while he climbs the woody hill,
The cry grows weak—and weaker still ;
And now at last it dies away.

So with his freight the Creature turns
Into a gloomy grove of beech,
Along the shade with footsteps true
Descending slowly, till the two
The open moonlight reach.

And there, along the narrow dell,
A fair smooth pathway you discern.
A length of green and open road—
As if it from a fountain flowed—
Winding away between the fern.

The rocks that tower on either side
Build up a wild fantastic scene ;
Temples like those among the Hindoos,
And mosques, and spires, and abbey windows,
And castles all with ivy green !

And, while the Ass pursues his way,
Along this solitary dell,
As pensively his steps advance,
The mosques and spires change countenance
And look at Peter Bell !

That unintelligible cry
Hath left him high in preparation,—
Convinced that he, or soon or late,
This very night will meet his fate—
And so he sits in expectation !

The strenuous Animal hath clomb
With the green path ; and now he wends
Where, shining like the smoothest sea,
In undisturbed immensity
A level plain extends.

But whence this faintly-rustling sound
By which the journeying pair are chased ?
—A withered leaf is close behind,
Light plaything for the sportive wind
Upon that solitary waste.

When Peter spied the moving thing,
It only doubled his distress ;
" Where there is not a bush or tree,
The very leaves they follow me—
So huge hath been my wickedness ! "

To a close lane they now are come,
Where, as before, the enduring Ass

Moves on without a moment's stop,
Nor once turns round his head to crop
A bramble-leaf or blade of grass.

Between the hedges as they go,
The white dust sleeps upon the lane ;
And Peter, ever and anon
Back-looking, sees, upon a stone,
Or in the dust, a crimson stain.

A stain—as of a drop of blood
By moonlight made more faint and wan ;
Ha ! why these sinkings of despair ?
He knows not how the blood comes there—
And Peter is a wicked man.

At length he spies a bleeding wound,
Where he had struck the Ass's head ;
He sees the blood, knows what it is,—
A glimpse of sudden joy was his,
But then it quickly fled ;

Of him whom sudden death had seized
He thought,—of thee, O faithful Ass !
And once again those ghastly pains
Shoot to and fro through heart and reins,
And through his brain like lightning pass.

PART THIRD

I'VE heard of one, a gentle Soul,
Though given to sadness and to gloom,
And for the fact will vouch,—one night
It chanced that by a taper's light
This man was reading in his room ;

Bending, as you or I might bend
At night o'er any pious book.

When sudden blackness overspread
The snow-white page on which he read,
And made the good man round him look.

The chamber walls were dark all round,—
And to his book he turned again ;
—The light had left the lonely taper,
And formed itself upon the paper
Into large letters—bright and plain !

The godly book was in his hand—
And, on the page, more black than coal,
Appeared, set forth in strange array,
A *word*—which to his dying day
Perplexed the good man's gentle soul.

The ghostly word, thus plainly seen,
Did never from his lips depart ;
But he hath said, poor gentle wight !
It brought full many a sin to light
Out of the bottom of his heart.

Dread Spirits ! to confound the meek
Why wander from your course so far,
Disordering colour, form, and stature !
—Let good men feel the soul of nature,
And see things as they are.

Yet, potent Spirits ! well I know,
How ye, that play with soul and sense,
Are not unused to trouble friends
Of goodness, for most gracious ends—
And this I speak in reverence !

But might I give advice to you,
Whom in my fear I love so well ;
From men of pensive virtue go,
Dread Beings ! and your empire show
On hearts like that of Peter Bell.

Your presence often have I felt
In darkness and the stormy night ;
And, with like force, if need there be,
Ye can put forth your agency
When earth is calm, and heaven is bright.

Then, coming from the wayward world,
That powerful world in which ye dwell,
Come, Spirits of the Mind ! and try
To-night, beneath the moonlight sky,
What may be done with Peter Bell !

—O, would that some more skilful voice
My further labour might prevent !
Kind Listeners, that around me sit,
I feel that I am all unfit
For such high argument.

I've played, I've danced, with my narration ;
I loitered long ere I began :
Ye waited then on my good pleasure ;
Pour out indulgence still, in measure
As liberal as ye can !

Our Travellers, ye remember well,
Are thridding a sequestered lane ;
And Peter many tricks is trying,
And many anodynes applying,
To ease his conscience of its pain.

By this his heart is lighter far ;
And, finding that he can account
So snugly for that crimson stain,
His evil spirit up again
Does like an empty bucket mount.

And Peter is a deep logician
Who hath no lack of wit mercurial ;

" Blood drops—leaves rustle—yet," quoth he,
" This poor man never, but for me,
Could have had Christian burial.

" And, say the best you can, 'tis plain,
That here has been some wicked dealing;
No doubt the devil in me wrought;
I'm not the man who could have thought
An Ass like this was worth the stealing!"

So from his pocket Peter takes
His shining horn tobacco-box;
And, in a light and careless way,
As men who with their purpose play,
Upon the lid he knocks.

Let them whose voice can stop the clouds,
Whose cunning eye can see the wind,
Tell to a curious world the cause
Why, making here a sudden pause,
The Ass turned round his head, and *grinned*.

Appalling process! I have marked
The like on heath, in lonely wood;
And, verily, have seldom met
A spectacle more hideous—yet
It suited Peter's present mood.

And, grinning in his turn, his teeth
He in jocose defiance showed—
When, to upset his spiteful mirth,
A murmur, pent within the earth,
In the dead earth beneath the road

Rolled audibly! it swept along,
A muffled noise—a rumbling sound!—
'Twas by a troop of miners made,
Plying with gunpowder their trade,
Some twenty fathoms under ground.

Small cause of dire effect ! for, surely,
If ever mortal, King or Cotter,
Believed that earth was charged to quake
And yawn for his unworthy sake,
'Twas Peter Bell the Potter.

But, as an oak in breathless air
Will stand though to the centre hewn ;
Or as the weakest things, if frost
Have stiffened them, maintain their post ;
So he, beneath the gazing moon !—

The Beast bestriding thus, he reached
A spot where, in a sheltering cove,
A little chapel stands alone,
With greenest ivy overgrown,
And tufted with an ivy grove ;

Dying insensibly away
From human thoughts and purposes,
It seemed—wall, window, roof and tower
To bow to some transforming power,
And blend with the surrounding trees.

As ruinous a place it was,
Thought Peter, in the shire of Fife
That served my turn, when following still
From land to land a reckless will
I married my sixth wife !

The unheeding Ass moves slowly on,
And now is passing by an inn
Brim-full of a carousing crew,
That make, with curses not a few,
An uproar and a drunken din.

I cannot well express the thoughts
Which Peter in those noises found ;—

A stifling power compressed his frame,
While-as a swimming darkness came
Over that dull and dreary sound.

For well did Peter know the sound ;
The language of those drunken joys
To him, a jovial soul, I ween,
But a few hours ago, had been
A gladsome and a welcome noise.

Now, turned adrift into the past,
He finds no solace in his course ;
Like planet-stricken men of yore,
He trembles, smitten to the core
By strong compunction and remorse.

But, more than all, his heart is stung
To think of one, almost a child ;
A sweet and playful Highland girl,
As light and beauteous as a squirrel,
As beauteous and as wild !

Her dwelling was a lonely house,
A cottage in a heathy dell ;
And she put on her gown of green,
And left her mother at sixteen,
And followed Peter Bell.

But many good and pious thoughts
Had she ; and, in the kirk to pray,
Two long Scotch miles, through rain or snow
To kirk she had been used to go,
Twice every Sabbath-day.

And, when she followed Peter Bell,
It was to lead an honest life ;
For he, with tongue not used to falter,
Had pledged his troth before the altar
To love her as his wedded wife.

A mother's hope is hers ;—but soon
She drooped and pined like one forlorn ;—
From Scripture she a name did borrow ;
Benoni, or the child of sorrow,
She called her babe unborn.

For she had learned how Peter lived,
And took it in most grievous part ;
She to the very bone was worn,
And, ere that little child was born,
Died of a broken heart.

And now the Spirits of the Mind
Are busy with poor Peter Bell ;
Upon the rights of visual sense
Usurping, with a prevalence
More terrible than magic spell.

Close by a brake of flowering furze
(Above it shivering aspens play)
He sees an unsubstantial creature,
His very self in form and feature,
Not four yards from the broad highway :

And stretched beneath the furze he sees
The Highland girl—it is no other ;
And hears her crying as she cried,
The very moment that she died,
" My mother ! oh my mother ! "

The sweat pours down from Peter's face,
So grievous is his heart's contrition ;
With agony his eye-balls ache
While he beholds by the furze-brake
This miserable vision !

Calm is the well-deserving brute,
His peace hath no offence betrayed ;

But now, while down that slope he wends
A voice to Peter's ear ascends,
Resounding from the woody glade :

The voice, though clamorous as a horn
Re-echoed by a naked rock,
Comes from that tabernacle—List !
Within, a fervent Methodist
Is preaching to no heedless flock !

" Repent ! repent ! " he cries aloud,
" While yet ye may find mercy ;—strive
To love the Lord with all your might ;
Turn to him, seek him day and night,
And save your souls alive !

" Repent ! repent ! though ye have gone,
Through paths of wickedness and woe,
After the Babylonian harlot ;
And, though your sins be red as scarlet,
They shall be white as snow ! "

Even as he passed the door, these words
Did plainly come to Peter's ears ;
And they such joyful tidings were,
The joy was more than he could bear !—
He melted into tears.

Sweet tears of hope and tenderness !
And fast they fell, a plenteous shower !
His nerves, his sinews seemed to melt ;
Through all his iron frame was felt
A gentle, a relaxing, power !

Each fibre of his frame was weak ;
Weak all the animal within ;
But, in its helplessness, grew mild
And gentle as an infant child,
An infant that has known no sin.

'Tis said, meek Beast! that, through Heaven's grace,
He not unmoved did notice now
The cross upon thy shoulder scored,
For lasting impress, by the Lord
To whom all human-kind shall bow;

Memorial of his touch—that day
When Jesus humbly deigned to ride,
Entering the proud Jerusalem,
By an immeasurable stream
Of shouting people deified!

Meanwhile the persevering Ass
Turned towards a gate that hung in view
Across a shady lane; his chest
Against the yielding gate he pressed
And quietly passed through.

And up the stony lane he goes;
No ghost more softly ever trod;
Among the stones and pebbles, he
Sets down his hoofs inaudibly,
As if with felt his hoofs were shod.

Along the lane the trusty Ass
Went twice two hundred yards or more,
And no one could have guessed his aim,—
Till to a lonely house he came,
And stopped beside the door.

Thought Peter, 'tis the poor man's home!
He listens—not a sound is heard
Save from the trickling household rill;
But, stepping o'er the cottage-sill,
Forthwith a little Girl appeared.

She to the Meeting-house was bound
In hopes some tidings there to gather:

No glimpse it is, no doubtful gleam ;
She saw—and uttered with a scream,
" My father ! here's my father ! "

The very word was plainly heard,
Heard plainly by the wretched Mother—
Her joy was like a deep affright :
And forth she rushed into the light,
And saw it was another !

And, instantly, upon the earth,
Beneath the full moon shining bright,
Close to the Ass's feet she fell ;
At the same moment Peter Bell
Dismounts in most unhappy plight.

As he beheld the Woman lie
Breathless and motionless, the mind
Of Peter sadly was confused ;
But, though to such demands unused,
And helpless almost as the blind,

He raised her up ; and, while he held
Her body propped against his knee,
The Woman waked—and when she spied
The poor Ass standing by her side,
She moaned most bitterly.

" Oh ! God be praised—my heart's at ease—
For he is dead—I know it well ! "
—At this she wept a bitter flood ;
And, in the best way that he could,
His tale did Peter tell.

He trembles—he is pale as death ;
His voice is weak with perturbation ;
He turns aside his head, he pauses ;
Poor Peter, from a thousand causes,
Is crippled sore in his narration.

At length she learned how he espied
The Ass in that small meadow-ground ;
And that her Husband now lay dead,
Beside that luckless river's bed
In which he had been drowned.

A piercing look the Widow cast
Upon the Beast that near her stands ;
She sees 'tis he, that 'tis the same ;
She calls the poor Ass by his name,
And wrings, and wrings her hands.

" O wretched loss—untimely stroke !
If he had died upon his bed !
He knew not one forewarning pain ;
He never will come home again—
Is dead, for ever dead ! "

Beside the woman Peter stands ;
His heart is opening more and more ;
A holy sense pervades his mind ;
He feels what he for human kind
Had never felt before.

At length, by Peter's arm sustained,
The Woman rises from the ground—
" Oh, mercy ! something must be done,
My little Rachel, you must run,—
Some willing neighbour must be found.

" Make haste—my little Rachel—do,
The first you meet with—bid him come,
Ask him to lend his horse to-night,
And this good Man, whom Heaven requite,
Will help to bring the body home."

Away goes Rachel weeping loud ;—
An Infant, waked by her distress,

Makes in the house a piteous cry ;
And Peter hears the Mother sigh,
" Seven are they, and all fatherless ! "

And now is Peter taught to feel
That man's heart is a holy thing ;
And Nature, through a world of death,
Breathes into him a second breath,
More searching than the breath of spring.

Upon a stone the Woman sits
In agony of silent grief—
From his own thoughts did Peter start ;
He longs to press her to his heart,
From love that cannot find relief.

But roused, as if through every limb
Had past a sudden shock of dread,
The Mother o'er the threshold flies,
And up the cottage stairs she hies,
And on the pillow lays her burning head.

And Peter turns his steps aside
Into a shade of darksome trees,
Where he sits down, he knows not how,
With his hands pressed against his brow,
His elbows on his tremulous knees.

There, self-involved, does Peter sit
Until no sign of life he makes,
As if his mind were sinking deep
Through years that have been long asleep.
The trance is passed away—he wakes ;

He lifts his head—and sees the Ass
Yet standing in the clear moonshine ;
" When shall I be as good as thou ?
Oh ! would, poor beast, that I had now
A heart but half as good as thine ! "

But *He*—who deviously hath sought
His Father through the lonesome woods,
Hath sought, proclaiming to the ear
Of night his grief and sorrowful fear—
He comes, escaped from fields and floods ;—

With weary pace is drawing nigh ;
He sees the Ass—and nothing living
Had ever such a fit of joy
As hath this little orphan Boy,
For he has no misgiving !

Forth to the gentle Ass he springs,
And up about his neck he climbs ;
In loving words he talks to him,
He kisses, kisses face and limb,—
He kisses him a thousand times !

This Peter sees, while in the shade
He stood beside the cottage-door ;
And Peter Bell, the ruffian wild,
Sobs loud, he sobs even like a child,
" O God ! I can endure no more ! "

—Here ends my Tale : for in a trice
Arrived a neighbour with his horse ;
Peter went forth with him straightway :
And, with due care, ere break of day,
Together they brought back the Corse.

And many years did this poor Ass,
Whom once it was my luck to see
Cropping the shrubs of Leming-Lane,
Help by his labour to maintain
The Widow and her family.

And Peter Bell, who, till that night,
Had been the wildest of his clan,

Forsook his crimes, renounced his folly,
And, after ten months' melancholy,
Became a good and honest man.

THE WHITE DOE OF RYLSTONE *

OR, THE FATE OF THE NORTONS

ADVERTISEMENT

During the Summer of 1807 I visited, for the first time,
the beautiful country that surrounds Bolton Priory, in
Yorkshire; and the Poem of "The White Doe," founded
upon a Tradition connected with that place, was composed
at the close of the same year.

DEDICATION

In trellised shed with clustering roses gay,
And, MARY! oft beside our blazing fire,
When years of wedded life were as a day
Whose current answers to the heart's desire,
Did we together read in Spenser's Lay
How Una, sad of soul—in sad attire,
The gentle Una, of celestial birth,
To seek her Knight went wandering o'er the earth.

---

* The Poem of the White Doe of Rylstone is founded on a local
tradition, and on the Ballad in Percy's Collection, entitled "The Rising of the North." The tradition is as follows :—" About this time,"
not long after the Dissolution, "a White Doe," say the aged people of
the neighbourhood, "long continued to make a weekly pilgrimage
from Rylstone over the fells of Bolton, and was constantly found in
the Abbey Churchyard during divine service ; after the close of which
she returned home as regularly as the rest of the congregation."—
DR. WHITAKER's *History of the Deanery of Craven.*—Rylstone was the
property and residence of the Nortons, distinguished in that ill-advised
and unfortunate Insurrection ; which led me to connect with this
tradition the principal circumstances of their fate, as recorded in the
Ballad.
    "Bolton Priory," says Dr. Whitaker in his excellent book, *The
History and Antiquities of the Deanery of Craven,* "stands upon a
beautiful curvature of the Wharf, on a level sufficiently elevated to
protect it from inundations, and low enough for every purpose of
picturesque effect.

Ah, then, Belovèd ! pleasing was the smart,
And the tear precious in compassion shed
For Her, who, pierced by sorrow's thrilling dart,
Did meekly bear the pang unmerited ;
Meek as that emblem of her lowly heart
The milk-white Lamb which in a line she led,—
And faithful, loyal in her innocence,
Like the brave Lion slain in her defence.

"Opposite to the East window of the Priory Church, the river washes the foot of a rock nearly perpendicular, and of the richest purple, where several of the mineral beds, which break out instead of maintaining their usual inclination to the horizon, are twisted by some inconceivable process into undulating and spiral lines. To the South all is soft and delicious ; the eye reposes upon a few rich pastures, a moderate reach of the river, sufficiently tranquil to form a mirror to the sun, and the bounding hills beyond, neither too near nor too lofty to exclude, even in winter, any portion of his rays.

"But after all, the glories of Bolton are on the North. Whatever the most fastidious taste could require to constitute a perfect landscape, is not only found here, but in its proper place. In front, and immediately under the eye, is a smooth expanse of park-like enclosure, spotted with native elm, ash, etc., of the finest growth : on the right a skirting oak wood, with jutting points of grey rock ; on the left a rising copse. Still forward are seen the aged groves of Bolton Park, the growth of centuries ; and farther yet, the barren and rocky distances of Simon-seat and Barden Fell contrasted with the warmth, fertility, and luxuriant foliage of the valley below.

"About half a mile above Bolton the valley closes, and either side of the Wharf is overhung by solemn woods, from which huge perpendicular masses of grey rock jut out at intervals.

"This sequestered scene was almost inaccessible till of late, that ridings have been cut out on both sides of the river, and the most interesting points laid open by judicious thinnings in the woods. Here a tributary stream rushes from a waterfall, and bursts through a woody glen to mingle its waters with the Wharf : there the Wharf itself is nearly lost in a deep cleft in the rock, and next becomes a horned flood enclosing a woody island—sometimes it reposes for a moment, and then resumes its native character, lively, irregular, and impetuous.

"The cleft mentioned above is the tremendous STRID. This chasm, being incapable of receiving the winter floods, has formed on either side a broad strand of naked gritstone full of rock-basins, or ' pots of the Linn,' which bear witness to the restless impetuosity of so many Northern torrents. But, if here Wharf is lost to the eye, it amply repays another sense by its deep and solemn roar, like 'the Voice of the angry Spirit of the Waters,' heard far above and beneath, amidst the silence of the surrounding woods.

"The terminating object of the landscape is the remains of Barden Tower, interesting from their form and situation, and still more so from the recollections which they excite."

Notes could we hear as of a faery shell
Attuned to words with sacred wisdom fraught ;
Free Fancy prized each specious miracle,
And all its finer inspiration caught ;
Till in the bosom of our rustic Cell,
We by a lamentable change were taught
That " bliss with mortal Man may not abide : "
How nearly joy and sorrow are allied !

For us the stream of fiction ceased to flow,
For us the voice of melody was mute.
—But, as soft gales dissolve the dreary snow,
And give the timid herbage leave to shoot,
Heaven's breathing influence failed not to bestow
A timely promise of unlooked-for fruit,
Fair fruit of pleasure and serene content
From blossoms wild of fancies innocent.

It soothed us—it beguiled us—then, to hear
Once more of troubles wrought by magic spell ;
And griefs whose aery motion comes not near
The pangs that tempt the Spirit to rebel :
Then, with mild Una in her sober cheer,
High over hill and low adown the dell
Again we wandered, willing to partake
All that she suffered for her dear Lord's sake.

Then, too, this Song *of mine* once more could please,
Where anguish, strange as dreams of restless sleep,
Is tempered and allayed by sympathies
Aloft ascending, and descending deep,
Even to the inferior Kinds ; whom forest-trees
Protect from beating sunbeams, and the sweep
Of the sharp winds ;—fair Creatures !—to whom Heaven
A calm and sinless life, with love, hath given.

This tragic Story cheered us ; for it speaks
Of female patience winning firm repose ;
And, of the recompense that conscience seeks,
A bright, encouraging, example shows ;
Needful when o'er wide realms the tempest breaks,
Needful amid life's ordinary woes ;—
Hence, not for them unfitted who would bless
A happy hour with holier happiness.

He serves the Muses erringly and ill,
Whose aim is pleasure light and fugitive :
Oh, that my mind were equal to fulfil
The comprehensive mandate which they give—
Vain aspiration of an earnest will !
Yet in this moral Strain a power may live,
Belovèd Wife ! such solace to impart
As it hath yielded to thy tender heart.

RYDAL MOUNT, WESTMORELAND,
    April 20, 1815.

———

' Action is transitory—a step, a blow,
The motion of a muscle—this way or that—
'Tis done ; and in the after-vacancy
We wonder at ourselves like men betrayed :
Suffering is permanent, obscure and dark,
And has the nature of infinity.
Yet through that darkness (infinite though it seem
And irremoveable) gracious openings lie,
By which the soul—with patient steps of thought
Now toiling, wafted now on wings of prayer—
May pass in hope, and, though from mortal bonds
Yet undelivered, rise with sure ascent
Even to the fountain-head of peace divine.''

———

" They that deny a God, destroy Man's nobility: for certainly Man is of kinn to the Beast by his Body ; and if he be not of kinn to God by his Spirit, he is a base, ignoble Creature. It destroys likewise Magnanimity, and the raising of humane Nature : for take an example of a Dogg, and mark what a generosity and courage he will put on, when he finds himself maintained by a Man, who to him is instead of a God, or Melior Natura. Which courage is manifestly such, as that Creature without that confidence of a better Nature than his own could never attain. So Man, when he resteth and assureth himself upon Divine protection and favour, gathereth a force and faith which human Nature in itself could not obtain."—LORD BACON.

CANTO FIRST

FROM Bolton's old monastic tower
The bells ring loud with gladsome power ;
The sun shines bright ; the fields are gay
With people in their best array
Of stole and doublet, hood and scarf,
Along the banks of crystal Wharf,
Through the Vale retired and lowly,
Trooping to that summons holy.
And, up among the moorlands, see
What sprinklings of blithe company !
Of lasses and of shepherd grooms,
That down the steep hills force their way,
Like cattle through the budded brooms ;
Path, or no path, what care they ?
And thus in joyous mood they hie
To Bolton's mouldering Priory.
  What would they there ?—Full fifty years
That sumptuous Pile, with all its peers,
Too harshly hath been doomed to taste
The bitterness of wrong and waste :
Its courts are ravaged ; but the tower
Is standing with a voice of power,
That ancient voice which wont to call
To mass or some high festival ;
And in the shattered fabric's heart
Remaineth one protected part ;
A Chapel, like a wild-bird's nest,
Closely embowered and trimly drest ;
And thither young and old repair,
This Sabbath-day, for praise and prayer.
  Fast the churchyard fills ;—anon
Look again, and they all are gone ;
The cluster round the porch, and the folk
Who sate in the shade of the Prior's Oak !
And scarcely have they disappeared

Ere the prelusive hymn is heard :—
With one consent the people rejoice,
Filling the church with a lofty voice !
They sing a service which they feel :
For 'tis the sunrise now of zeal ;
Of a pure faith the vernal prime—
In great Eliza's golden time.
   A moment ends the fervent din,
And all is hushed, without and within ;
For though the priest, more tranquilly,
Recites the holy liturgy,
The only voice which you can hear
Is the river murmuring near.
—When soft !—the dusky trees between,
And down the path through the open green,
Where is no living thing to be seen ;
And through yon gateway, where is found,
Beneath the arch with ivy bound,
Free entrance to the churchyard ground—
Comes gliding in with lovely gleam,
Comes gliding in serene and slow,
Soft and silent as a dream,
A solitary Doe !
White she is as lily of June,
And beauteous as the silver moon
When out of sight the clouds are driven
And she is left alone in heaven ;
Or like a ship some gentle day
In sunshine sailing far away,
A glittering ship, that hath the plain
Of ocean for her own domain.
   Lie silent in your graves, ye dead !
Lie quiet in your churchyard bed !
Ye living, tend your holy cares ;
Ye multitude, pursue your prayers ;
And blame not me if my heart and sight
Are occupied with one delight !
'Tis a work for sabbath hours

If I with this bright Creature go :
Whether she be of forest bowers,
From the bowers of earth below ;
Or a Spirit for one day given,
A pledge of grace from purest heaven.

What harmonious pensive changes
Wait upon her as she ranges
Round and through this Pile of state
Overthrown and desolate !
Now a step or two her way
Leads through space of open day,
Where the enamoured sunny light
Brightens her that was so bright ;
Now doth a delicate shadow fall,
Falls upon her like a breath,
From some lofty arch or wall,
As she passes underneath :
Now some gloomy nook partakes
Of the glory that she makes,—
High-ribbed vault of stone, or cell,
With perfect cunning framed as well
Of stone, and ivy, and the spread
Of the elder's bushy head ;
Some jealous and forbidding cell,
That doth the living stars repel,
And where no flower hath leave to dwell.

The presence of this wandering Doe
Fills many a damp obscure recess
With lustre of a saintly show ;
And, reappearing, she no less
Sheds on the flowers that round her blow
A more than sunny liveliness.
But say, among these holy places,
Which thus assiduously she paces,
Comes she with a votary's task,
Rite to perform, or boon to ask ?
Fair Pilgrim ! harbours she a sense
Of sorrow, or of reverence ?

Can she be grieved for quire or shrine,
Crushed as if by wrath divine ?
For what survives of house where God
Was worshipped, or where Man abode ;
For old magnificence undone ;
Or for the gentler work begun
By Nature, softening and concealing,
And busy with a hand of healing ?
Mourns she for lordly chamber's hearth
That to the sapling ash gives birth ;
For dormitory's length laid bare
Where the wild rose blossoms fair ;
Or altar, whence the cross was rent,
Now rich with mossy ornament ?
—She sees a warrior carved in stone,
Among the thick weeds, stretched alone ;
A warrior, with his shield of pride
Cleaving humbly to his side,
And hands in resignation prest,
Palm to palm, on his tranquil breast ;
As little she regards the sight
As a common creature might :
If she be doomed to inward care,
Or service, it must lie elsewhere.
—But hers are eyes serenely bright,
And on she moves—with pace how light !
Nor spares to stoop her head, and taste
The dewy turf with flowers bestrown ;
And thus she fares, until at last
Beside the ridge of a grassy grave
In quietness she lays her down ;
Gentle as a weary wave
Sinks, when the summer breeze hath died,
Against an anchored vessel's side ;
Even so, without distress, doth she
Lie down in peace, and lovingly.
  The day is placid in its going,
To a lingering motion bound,

Like the crystal stream now flowing
With its softest summer sound :
So the balmy minutes pass,
While this radiant Creature lies
Couched upon the dewy grass,
Pensively with downcast eyes.
—But now again the people raise
With awful cheer a voice of praise :
It is the last, the parting song ;
And from the temple forth they throng,
And quickly spread themselves abroad,
While each pursues his several road.
But some—a variegated band
Of middle-aged, and old, and young,
And little children by the hand
Upon their leading mothers hung—
With mute obeisance gladly paid
Turn towards the spot, where, full in view,
The white Doe, to her service true,
Her sabbath couch has made.
    It was a solitary mound ;
Which two spears' length of level ground
Did from all other graves divide :
As if in some respect of pride ;
Or melancholy's sickly mood,
Still shy of human neighbourhood ;
Or guilt, that humbly would express
A penitential loneliness.
    " Look, there she is, my Child ! draw near ;
She fears not, wherefore should we fear ?
She means no harm ; "—but still the Boy,
To whom the words were softly said,
Hung back, and smiled, and blushed for joy,
A shame-faced blush of glowing red !
Again the Mother whispered low,
" Now you have seen the famous Doe ;
From Rylstone she hath found her way
Over the hills this sabbath day.

Her work, whate'er it be, is done,
And she will depart when we are gone ;
Thus doth she keep, from year to year,
Her sabbath morning, foul or fair."

Bright was the Creature, as in dreams
The Boy had seen her, yea, more bright ;
But is she truly what she seems ?
He asks with insecure delight,
Asks of himself, and doubts,—and still
The doubt returns against his will :
Though he, and all the standers-by,
Could tell a tragic history
Of facts divulged, wherein appear
Substantial motive, reason clear,
Why thus the milk-white Doe is found
Couchant beside that lonely mound ;
And why she duly loves to pace
The circuit of this hallowed place.
Nor to the Child's inquiring mind
Is such perplexity confined :
For, spite of sober Truth that sees
A world of fixed remembrances
Which to this mystery belong,
If, undeceived, my skill can trace
The characters of every face,
There lack not strange delusion here,
Conjecture vague, and idle fear,
And superstitious fancies strong,
Which do the gentle Creature wrong.

That bearded, staff-supported Sire—
Who in his boyhood often fed
Full cheerily on convent-bread
And heard old tales by the convent-fire,
And to his grave will go with scars,
Relics of long and distant wars—
That Old Man, studious to expound
The spectacle, is mounting high
To days of dim antiquity ;

When Lady Aäliza mourned
Her Son, and felt in her despair
The pang of unavailing prayer ;
Her Son in Wharf's abysses drowned,
The noble Boy of Egremound.
From which affliction—when the grace
Of God had in her heart found place—
A pious structure, fair to see,
Rose up, this stately Priory !
The Lady's work ;—but now laid low ;
To the grief of her soul that doth come and go,
In the beautiful form of this innocent Doe :
Which, though seemingly doomed in its breast to
    sustain
A softened remembrance of sorrow and pain,
Is spotless, and holy, and gentle, and bright ;
And glides o'er the earth like an angel of light.
  Pass, pass who will, yon chantry door ;
And, through the chink in the fractured floor
Look down, and see a griesly sight ;
A vault where the bodies are buried upright !
There, face by face, and hand by hand,
The Claphams and Mauleverers stand ;
And, in his place, among son and sire,
Is John de Clapham, that fierce Esquire,
A valiant man, and a name of dread
In the ruthless wars of the White and Red ;
Who dragged Earl Pembroke from Banbury
    church
And smote off his head on the stones of the
    porch !
Look down among them, if you dare ;
Oft does the White Doe loiter there,
Prying into the darksome rent ;
Nor can it be with good intent :
So thinks that Dame of haughty air,
Who hath a Page her book to hold,
And wears a frontlet edged with gold.

Harsh thoughts with her high mood agree—
Who counts among her ancestry
Earl Pembroke, slain so impiously!
  That slender Youth, a scholar pale,
From Oxford come to his native vale,
He also hath his own conceit:
It is, thinks he, the gracious Fairy,
Who loved the Shepherd-lord to meet
In his wanderings solitary:
Wild notes she in his hearing sang,
A song of Nature's hidden powers;
That whistled like the wind, and rang
Among the rocks and holly bowers.
'Twas said that She all shapes could wear;
And oftentimes before him stood,
Amid the trees of some thick wood,
In semblance of a lady fair;
And taught him signs, and showed him sights,
In Craven's dens, on Cumbrian heights;
When under cloud of fear he lay,
A shepherd clad in homely grey;
Nor left him at his later day.
And hence, when he, with spear and shield,
Rode full of years to Flodden-field,
His eye could see the hidden spring,
And how the current was to flow;
The fatal end of Scotland's King,
And all that hopeless overthrow.
But not in wars did he delight,
This Clifford wished for worthier might;
Nor in broad pomp, or courtly state;
Him his own thoughts did elevate,—
Most happy in the shy recess
Of Barden's lowly quietness.
And choice of studious friends had he
Of Bolton's dear fraternity;
Who, standing on this old church tower,
In many a calm propitious hour,

Perused, with him, the starry sky ;
Or, in their cells, with him did pry
For other lore,—by keen desire
Urged to close toil with chemic fire ;
In quest belike of transmutations
Rich as the mine's most bright creations.
But they and their good works are fled,
And all is now disquieted—
And peace is none, for living or dead !

Ah, pensive Scholar, think not so,
But look again at the radiant Doe !
What quiet watch she seems to keep,
Alone, beside that grassy heap !
Why mention other thoughts unmeet
For vision so composed and sweet ?
While stand the people in a ring,
Gazing, doubting, questioning ;
Yea, many overcome in spite
Of recollections clear and bright ;
Which yet do unto some impart
An undisturbed repose of heart.
And all the assembly own a law
Of orderly respect and awe ;
But see—they vanish one by one,
And last, the Doe herself is gone.

Harp ! we have been full long beguiled
By vague thoughts, lured by fancies wild ;
To which, with no reluctant strings,
Thou hast attuned thy murmurings ;
And now before this Pile we stand
In solitude, and utter peace :
But, Harp ! thy murmurs may not cease—
A Spirit, with his angelic wings,
In soft and breeze-like visitings,
Has touched thee—and a Spirit's hand :
A voice is with us—a command
To chant, in strains of heavenly glory,
A tale of tears, a mortal story !

CANTO SECOND

The Harp in lowliness obeyed ;
And first we sang of the greenwood shade
And a solitary Maid ;
Beginning, where the song must end,
With her, and with her sylvan Friend ;
The Friend who stood before her sight,
Her only unextinguished light ;
Her last companion in a dearth
Of love, upon a hopeless earth.

For She it was—this Maid, who wrought
Meekly, with foreboding thought,
In vermeil colours and in gold
An unblest work ; which, standing by,
Her Father did with joy behold,—
Exulting in its imagery ;
A Banner, fashioned to fulfil
Too perfectly his headstrong will :
For on this Banner had her hand
Embroidered (such her Sire's command)
The sacred Cross ; and figured there
The five dear wounds our Lord did bear ;
Full soon to be uplifted high,
And float in rueful company !

It was the time when England's Queen
Twelve years had reigned, a Sovereign dread ;
Nor yet the restless crown had been
Disturbed upon her virgin head ;
But now the inly-working North
Was ripe to send its thousands forth,
A potent vassalage, to fight
In Percy's and in Neville's right,
Two Earls fast leagued in discontent,
Who gave their wishes open vent ;
And boldly urged a general plea,
The rites of ancient piety
To be triumphantly restored,

By the stern justice of the sword !
And that same Banner, on whose breast
The blameless Lady had exprest
Memorials chosen to give life
And sunshine to a dangerous strife ;
That Banner, waiting for the Call,
Stood quietly in Rylstone-hall.

    It came ; and Francis Norton said,
" O Father ! rise not in this fray—
The hairs are white upon your head ;
Dear Father, hear me when I say
It is for you too late a day !
Bethink you of your own good name :
A just and gracious Queen have we,
A pure religion, and the claim
Of peace on our humanity.—
'Tis meet that I endure your scorn ;
I am your son, your eldest born ;
But not for lordship or for land,
My Father, do I clasp your knees ;
The Banner touch not, stay your hand,
This multitude of men disband,
And live at home in blameless ease ;
For these my brethren's sake, for me ;
And, most of all, for Emily ! "

    Tumultuous noises filled the hall ;
And scarcely could the Father hear
That name—pronounced with a dying fall—
The name of his only Daughter dear,
As on the banner which stood near
He glanced a look of holy pride,
And his moist eyes were glorified ;
Then did he seize the staff, and say :
" Thou, Richard, bear'st thy father's name,
Keep thou this ensign till the day
When I of thee require the same :
Thy place be on my better hand ;—
And seven as true as thou, I see,

Will cleave to this good cause and me."
He spake, and eight brave sons straightway
All followed him, a gallant band !
    Thus, with his sons, when forth he came
The sight was hailed with loud acclaim
And din of arms and minstrelsy,
From all his warlike tenantry,
All horsed and harnessed with him to ride,—
A voice to which the hills replied !
    But Francis, in the vacant hall,
Stood silent under dreary weight,—
A phantasm, in which roof and wall
Shook, tottered, swam before his sight ;
A phantasm like a dream of night !
Thus overwhelmed, and desolate,
He found his way to a postern gate ;
And, when he waked, his languid eye
Was on the calm and silent sky ;
With air about him breathing sweet,
And earth's green grass beneath his feet ;
Nor did he fail ere long to hear
A sound of military cheer,
Faint—but it reached that sheltered spot ;
He heard, and it disturbed him not.
    There stood he, leaning on a lance
Which he had grasped unknowingly,
Had blindly grasped in that strong trance,
That dimness of heart-agony ;
There stood he, cleansed from the despair
And sorrow of his fruitless prayer.
The past he calmly hath reviewed :
But where will be the fortitude
Of this brave man, when he shall see
That Form beneath the spreading tree,
And know that it is Emily ?
    He saw her where in open view
She sate beneath the spreading yew—
Her head upon her lap, concealing

In solitude her bitter feeling :
" Might ever son *command* a sire,
The act were justified to-day."
This to himself—and to the Maid,
Whom now he had approached, he said—
" Gone are they,—they have their desire ;
And I with thee one hour will stay,
To give thee comfort if I may."

She heard, but looked not up, nor spake ;
And sorrow moved him to partake
Her silence ; then his thoughts turned round,
And fervent words a passage found.

" Gone are they, bravely, though misled ;
With a dear Father at their head !
The Sons obey a natural lord ;
The Father had given solemn word
To noble Percy ; and a force
Still stronger, bends him to his course.
This said, our tears to-day may fall
As at an innocent funeral.
In deep and awful channel runs
This sympathy of Sire and Sons ;
Untried our Brothers have been loved
With heart by simple nature moved ;
And now their faithfulness is proved :
For faithful we must call them, bearing
That soul of conscientious daring.
—There were they all in circle—there
Stood Richard, Ambrose, Christopher,
John with a sword that will not fail,
And Marmaduke in fearless mail,
And those bright Twins were side by side ;
And there, by fresh hopes beautified,
Stood He, whose arm yet lacks the power
Of man, our youngest, fairest flower !
I, by the right of eldest born,
And in a second father's place,
Presumed to grapple with their scorn,

And meet their pity face to face ;
Yea, trusting in God's holy aid,
I to my Father knelt and prayed ;
And one, the pensive Marmaduke,
Methought, was yielding inwardly,
And would have laid his purpose by,
But for a glance of his Father's eye,
Which I myself could scarcely brook.
    Then be we, each and all, forgiven !
Thou, chiefly thou, my Sister dear,
Whose pangs are registered in heaven—
The stifled sigh, the hidden tear,
And smiles, that dared to take their place,
Meek filial smiles, upon thy face,
As that unhallowed Banner grew
Beneath a loving old Man's view.
Thy part is done—thy painful part ;
Be thou then satisfied in heart !
A further, though far easier, task
Than thine hath been, my duties ask ;
With theirs my efforts cannot blend,
I cannot for such cause contend ;
Their aims I utterly forswear ;
But I in body will be there.
Unarmed and naked will I go,
Be at their side, come weal or woe :
On kind occasions I may wait,
See, hear, obstruct, or mitigate.
Bare breast I take and an empty hand." *—
Therewith he threw away the lance,
Which he had grasped in that strong trance,
Spurned it, like something that would stand
Between him and the pure intent
Of love on which his soul was bent.
    " For thee, for thee, is left the sense
Of trial past without offence

* See the old ballad : " The Rising of the North."

To God or man ; such innocence,
Such consolation, and the excess
Of an unmerited distress ;
In that thy very strength must lie.
—O Sister, I could prophesy !
The time is come that rings the knell
Of all we loved, and loved so well :
Hope nothing, if I thus may speak
To thee, a woman, and thence weak :
Hope nothing, I repeat ; for we
Are doomed to perish utterly :
'Tis meet that thou with me divide
The thought while I am by thy side,
Acknowledging a grace in this,
A comfort in the dark abyss.
But look not for me when I am gone,
And be no farther wrought upon :
Farewell all wishes, all debate,
All prayers for this cause, or for that !
Weep, if that aid thee ; but depend
Upon no help of outward friend ;
Espouse thy doom at once, and cleave
To fortitude without reprieve.
For we must fall, both we and ours—
This Mansion and these pleasant bowers,
Walks, pools, and arbours, homestead, hall—
Our fate is theirs, will reach them all ;
The young horse must forsake his manger,
And learn to glory in a Stranger ;
The hawk forget his perch ; the hound
Be parted from his ancient ground :
The blast will sweep us all away—
One desolation, one decay !
And even this Creature ! " which words saying,
He pointed to a lovely Doe,
A few steps distant, feeding, straying ;
Fair creature, and more white than snow !
" Even she will to her peaceful woods

Return, and to her murmuring floods,
And be in heart and soul the same
She was before she hither came ;
Ere she had learned to love us all,
Herself beloved in Rylstone-hall.
—But thou, my Sister, doomed to be
The last leaf on a blasted tree ;
If not in vain we breathed the breath
Together of a purer faith ;
If hand in hand we have been led,
And thou, (O happy thought this day :)
Not seldom foremost in the way ;
If on one thought our minds have fed,
And we have in one meaning read ;
If, when at home our private weal
Hath suffered from the shock of zeal,
Together we have learned to prize
Forbearance and self-sacrifice ;
If we like combatants have fared,
And for this issue been prepared ;
If thou art beautiful, and youth
And thought enduc thee with all truth—
Be strong ;—be worthy of the grace
Of God, and fill thy destined place :
A Soul, by force of sorrows high,
Uplifted to the purest sky
Of undisturbed humanity ! ”
    He ended,—or she heard no more ;
He led her from the yew-tree shade,
And at the mansion's silent door,
He kissed the consecrated Maid ;
And down the valley then pursued,
Alone, the armèd Multitude.

CANTO THIRD

Now joy for you who from the towers
Of Brancepeth look in doubt and fear,
Telling melancholy hours !
Proclaim it, let your Masters hear
That Norton with his band is near !
The watchmen from their station high
Pronounced the word,—and the Earls descry,
Well-pleased, the armèd Company
Marching down the banks of Were.
    Said fearless Norton to the pair
Gone forth to greet him on the plain—
" This meeting, noble Lords ! looks fair,
I bring with me a goodly train ;
Their hearts are with you : hill and dale
Have helped us : Ure we crossed, and Swale,
And horse and harness followed—see
The best part of their Yeomanry !
—Stand forth, my Sons !—these eight are mine,
Whom to this service I commend ;
Which way soe'er our fate incline,
These will be faithful to the end ;
They are my all "—voice failed him here—
" My all save one, a Daughter dear !
Whom I have left, Love's mildest birth,
The meekest Child on this blessed earth.
I had—but these are by my side,
These Eight, and this is a day of pride !
The time is ripe.   With festive din
Lo ! how the people are flocking in,—
Like hungry fowl to the feeder's hand
When snow lies heavy upon the land."
    He spake bare truth ; for far and near
From every side came noisy swarms
Of Peasants in their homely gear ;
And, mixed with these, to Brancepeth came

Grave Gentry of estate and name,
And Captains known for worth in arms
And prayed the Earls in self-defence
To rise, and prove their innocence.—
" Rise, noble Earls, put forth your might
For holy Church, and the People's right ! "
    The Norton fixed, at this demand,
His eye upon Northumberland,
And said ; " The Minds of Men will own
No loyal rest while England's Crown
Remains without an Heir, the bait
Of strife and factions desperate ;
Who, paying deadly hate in kind
Through all things else, in this can find
A mutual hope, a common mind ;
And plot, and pant to overwhelm
All ancient honour in the realm.
—Brave Earls ! to whose heroic veins
Our noblest blood is given in trust,
To you a suffering State complains,
And ye must raise her from the dust.
With wishes of still bolder scope
On you we look, with dearest hope ;
Even for our Altars—for the prize,
In Heaven, of life that never dies ;
For the old and holy Church we mourn,
And must in joy to her return.
Behold ! "—and from his Son whose stand
Was on his right, from that guardian hand
He took the Banner, and unfurled
The precious folds—" behold," said he,
" The ransom of a sinful world ;
Let this your preservation be ;
The wounds of hands and feet and side,
And the sacred Cross on which Jesus died.
—This bring I from an ancient hearth,
These Records wrought in pledge of love
By hands of no ignoble birth,

A Maid o'er whom the blessed Dove
Vouchsafed in gentleness to brood
While she the holy work pursued."
" Uplift the Standard ! " was the cry
From all the listeners that stood round,
" Plant it,—by this we live or die."
The Norton ceased not for that sound,
But said ; " The prayer which ye have heard,
Much-injured Earls ! by these preferred,
Is offered to the Saints, the sigh
Of tens of thousands, secretly."
" Uplift it ! " cried once more the Band,
And then a thoughtful pause ensued :
" Uplift it ! " said Northumberland—
Whereat, from all the multitude
Who saw the Banner reared on high
In all its dread emblazonry,
A voice of uttermost joy brake out :
The transport was rolled down the river of Were,
And Durham, the time-honoured Durham, did hear,
And the towers of Saint Cuthbert were stirred by
      the shout !
   Now was the North in arms :—they shine
In warlike trim from Tweed to Tyne,
At Percy's voice : and Neville sees
His Followers gathering in from Tees,
From Were, and all the little rills
Concealed among the forkèd hills—
Seven hundred Knights, Retainers all
Of Neville, at their Master's call
Had sate together in Raby Hall !
Such strength that Earldom held of yore ;
Nor wanted at this time rich store
Of well-appointed chivalry.
—Not loth the sleepy lance to wield,
And greet the old paternal shield,
They heard the summons ;—and, furthermore,
Horsemen and Foot of each degree,

Unbound by pledge of fealty,
Appeared, with free and open hate
Of novelties in Church and State ;
Knight, burgher, yeoman, and esquire ;
And Romish priest, in priest's attire.
And thus, in arms, a zealous Band
Proceeding under joint command,
To Durham first their course they bear ;
And in Saint Cuthbert's ancient seat
Sang mass,—and tore the book of prayer,—
And trod the bible beneath their feet.
   Thence marching southward smooth and free
" They mustered their host at Wetherby,
Full sixteen thousand fair to see," *
The Choicest Warriors of the North !
But none for beauty and for worth
Like those eight Sons—who, in a ring,
(Ripe men, or blooming in life's spring)
Each with a lance, erect and tall,
A falchion, and a buckler small,
Stood by their Sire, on Clifford-moor,
To guard the Standard which he bore.
On foot they girt their Father round ;
And so will keep the appointed ground
Where'er their march : no steed will he
Henceforth bestride ;—triumphantly,
He stands upon the grassy sod,
Trusting himself to the earth, and God.
Rare sight to embolden and inspire !
Proud was the field of Sons and Sire ;
Of him the most ; and, sooth to say,
No shape of man in all the array
So graced the sunshine of that day.
The monumental pomp of age
Was with this goodly Personage ;
A stature undepressed in size,

* From the old ballad.

Unbent, which rather seemed to rise,
In open victory o'er the weight
Of seventy years, to loftier height ;
Magnific limbs of withered state ;
A face to fear and venerate ;
Eyes dark and strong ; and on his head
Bright locks of silver hair, thick spread,
Which a brown morion half-concealed,
Light as a hunter's of the field ;
And thus, with girdle round his waist,
Whereon the Banner-staff might rest
At need, he stood, advancing high
The glittering, floating Pageantry.
    Who sees him ?—thousands see, and One
With unparticipated gaze ;
Who, 'mong those thousands, friend hath none,
And treads in solitary ways.
He, following wheresoe'er he might,
Hath watched the Banner from afar,
As shepherds watch a lonely star,
Or mariners the distant light
That guides them through a stormy night.
And now, upon a chosen plot
Of rising ground, yon heathy spot !
He takes alone his far-off stand,
With breast unmailed, unweaponed hand.
Bold is his aspect ; but his eye
Is pregnant with anxiety,
While, like a tutelary Power,
He there stands fixed from hour to hour :
Yet sometimes in more humble guise,
Upon the turf-clad height he lies
Stretched, herdsman-like, as if to bask
In sunshine were his only task,
Or by his mantle's help to find
A shelter from the nipping wind :
And thus, with short oblivion blest,
His weary spirits gather rest.

Again he lifts his eyes ; and lo !
The pageant glancing to and fro ;
And hope is wakened by the sight,
He thence may learn, ere fall of night,
Which way the tide is doomed to flow.
   To London were the Chieftains bent ;
But what avails the bold intent ?
A Royal army is gone forth
To quell the RISING OF THE NORTH ;
They march with Dudley at their head,
And, in seven days' space, will to York be led !—
Can such a mighty Host be raised
Thus suddenly, and brought so near ?
The Earls upon each other gazed,
And Neville's cheek grew pale with fear ;
For, with a high and valiant name,
He bore a heart of timid frame ;
And bold if both had been, yet they
" Against so many may not stay." *
Back therefore will they hie to seize
A strong Hold on the banks of Tees ;
There wait a favourable hour,
Until Lord Dacre with his power
From Naworth come ; and Howard's aid
Be with them openly displayed.
   While through the Host, from man to man,
A rumour of this purpose ran,
The Standard trusting to the care
Of him who heretofore did bear
That charge, impatient Norton sought
The Chieftains to unfold his thought,
And thus abruptly spake ;—" We yield
(And can it be ?) an unfought field !—
How oft has strength, the strength of heaven,
To few triumphantly been given !
Still do our very children boast

* From the old ballad.

Of mitred Thurston—what a Host
He conquered !—Saw we not the Plain
(And flying shall behold again)
Where faith was proved ?—while to battle moved
The Standard, on the Sacred Wain
That bore it, compassed round by a bold
Fraternity of Barons old ;
And with those grey-haired champions stood,
Under the saintly ensigns three,
The infant Heir of Mowbray's blood—
All confident of victory !—
Shall Percy blush, then, for his name ?
Must Westmoreland be asked with shame
Whose were the numbers, where the loss,
In that other day of Neville's Cross ?
When the Prior of Durham with holy hand
Raised, as the Vision gave command,
Saint Cuthbert's Relic—far and near
Kenned on the point of a lofty spear ;
While the Monks prayed in Maiden's Bower
To God descending in his power.
Less would not at our need be due
To us, who war against the Untrue ;—
The delegates of Heaven we rise,
Convoked the impious to chastise :
We, we, the sanctities of old
Would re-establish and uphold :
Be warned ''—His zeal the Chiefs confounded,
But word was given, and the trumpet sounded :
Back through the melancholy Host
Went Norton, and resumed his post.
Alas ! thought he, and have I borne
This Banner raised with joyful pride,
This hope of all posterity,
By those dread symbols sanctified ;
Thus to become at once the scorn
Of babbling winds as they go by,
A spot of shame to the sun's bright eye,

To the light clouds a mockery !
—" Even these poor eight of mine would stem—"
Half to himself, and half to them
He spake—" would stem, or quell, a force
Ten times their number, man and horse :
This by their own unaided might,
Without their father in their sight,
Without the Cause for which they fight ;
A Cause, which on a needful day
Would breed us thousands brave as they."
—So speaking, he his reverend head
Raised towards that Imagery once more :
But the familiar prospect shed
Despondency unfelt before :
A shock of intimations vain,
Dismay, and superstitious pain,
Fell on him, with the sudden thought
Of her by whom the work was wrought :—
Oh wherefore was her countenance bright
With love divine and gentle light ?
She would not, could not, disobey,
But her Faith leaned another way.
Ill tears she wept ; I saw them fall,
I overheard her as she spake
Sad words to that mute Animal,
The White Doe, in the hawthorn brake ;
She steeped, but not for Jesu's sake,
This Cross in tears : by her, and One
Unworthier far we are undone—
Her recreant Brother—he prevailed
Over that tender Spirit—assailed
Too oft, alas ! by her whose head
In the cold grave hath long been laid :
She first, in reason's dawn beguiled
Her docile, unsuspecting Child :
Far back—far back my mind must go
To reach the well-spring of this woe !
  While thus he brooded, music sweet

Of border tunes was played to cheer
The footsteps of a quick retreat ;
But Norton lingered in the rear,
Stung with sharp thoughts ; and ere the last
From his distracted brain was cast,
Before his Father, Francis stood,
And spake in firm and earnest mood.

" Though here I bend a suppliant knee
In reverence, and unarmed, I bear
In your indignant thoughts my share ;
Am grieved this backward march to see
So careless and disorderly.
I scorn your Chiefs—men who would lead,
And yet want courage at their need :
Then look at them with open eyes !
Deserve they further sacrifice ?—
If—when they shrink, nor dare oppose
In open field their gathering foes,
(And fast, from this decisive day,
Yon multitude must melt away ;)
If now I ask a grace not claimed
While ground was left for hope ; unblamed
Be an endeavour that can do
No injury to them or you.
My Father ! I would help to find
A place of shelter, till the rage
Of cruel men do like the wind
Exhaust itself and sink to rest ;
Be Brother now to Brother joined !
Admit me in the equipage
Of your misfortunes, that at least,
Whatever fate remain behind,
I may bear witness in my breast
To your nobility of mind ! "

" Thou Enemy, my bane and blight !
Oh ! bold to fight the Coward's fight
Against all good "—but why declare,
At length, the issue of a prayer

Which love had prompted, yielding scope
Too free to one bright moment's hope ?
Suffice it that the Son, who strove
With fruitless effort to allay
That passion, prudently gave way ;
Nor did he turn aside to prove
His Brothers' wisdom or their love—
But calmly from the spot withdrew ;
His best endeavours to renew,
Should e'er a kindlier time ensue.

Canto Fourth

'Tis night : in silence looking down,
The Moon, from cloudless ether, sees
A Camp, and a beleaguered Town,
And Castle, like a stately crown
On the steep rocks of winding Tees ;—
And southward far, with moor between,
Hill-top, and flood, and forest green,
The bright Moon sees that valley small
Where Rylstone's old sequestered Hall
A venerable image yields
Of quiet to the neighbouring fields ;
While from one pillared chimney breathes
The smoke, and mounts in silver wreaths.
—The courts are hushed ;—for timely sleep
The greyhounds to their kennel creep ;
The peacock in the broad ash tree
Aloft is roosted for the night,
He who in proud prosperity
Of colours manifold and bright
Walked round, affronting the daylight ;
And higher still, above the bower
Where he is perched, from yon lone Tower
The hall-clock in the clear moonshine
With glittering finger points at nine.

Ah ! who could think that sadness here
Hath any sway ? or pain, or fear ?
A soft and lulling sound is heard
Of streams inaudible by day ;
The garden pool's dark surface, stirred
By the night insects in their play,
Breaks into dimples small and bright ;
A thousand, thousand rings of light
That shape themselves and disappear
Almost as soon as seen :—and lo !
Not distant far, the milk-white Doe—
The same who quietly was feeding
On the green herb, and nothing heeding,
When Francis, uttering to the Maid
His last words in the yew-tree shade,
Involved whate'er by love was brought
Out of his heart, or crossed his thought,
Or chance presented to his eye,
In one sad sweep of destiny—
The same fair Creature, who hath found
Her way into forbidden ground ;
Where now—within this spacious plot
For pleasure made, a goodly spot,
With lawns and beds of flowers, and shades
Of trellis-work in long arcades,
And cirque and crescent framed by wall
Of close-clipt foliage green and tall,
Converging walks, and fountains gay,
And terraces in trim array—
Beneath yon cypress spiring high,
With pine and cedar spreading wide
Their darksome boughs on either side,
In open moonlight doth she lie ;
Happy as others of her kind,
That, far from human neighbourhood,
Range unrestricted as the wind,
Through park, or chase, or savage wood.
But see the consecrated Maid

Emerging from a cedar shade
To open moonshine, where the Doe
Beneath the cypress-spire is laid ;
Like a patch of April snow—
Upon a bed of herbage green,
Lingering in a woody glade
Or behind a rocky screen—
Lonely relic ! which, if seen
By the shepherd, is passed by
With an inattentive eye.
Nor more regard doth She bestow
Upon the uncomplaining Doe
Now couched at ease, though oft this day
Not unperplexed nor free from pain,
When she had tried, and tried in vain,
Approaching in her gentle way,
To win some look of love, or gain
Encouragement to sport or play ;
Attempts which still the heart-sick Maid
Rejected, or with slight repaid.
    Yet Emily is soothed ;—the breeze
Came fraught with kindly sympathies.
As she approached yon rustic Shed
Hung with late-flowering woodbine, spread
Along the walls and overhead,
The fragrance of the breathing flowers
Revived a memory of those hours
When here, in this remote alcove,
(While from the pendent woodbine came
Like odours, sweet as if the same)
A fondly-anxious Mother strove
To teach her salutary fears
And mysteries above her years.
Yes, she is soothed : an Image faint,
And yet not faint—a presence bright
Returns to her—that blessèd Saint
Who with mild looks and language mild
Instructed here her darling Child

While yet a prattler on the knee,
To worship in simplicity
The invisible God, and take for guide
The faith reformed and purified.
  'Tis flown—the Vision, and the sense
Of that beguiling influence,
" But oh ! thou Angel from above,
Mute Spirit of maternal love,
That stood'st before my eyes, more clear
Than ghosts are fabled to appear
Sent upon embassies of fear ;
As thou thy presence hast to me
Vouchsafed, in radiant ministry
Descend on Francis ; nor forbear
To greet him with a voice, and say ;—
' If hope be a rejected stay,
' Do thou, my christian Son, beware
' Of that most lamentable snare,
' The self-reliance of despair ! ' "
  Then from within the embowered retreat
Where she had found a grateful seat
Perturbed she issues.   She will go !
Herself will follow to the war,
And clasp her Father's knees ;—ah, no !
She meets the insuperable bar,
The injunction by her Brother laid ;
His parting charge—but ill obeyed—
That interdicted all debate,
All prayer for this cause or for that ;
All efforts that would turn aside
The headstrong current of their fate :
Her duty is to stand and wait ;
In resignation to abide
The shock, AND FINALLY SECURE
O'ER PAIN AND GRIEF A TRIUMPH PURE.
—She feels it, and her pangs are checked.
But now, as silently she paced
The turf, and thought by thought was chased,

Came One who, with sedate respect,
Approached, and, greeting her, thus spake;
" An old man's privilege I take :
Dark is the time—a woeful day !
Dear daughter of affliction, say
How can I serve you ? point the way."

   " Rights have you, and may well be bold ;
You with my Father have grown old
In friendship—strive—for his sake go—
Turn from us all the coming woe :
This would I beg ; but on my mind
A passive stillness is enjoined.
On you, if room for mortal aid
Be left, is no restriction laid ;
You not forbidden to recline
With hope upon the Will divine."

   " Hope," said the old Man, " must abide
With all of us, whate'er betide.
In Craven's Wilds is many a den,
To shelter persecuted men :
Far under ground is many a cave,
Where they might lie as in the grave,
Until this storm hath ceased to rave :
Or let them cross the River Tweed,
And be at once from peril freed ! "

   " Ah tempt me not ! " she faintly sighed ;
" I will not counsel nor exhort,
With my condition satisfied ;
But you, at least, may make report
Of what befalls ;—be this your task—
This may be done ;—'tis all I ask ! "

   She spake—and from the Lady's sight
The Sire, unconscious of his age,
Departed promptly as a Page
Bound on some errand of delight.
—The noble Francis—wise as brave,
Thought he, may want not skill to save.
With hopes in tenderness concealed,

Unarmed he followed to the field ;
Him will I seek : the insurgent Powers
Are now besieging Barnard's Towers,—
" Grant that the Moon which shines this night
May guide them in a prudent flight ! "
    But quick the turns of chance and change,
And knowledge has a narrow range ;
Whence idle fears, and needless pain,
And wishes blind, and efforts vain.—
The Moon may shine, but cannot be
Their guide in flight—already she
Hath witnessed their captivity.
She saw the desperate assault
Upon that hostile castle made ;—
But dark and dismal is the vault
Where Norton and his sons are laid !
Disastrous issue !—he had said
" This night yon faithless Towers must yield,
Or we for ever quit the field.
—Neville is utterly dismayed,
For promise fails of Howard's aid ;
And Dacre to our call replies
That *he* is unprepared to rise.
My heart is sick ;—this weary pause
Must needs be fatal to our cause.
The breach is open—on the wall,
This night, the Banner shall be planted ! "
—'Twas done : his Sons were with him—all ;
They belt him round with hearts undaunted
And others follow ;—Sire and Son
Leap down into the court ;—" 'Tis won "—
They shout aloud—but Heaven decreed
That with their joyful shout should close
The triumph of a desperate deed
Which struck with terror friends and foes !
The friend shrinks back—the foe recoils
From Norton and his filial band ;
But they, now caught within the toils,

Against a thousand cannot stand ;—
The foe from numbers courage drew,
And overpowered that gallant few.
" A rescue for the Standard ! " cried
The Father from within the walls ;
But, see, the sacred Standard falls !—
Confusion through the Camp spread wide :
Some fled ; and some their fears detained :
But ere the Moon had sunk to rest
In her pale chambers of the west,
Of that rash levy nought remained.

CANTO FIFTH

HIGH on a point of rugged ground
Among the wastes of Rylstone Fell
Above the loftiest ridge or mound
Where foresters or shepherds dwell,
An edifice of warlike frame
Stands single—Norton Tower its name—
It fronts all quarters, and looks round
O'er path and road, and plain and dell,
Dark moor, and gleam of pool and stream,
Upon a prospect without bound.
    The summit of this bold ascent—
Though bleak and bare, and seldom free
As Pendle-hill or Pennygent
From wind, or frost, or vapours wet—
Had often heard the sound of glee
When there the youthful Nortons met,
To practise games and archery :
How proud and happy they ! the crowd
Of Lookers-on how pleased and proud !
And from the scorching noon-tide sun,
From showers, or when the prize was won,
They to the Tower withdrew, and there
Would mirth run round, with generous fare ;

And the stern old Lord of Rylstone-hall
Was happiest, proudest, of them all !

But now, his Child, with anguish pale,
Upon the height walks to and fro ;
'Tis well that she hath heard the tale,
Received the bitterness of woe :
For she *had* hoped, had hoped and feared,
Such rights did feeble nature claim ;
And oft her steps had hither steered,
Though not unconscious of self-blame ;
For she her brother's charge revered,
His farewell words ; and by the same,
Yea by her brother's very name,
Had, in her solitude, been cheered.

Beside the lonely watch-tower stood
That grey-haired Man of gentle blood,
Who with her Father had grown old
In friendship ; rival hunters they,
And fellow warriors in their day ;
To Rylstone he the tidings brought ;
Then on this height the Maid had sought.
And, gently as he could, had told
The end of that dire Tragedy,
Which it had been his lot to see.

To him the Lady turned : " You said
That Francis lives, *he* is not dead ? "
" Your noble brother hath been spared ;
To take his life they have not dared ;
On him and on his high endeavour
The light of praise shall shine for ever !
Nor did he (such Heaven's will) in vain
His solitary course maintain ;
Not vainly struggled in the might
Of duty, seeing with clear sight ;
He was their comfort to the last,
Their joy till every pang was past
I witnessed when to York they came—
What, Lady, if their feet were tied ;

They might deserve a good Man's blame ;
But marks of infamy and shame—
These were their triumph, these their pride ;
Nor wanted 'mid the pressing crowd
Deep feeling, that found utterance loud,
' Lo, Francis comes,' there were who cried,
' A Prisoner once, but now set free !
'Tis well, for he the worst defied
Through force of natural piety ;
He rose not in this quarrel ; he,
For concord's sake and England's good,
Suit to his Brothers often made
With tears, and of his Father prayed—
And when he had in vain withstood
Their purpose—then did he divide,
He parted from them ; but at their side
Now walks in unanimity.
Then peace to cruelty and scorn,
While to the prison they are borne,
Peace, peace to all indignity ! '
   And so in Prison were they laid—
Oh hear me, hear me, gentle Maid,
For I am come with power to bless,
By scattering gleams, through your distress,
Of a redeeming happiness.
Me did a reverent pity move
And privilege of ancient love ;
And, in your service, making bold,
Entrance I gained to that stronghold.
   Your Father gave me cordial greeting ;
But to his purposes, that burned
Within him, instantly returned :
He was commanding and entreating,
And said—' We need not stop, my Son !
Thoughts press, and time is hurrying on '—
And so to Francis he renewed
His words, more calmly thus pursued.
   ' Might this our enterprise have sped,

Change wide and deep the Land had seen,
A renovation from the dead,
A spring-tide of immortal green :
The darksome altars would have blazed
Like stars when clouds are rolled away ;
Salvation to all eyes that gazed,
Once more the Rood had been upraised
To spread its arms, and stand for aye.
Then, then—had I survived to see
New life in Bolton Priory ;
The voice restored, the eye of Truth
Re-opened that inspired my youth ;
To see her in her pomp arrayed—
This Banner (for such vow I made)
Should on the consecrated breast
Of that same Temple have found rest :
I would myself have hung it high,
Fit offering of glad victory !
    A shadow of such thought remains
To cheer this sad and pensive time ;
A solemn fancy yet sustains
One feeble Being—bids me climb
Even to the last—one effort more
To attest my Faith, if not restore.
    Hear then,' said he, ' while I impart,
My Son, the last wish of my heart.
The Banner strive thou to regain ;
And, if the endeavour prove not vain,
Bear it—to whom if not to thee
Shall I this lonely thought consign ?—
Bear it to Bolton Priory,
And lay it on Saint Mary's shrine ;
To wither in the sun and breeze
'Mid those decaying sanctities.
There let at least the gift be laid,
The testimony there displayed ;
Bold proof that with no selfish aim,
But for lost Faith and Christ's dear name,

I helmeted a brow though white,
And took a place in all men's sight ;
Yea offered up this noble Brood,
This fair unrivalled Brotherhood,
And turned away from thee, my Son !
And left—but be the rest unsaid,
The name untouched, the tear unshed ;—
My wish is known, and I have done :
Now promise, grant this one request,
This dying prayer, and be thou blest ! '
    Then Francis answered—' Trust thy Son,
For, with God's will, it shall be done ! '—
    The pledge obtained, the solemn word
Thus scarcely given, a noise was heard,
And Officers appeared in state
To lead the prisoners to their fate.
They rose, oh ! wherefore should I fear
To tell, or, Lady, you to hear ?
They rose—embraces none were given—
They stood like trees when earth and heaven
Are calm ; they knew each other's worth,
And reverently the Band went forth.
They met, when they had reached the door,
One with profane and harsh intent
Placed there—that he might go before
And, with that rueful Banner borne
Aloft in sign of taunting scorn,
Conduct them to their punishment :
So cruel Sussex, unrestrained
By human feeling, had ordained.
The unhappy Banner Francis saw,
And, with a look of calm command
Inspiring universal awe,
He took it from the soldier's hand ;
And all the people that stood round
Confirmed the deed in peace profound.
—High transport did the Father shed
Upon his Son—and they were led,

Led on, and yielded up their breath :
Together died, a happy death !—
But Francis, soon as he had braved
That insult, and the Banner saved,
Athwart the unresisting tide
Of the spectators occupied
In admiration or dismay,
Bore instantly his Charge away."
   These things, which thus had in the sight
And hearing passed of Him who stood
With Emily, on the Watch-tower height,
In Rylstone's woeful neighbourhood,
He told ; and oftentimes with voice
Of power to comfort or rejoice ;
For deepest sorrows that aspire,
Go high, no transport ever higher.
" Yes—God is rich in mercy," said
The old Man to the silent Maid,
" Yet, Lady ! shines, through this black night,
One star of aspect heavenly bright ;
Your Brother lives—he lives—is come
Perhaps already to his home ;
Then let us leave this dreary place."
She yielded, and with gentle pace,
Though without one uplifted look,
To Rylstone-hall her way she took.

CANTO SIXTH

WHY comes not Francis ?—From the doleful City
He fled,—and, in his flight, could hear
The death-sounds of the Minster-bell :
That sullen stroke pronounced farewell
To Marmaduke, cut off from pity !
To Ambrose that ! and then a knell
For him, the sweet half-opened Flower !
For all—all dying in one hour !

—Why comes not Francis ?   Thoughts of love
Should bear him to his Sister dear
With the fleet motion of a dove ;
Yea, like a heavenly messenger
Of speediest wing, should he appear.
Why comes he not ?—for westward fast
Along the plain of York he past :
Reckless of what impels or leads,
Unchecked he hurries on ;—nor heeds
The sorrow, through the Villages,
Spread by triumphant cruelties
Of vengeful military force,
And punishment without remorse.
He marked not, heard not, as he fled
All but the suffering heart was dead
For him, abandoned to blank awe,
To vacancy, and horror strong :
And the first object which he saw,
With conscious sight, as he swept along—
It was the Banner in his hand !
He felt—and made a sudden stand.

He looked about like one betrayed :
What hath he done ? what promise made ?
Oh weak, weak moment ! to what end
Can such a vain oblation tend,
And he the Bearer ?—Can he go
Carrying this instrument of woe,
And find, find anywhere, a right
To excuse him in his Country's sight ?
No ; will not all men deem the change
A downward course, perverse and strange ?
Here is it ;—but how ? when ? must she,
The unoffending Emily,
Again this piteous object see ?

Such conflict long did he maintain,
Nor liberty nor rest could gain :
His own life into danger brought
By this sad burden—even that thought,

Exciting self-suspicion strong,
Swayed the brave man to his wrong.
And how—unless it were the sense
Of all-disposing Providence,
Its will unquestionably shown—
How has the Banner clung so fast
To a palsied, and unconscious hand ;
Clung to the hand to which it passed
Without impediment ?   And why,
But that Heaven's purpose might be known,
Doth now no hindrance meet his eye,
No intervention, to withstand
Fulfilment of a Father's prayer
Breathed to a Son forgiven, and blest
When all resentments were at rest,
And life in death laid the heart bare ?—
Then, like a spectre sweeping by,
Rushed through his mind the prophecy
Of utter desolation made
To Emily in the yew-tree shade :
He sighed, submitting will and power
To the stern embrace of that grasping hour.
" No choice is left, the deed is mine—
Dead are they, dead !—and I will go,
And, for their sakes, come weal or woe,
Will lay the Relic on the shrine."
     So forward with a steady will
He went, and traversed plain and hill ;
And up the vale of Wharf his way
Pursued ;—and, at the dawn of day,
Attained a summit whence his eyes
Could see the Tower of Bolton rise.
There Francis for a moment's space
Made halt—but hark ! a noise behind
Of horsemen at an eager pace !
He heard, and with misgiving mind.
—'Tis Sir George Bowes who leads the Band :
They come, by cruel Sussex sent ;

Who, when the Nortons from the hand
Of death had drunk their punishment,
Bethought him, angry and ashamed,
How Francis, with the Banner claimed
As his own charge, had disappeared,
By all the standers-by revered.
His whole bold carriage (which had quelled
Thus far the Opposer, and repelled
All censure, enterprise so bright
That even bad men had vainly striven
Against that overcoming light)
Was then reviewed, and prompt word given
That to what place soever fled
He should be seized, alive or dead.

The troop of horse have gained the height
Where Francis stood in open sight.
They hem him round—" Behold the proof,"
They cried, " the Ensign in his hand !
He did not arm, he walked aloof !
For why ?—to save his Father's land ;—
Worst Traitor of them all is he,
A Traitor dark and cowardly ! "
" I am no Traitor," Francis said,
" Though this unhappy freight I bear ;
And must not part with.   But beware ;—
Err not by hasty zeal misled,
Nor do a suffering Spirit wrong,
Whose self-reproaches are too strong ! "
At this he from the beaten road
Retreated towards a brake of thorn,
That like a place of vantage showed ;
And there stood bravely, though forlorn.
In self-defence with warlike brow
He stood,—nor weaponless was now ;
He from a Soldier's hand had snatched
A spear,—and, so protected, watched
The Assailants, turning round and round ;
But from behind with treacherous wound

A Spearman brought him to the ground.
The guardian lance, as Francis fell,
Dropped from him ; but his other hand
The Banner clenched ; till, from out the Band,
One, the most eager for the prize,
Rushed in ; and—while, O grief to tell !
A glimmering sense still left, with eyes
Unclosed the noble Francis lay—
Seized it, as hunters seize their prey ;
But not before the warm life-blood
Had tinged more deeply, as it flowed,
The wounds the broidered Banner showed,
Thy fatal work, O Maiden, innocent as good !
　　Proudly the Horsemen bore away
The Standard ; and where Francis lay
There was he left alone, unwept,
And for two days unnoticed slept.
For at that time bewildering fear
Possessed the country, far and near ;
But, on the third day, passing by
One of the Norton Tenantry
Espied the uncovered Corse ; the Man
Shrunk as he recognised the face,
And to the nearest homesteads ran
And called the people to the place.
—How desolate is Rylstone-hall !
This was the instant thought of all ;
And if the lonely Lady there
Should be ; to her they cannot bear
This weight of anguish and despair.
So, when upon sad thoughts had prest
Thoughts sadder still, they deemed it best
That, if the Priest should yield assent
And no one hinder their intent,
Then, they, for Christian pity's sake,
In holy ground a grave would make ;
And straightway buried he should be
In the Churchyard of the Priory.

Apart, some little space, was made
The grave where Francis must be laid.
In no confusion or neglect
This did they,—but in pure respect
That he was born of gentle blood ;
And that there was no neighbourhood
Of kindred for him in that ground :
So to the Churchyard they are bound,
Bearing the body on a bier ;
And psalms they sing—a holy sound
That hill and vale with sadness hear.

But Emily hath raised her head,
And is again disquieted ;
She must behold !—so many gone,
Where is the solitary One ?
And forth from Rylstone-hall stepped she,—
To seek her Brother forth she went,
And tremblingly her course she bent
Toward Bolton's ruined Priory.
She comes, and in the vale hath heard
The funeral dirge ;—she sees the knot
Of people, sees them in one spot—
And darting like a wounded bird
She reached the grave, and with her breast
Upon the ground received the rest,—
The consummation, the whole ruth
And sorrow of this final truth !

CANTO SEVENTH

" Powers there are
That touch each other to the quick—in modes
Which the gross world no sense hath to perceive,
No soul to dream of."

THOU Spirit, whose angelic hand
Was to the harp a strong command,
Called the submissive strings to wake

In glory for this Maiden's sake,
Say, Spirit ! whither hath she fled
To hide her poor afflicted head ?
What mighty forest in its gloom
Enfolds her ?—is a rifted tomb
Within the wilderness her seat ?
Some island which the wild waves beat—
Is that the Sufferer's last retreat ?
Or some aspiring rock, that shrouds
Its perilous front in mists and clouds ?
High-climbing rock, low sunless dale,
Sea, desert, what do these avail ?
Oh take her anguish and her fears
Into a deep recess of years !

　　'Tis done ;—despoil and desolation
O'er Rylstone's fair domain have blown ;
Pools, terraces, and walks are sown
With weeds ; the bowers are overthrown,
Or have given way to slow mutation,
While, in their ancient habitation
The Norton name hath been unknown.
The lordly mansion of its pride
Is stripped ; the ravage hath spread wide
Through park and field, a perishing
That mocks the gladness of the Spring !
And, with this silent gloom agreeing,
Appears a joyless human Being,
Of aspect such as if the waste
Were under her dominion placed.
Upon a primrose bank, her throne
Of quietness, she sits alone ;
Among the ruins of a wood,
Erewhile a covert bright and green,
And where full many a brave tree stood,
That used to spread its boughs, and ring
With the sweet bird's carolling,
Behold her, like a virgin Queen,
Neglecting in imperial state

These outward images of fate,
And carrying inward a serene
And perfect sway, through many a thought
Of chance and change, that hath been brought
To the subjection of a holy,
Though stern and rigorous, melancholy !
The like authority, with grace
Of awfulness, is in her face,—
There hath she fixed it ; yet it seems
To o'ershadow by no native right
That face, which cannot lose the gleams,
Lose utterly the tender gleams,
Of gentleness and meek delight,
And loving-kindness ever bright :
Such is her sovereign mien :—her dress
(A vest with woollen cincture tied,
A hood of mountain-wool undyed)
Is homely,—fashioned to express
A wandering Pilgrim's humbleness.

And she *hath* wandered, long and far,
Beneath the light of sun and star ;
Hath roamed in trouble and in grief,
Driven forward like a withered leaf,
Yea like a ship at random blown
To distant places and unknown.
But now she dares to seek a haven
Among her native wilds of Craven ;
Hath seen again her Father's roof,
And put her fortitude to proof ;
The mighty sorrow hath been borne,
And she is thoroughly forlorn :
Her soul doth in itself stand fast,
Sustained by memory of the past
And strength of Reason ; held above
The infirmities of mortal love ;
Undaunted, lofty, calm, and stable,
And awfully impenetrable.

And so—beneath a mouldered tree,

A self-surviving leafless oak
By unregarded age from stroke
Of ravage saved—sate Emily.
There did she rest, with head reclined,
Herself most like a stately flower,
(Such have I seen) whom chance of birth
Hath separated from its kind,
To live and die in a shady bower,
Single on the gladsome earth.

When, with a noise like distant thunder,
A troop of deer came swooping by ;
And, suddenly, behold a wonder !
For One, among those rushing deer,
A single One, in mid career
Hath stopped, and fixed her large full eye
Upon the Lady Emily ;
A Doe most beautiful, clear-white,
A radiant creature, silver-bright !

Thus checked, a little while it stayed ;
A little thoughtful pause it made ;
And then advanced with stealth-like pace,
Drew softly near her, and more near—
Looked round—but saw no cause for fear ;
So to her feet the Creature came,
And laid its head upon her knee,
And looked into the Lady's face,
A look of pure benignity,
And fond unclouded memory.
It is, thought Emily, the same,
The very Doe of other years !—
The pleading look the Lady viewed,
And, by her gushing thoughts subdued,
She melted into tears—
A flood of tears, that flowed apace,
Upon the happy Creature's face.

Oh, moment ever blest ! O Pair
Beloved of Heaven, Heaven's chosen care,
This was for you a precious greeting ;

And may it prove a fruitful meeting !
Joined are they, and the sylvan Doe
Can she depart ? can she forego
The Lady, once her playful peer,
And now her sainted Mistress dear ?
And will not Emily receive
This lovely chronicler of things
Long past, delights and sorrowings ?
Lone Sufferer ! will not she believe
The promise in that speaking face ;
And welcome, as a gift of grace,
The saddest thought the Creature brings ?
   That day, the first of a re-union
Which was to teem with high communion,
That day of balmy April weather,
They tarried in the wood together.
And when, ere fall of evening dew,
She from her sylvan haunt withdrew,
The White Doe tracked with faithful pace
The Lady to her dwelling-place ;
That nook where, on paternal ground,
A habitation she had found,
The Master of whose humble board
Once owned her Father for his Lord ;
A hut, by tufted trees defended,
Where Rylstone brook with Wharf is blended.
   When Emily by morning light
Went forth, the Doe stood there in sight.
She shrunk :—with one frail shock of pain
Received and followed by a prayer,
She saw the Creature once again ;
Shun will she not, she feels, will bear ;—
But, wheresoever she looked round,
All now was trouble-haunted ground ;
And therefore now she deems it good
Once more this restless neighbourhood
To leave.—Unwooed, yet unforbidden,
The White Doe followed up the vale,

Up to another cottage, hidden
In the deep fork of Amerdale ;
And there may Emily restore
Herself, in spots unseen before.
—Why tell of mossy rock, or tree,
By lurking Dernbrook's pathless side,
Haunts of a strengthening amity
That calmed her, cheered, and fortified ?
For she hath ventured now to read
Of time, and place, and thought, and deed—
Endless history that lies
In her silent Follower's eyes ;
Who with a power like human reason
Discerns the favourable season,
Skilled to approach or to retire,—
From looks conceiving her desire ;
From look, deportment, voice, or mien,
That vary to the heart within.
If she too passionately wreathed
Her arms, or over-deeply breathed,
Walked quick or slowly, every mood
In its degree was understood ;
Then well may their accord be true,
And kindliest intercourse ensue.
—Oh ! surely 'twas a gentle rousing
When she by sudden glimpse espied
The White Doe on the mountain browsing,
Or in the meadow wandered wide !
How pleased, when down the Straggler sank
Beside her, on some sunny bank !
How soothed, when in thick bower enclosed,
They, like a nested pair, reposed !
Fair Vision ! when it crossed the Maid
Within some rocky cavern laid,
The dark cave's portal gliding by,
White as whitest cloud on high
Floating through the azure sky.
—What now is left for pain or fear ?

That Presence, dearer and more dear,
While they, side by side, were straying,
And the shepherd's pipe was playing,
Did now a very gladness yield
At morning to the dewy field,
And with a deeper peace endued
The hour of moonlight solitude.

With her Companion, in such frame
Of mind, to Rylstone back she came ;
And, ranging through the wasted groves,
Received the memory of old loves,
Undisturbed and undistrest,
Into a soul which now was blest
With a soft spring-day of holy,
Mild, and grateful, melancholy :
Not sunless gloom or unenlightened,
But by tender fancies brightened.

When the bells of Rylstone played
Their sabbath music—" 𝔊𝔬𝔡 𝔲𝔰 𝔞𝔶𝔡𝔢 ! "
That was the sound they seemed to speak ;
Inscriptive legend which I ween
May on those holy bells be seen,
That legend and her Grandsire's name ;
And oftentimes the Lady meek
Had in her childhood read the same ;
Words which she slighted at that day ;
But now, when such sad change was wrought,
And of that lonely name she thought—
The bells of Rylstone seemed to say,
While she sate listening in the shade,
With vocal music, " 𝔊𝔬𝔡 𝔲𝔰 𝔞𝔶𝔢 ; "
And all the hills were glad to bear
Their part in this effectual prayer.

Nor lacked she Reason's firmest power ;
But with the White Doe at her side
Up would she climb to Norton Tower,
And thence look round her far and wide,
Her fate there measuring ;—all is stilled.—

The weak One hath subdued her heart ;
Behold the prophecy fulfilled,
Fulfilled, and she sustains her part !
But here her Brother's words have failed ;
Here hath a milder doom prevailed ;
That she, of him and all bereft,
Hath yet this faithful Partner left ;
This one Associate, that disproves
His words, remains for her, and loves.
If tears are shed, they do not fall
For loss of them—for one, or all ;
Yet, sometimes, sometimes doth she weep,
Moved gently in her soul's soft sleep ;
A few tears down her cheek descend
For this her last and living Friend.

Bless, tender Hearts, their mutual lot,
And bless for both this savage spot ;
Which Emily doth sacred hold
For reasons dear and manifold—
Here hath she, here before her sight,
Close to the summit of this height,
The grassy rock-encircled Pound
In which the Creature first was found.
So beautiful the timid Thrall
(A spotless Youngling white as foam)
Her youngest Brother brought it home ;
The youngest, then a lusty boy,
Bore it, or led, to Rylstone-hall
With heart brimful of pride and joy !

But most to Bolton's sacred Pile,
On favouring nights, she loved to go ;
There ranged through cloister, court, and aisle,
Attended by the soft-paced Doe ;
Nor feared she in the still moonshine
To look upon Saint Mary's shrine ;
Nor on the lonely turf that showed
Where Francis slept in his last abode.
For that she came ; there oft she sate

Forlorn, but not disconsolate :
And, when she from the abyss returned
Of thought, she neither shrunk nor mourned ;
Was happy that she lived to greet
Her mute Companion as it lay
In love and pity at her feet ;
How happy in its turn to meet
The recognition ! the mild glance
Beamed from that gracious countenance ;
Communication, like the ray
Of a new morning, to the nature
And prospects of the inferior Creature !
   A mortal Song we sing, by dower
Encouraged of celestial power ;
Power which the viewless Spirit shed
By whom we were first visited ;
Whose voice we heard, whose hand and wings
Swept like a breeze the conscious strings,
When, left in solitude, erewhile
We stood before this ruined Pile,
And, quitting unsubstantial dreams,
Sang in this Presence kindred themes ;
Distress and desolation spread
Through human hearts, and pleasure dead,—
Dead—but to live again on earth,
A second and yet nobler birth ;
Dire overthrow, and yet how high
The re-ascent in sanctity !
From fair to fairer ; day by day
A more divine and loftier way ?
Even such this blessèd Pilgrim trod,
By sorrow lifted towards her God ;
Uplifted to the purest sky
Of undisturbed mortality.
Her own thoughts loved she ; and could bend
A dear look to her lowly Friend ;
There stopped ; her thirst was satisfied
With what this innocent spring supplied :

Her sanction inwardly she bore,
And stood apart from human cares :
But to the world returned no more,
Although with no unwilling mind
Help did she give at need, and joined
The Wharfdale peasants in their prayers.
At length, thus faintly, faintly tied
To earth, she was set free, and died.
Thy soul, exalted Emily,
Maid of the blasted family,
Rose to the God from whom it came !
—In Rylstone Church her mortal frame
Was buried by her Mother's side.

  Most glorious sunset ! and a ray
Survives—the twilight of this day—
In that fair Creature whom the fields
Support, and whom the forest shields ;
Who, having filled a holy place,
Partakes, in her degree, Heaven's grace ;
And bears a memory and a mind
Raised far above the law of kind ;
Haunting the spots with lonely cheer
Which her dear Mistress once held dear :
Loves most what Emily loved most—
The enclosure of this churchyard ground ;
Here wanders like a gliding ghost,
And every sabbath here is found ;
Comes with the people when the bells
Are heard among the moorland dells,
Finds entrance through yon arch, where way
Lies open on the sabbath-day ;
Here walks amid the mournful waste
Of prostrate altars, shrines defaced,
And floors encumbered with rich show
Of fret-work imagery laid low ;
Paces softly, or makes halt,
By fractured cell, or tomb, or vault ;
By plate of monumental brass

Dim-gleaming among weeds and grass,
And sculptured Forms of Warriors brave :
But chiefly by that single grave,
That one sequestered hillock green,
The pensive visitant is seen.
There doth the gentle Creature lie
With those adversities unmoved ;
Calm spectacle, by earth and sky
In their benignity approved !
And aye, methinks, this hoary Pile,
Subdued by outrage and decay,
Looks down upon her with a smile,
A gracious smile, that seems to say—
" Thou, thou art not a Child of Time,
But Daughter of the Eternal Prime ! "

SIMON LEE

THE OLD HUNTSMAN ; WITH AN INCIDENT IN WHICH HE WAS CONCERNED

In the sweet shire of Cardigan,
Not far from pleasant Ivor-hall,
An old Man dwells, a little man,—
'Tis said he once was tall.
Full five and thirty years he lived
A running huntsman merry ;
And still the centre of his cheek
Is red as a ripe cherry.

No man like him the horn could sound,
And hill and valley rang with glee
When Echo bandied, round and round,
The halloo of Simon Lee.
In those proud days, he little cared
For husbandry or tillage ;
To blither tasks did Simon rouse
The sleepers of the village.

He all the country could outrun,
Could leave both man and horse behind ;
And often, ere the chase was done,
He reeled, and was stone-blind.
And still there's something in the world
At which his heart rejoices ;
For when the chiming hounds are out,
He dearly loves their voices !

But, oh the heavy change !—bereft
Of health, strength, friends, and kindred, see !
Old Simon to the world is left
In liveried poverty.
His Master's dead,—and no one now
Dwells in the Hall of Ivor ;
Men, dogs, and horses, all are dead ;
He is the sole survivor.

And he is lean and he is sick ;
His body, dwindled and awry,
Rests upon ankles swoln and thick ;
His legs are thin and dry.
One prop he has, and only one,
His wife, an aged woman,
Lives with him, near the waterfall,
Upon the village Common.

Beside their moss-grown hut of clay,
Not twenty paces from the door,
A scrap of land they have, but they
Are poorest of the poor.
This scrap of land he from the heath
Enclosed when he was stronger ;
But what to them avails the land
Which he can till no longer ?

Oft, working by her Husband's side,
Ruth does what Simon cannot do ;

For she, with scanty cause for pride,
Is stouter of the two.
And, though you with your utmost skill
From labour could not wean them,
'Tis little, very little—all
That they can do between them.

Few months of life has he in store,
As he to you will tell,
For still, the more he works, the more
Do his weak ankles swell.
My gentle Reader, I perceive
How patiently you've waited,
And now I fear that you expect
Some tale will be related.

O Reader ! had you in your mind
Such stores as silent thought can bring,
O gentle Reader ! you would find
A tale in every thing.
What more I have to say is short,
And you must kindly take it :
It is no tale ; but, should you think,
Perhaps a tale you'll make it.

One summer-day I chanced to see
This old Man doing all he could
To unearth the root of an old tree,
A stump of rotten wood.
The mattock tottered in his hand ;
So vain was his endeavour,
That at the root of the old tree
He might have worked for ever.

" You're overtasked, good Simon Lee,
Give me your tool," to him I said ;
And at the word right gladly he
Received my proffered aid.

I struck, and with a single blow
The tangled root I severed,
At which the poor old Man so long
And vainly had endeavoured.

The tears into his eyes were brought,
And thanks and praises seemed to run
So fast out of his heart, I thought
They never would have done.
—I've heard of hearts unkind, kind deeds
With coldness still returning ;
Alas ! the gratitude of men
Hath oftener left me mourning.

INCIDENT

CHARACTERISTIC OF A FAVOURITE DOG

On his morning rounds the Master
Goes to learn how all things fare ;
Searches pasture after pasture,
Sheep and cattle eyes with care ;
And, for silence or for talk,
He hath comrades in his walk ;
Four dogs, each pair of different breed,
Distinguished two for scent, and two for speed.

See a hare before him started !
—Off they fly in earnest chase ;
Every dog is eager-hearted,
All the four are in the race :
And the hare whom they pursue,
Knows from instinct what to do ;
Her hope is near : no turn she makes ;
But, like an arrow, to the river takes.

Deep the river was, and crusted
Thinly by a one night's frost ;
But the nimble Hare hath trusted
To the ice, and safely crost ;
She hath crost, and without heed
All are following at full speed,
When, lo ! the ice, so thinly spread,
Breaks—and the greyhound, DART, is overhead !

Better fate have PRINCE and SWALLOW—
See them cleaving to the sport !
MUSIC has no heart to follow,
Little MUSIC, she stops short.
She hath neither wish nor heart,
Hers is now another part :
A loving creature she, and brave !
And fondly strives her struggling friend to save.

From the brink her paws she stretches,
Very hands as you would say !
And afflicting moans she fetches,
As he breaks the ice away.
For herself she hath no fears,—
Him alone she sees and hears,—
Makes efforts with complainings ; nor gives o'er
Until her fellow sinks to reappear no more.

FIDELITY

A BARKING sound the Shepherd hears,
A cry as of a dog or fox ;
He halts—and searches with his eyes
Among the scattered rocks :
And now at distance can discern
A stirring in a brake of fern ;
And instantly a dog is seen,
Glancing through that covert green.

The Dog is not of mountain breed ;
Its motions, too, are wild and shy ;
With something, as the Shepherd thinks,
Unusual in its cry :
Nor is there any one in sight
All round, in hollow or on height ;
Nor shout, nor whistle strikes his ear ;
What is the creature doing here ?

It was a cove, a huge recess,
That keeps, till June, December's snow ;
A lofty precipice in front,
A silent tarn * below !
Far in the bosom of Helvellyn,
Remote from public road or dwelling,
Pathway, or cultivated land ;
From trace of human foot or hand.

There sometimes doth a leaping fish
Send through the tarn a lonely cheer ;
The crags repeat the raven's croak,
In symphony austere ;
Thither the rainbow comes—the cloud—
And mists that spread the flying shroud ;
And sunbeams ; and the sounding blast,
That, if it could, would hurry past ;
But that enormous barrier holds it fast.

Not free from boding thoughts, a while
The Shepherd stood ; then makes his way
O'er rocks and stones, following the Dog
As quickly as he may ;
Nor far had gone before he found
A human skeleton on the ground ;
The appalled Discoverer with a sigh
Looks round, to learn the history.

* Tarn is a *small* mere or lake, mostly high up in the mountains.

From those abrupt and perilous rocks
The Man had fallen, that place of fear !
At length upon the Shepherd's mind
It breaks, and all is clear :
He instantly recalled the name,
And who he was, and whence he came ;
Remembered, too, the very day
On which the Traveller passed this way.

But hear a wonder, for whose sake
This lamentable tale I tell !
A lasting monument of words
This wonder merits well.
The Dog, which still was hovering nigh,
Repeating the same timid cry,
This Dog, had been through three months' space
A dweller in that savage place.

Yes, proof was plain that, since the day
When this ill-fated Traveller died,
The Dog had watched about the spot,
Or by his master's side :
How nourished here through such long time
He knows, who gave that love sublime ;
And gave that strength of feeling, great
Above all human estimate !

THE FORCE OF PRAYER ; *

OR,

THE FOUNDING OF BOLTON PRIORY

A TRADITION

"𝔚𝔥𝔞𝔱 𝔦𝔰 𝔤𝔬𝔬𝔡 𝔣𝔬𝔯 𝔞 𝔟𝔬𝔬𝔱𝔩𝔢𝔰𝔰 𝔟𝔢𝔫𝔢 ?"
With these dark words begins my Tale ;
And their meaning is, whence can comfort spring
When Prayer is of no avail ?

* See "The White Doe of Rylstone."

" 𝔚hat is good for a bootless bene?"
The Falconer to the Lady said ;
And she made answer " ENDLESS SORROW ! "
For she knew that her Son was dead.

She knew it by the Falconer's words,
And from the look of the Falconer's eye,
And from the love which was in her soul
For her youthful Romilly.

—Young Romilly through Barden woods
Is ranging high and low ;
And holds a greyhound in a leash,
To let slip upon buck or doe.

The pair have reached that fearful chasm,
How tempting to bestride !
For lordly Wharf is there pent in
With rocks on either side.

This striding-place is called THE STRID,
A name which it took of yore :
A thousand years hath it borne that name,
And shall a thousand more.

And hither is young Romilly come,
And what may now forbid
That he, perhaps for the hundredth time,
Shall bound across THE STRID ?

He sprang in glee,—for what cared he
That the river was strong, and the rocks were steep?—
But the greyhound in the leash hung back,
And checked him in his leap.

The Boy is in the arms of Wharf,
And strangled by a merciless force ;
For never more was young Romilly seen
Till he rose a lifeless corse.

Now there is stillness in the vale,
And long, unspeaking, sorrow:
Wharf shall be to pitying hearts
A name more sad than Yarrow.

If for a lover the Lady wept,
A solace she might borrow
From death, and from the passion of death ;—
Old Wharf might heal her sorrow.

She weeps not for the wedding-day
Which was to be to-morrow :
Her hope was a further-looking hope,
And hers is a mother's sorrow.

He was a tree that stood alone,
And proudly did its branches wave ;
And the root of this delightful tree
Was in her husband's grave !

Long, long in darkness did she sit,
And her first words were, " Let there be
In Bolton, on the field of Wharf,
A stately Priory ! "

The stately Priory was reared ;
And Wharf, as he moved along,
To matins joined a mournful voice,
Nor failed at evensong.

And the Lady prayed in heaviness
That looked not for relief !
But slowly did her succour come,
And a patience to her grief.

Oh ! there is never sorrow of heart
That shall lack a timely end,
If but to God we turn, and ask
Of Him to be our friend !

PART III

SONNETS

SONNETS

"NUNS FRET NOT AT THEIR CONVENT'S NARROW ROOM"

Nuns fret not at their convent's narrow room;
And hermits are contented with their cells;
And students with their pensive citadels;
Maids at the wheel, the weaver at his loom,
Sit blithe and happy; bees that soar for bloom,
High as the highest Peak of Furness-fells,
Will murmur by the hour in foxglove bells:
In truth the prison, unto which we doom
Ourselves, no prison is: and hence for me,
In sundry moods, 'twas pastime to be bound
Within the Sonnet's scanty plot of ground;
Pleased if some Souls (for such there needs must be)
Who have felt the weight of too much liberty,
Should find brief solace there, as I have found.

TO SLEEP

A flock of sheep that leisurely pass by,
One after one; the sound of rain, and bees
Murmuring; the fall of rivers, winds and seas,
Smooth fields, white sheets of water, and pure sky;
I have thought of all by turns, and yet do lie
Sleepless! and soon the small birds' melodies
Must hear, first uttered from my orchard trees;
And the first cuckoo's melancholy cry.
Even thus last night, and two nights more, I lay,
And could not win thee, Sleep! by any stealth:
So do not let me wear to-night away:
Without Thee what is all the morning's wealth?
Come, blessed barrier between day and day,
Dear mother of fresh thoughts and joyous health!

TO THE RIVER DERWENT

AMONG the mountains were we nursed, loved Stream
Thou near the eagle's nest—within brief sail,
I, of his bold wing floating on the gale,
Where thy deep voice could lull me !   Faint the beam
Of human life when first allowed to gleam
On mortal notice.—Glory of the vale,
Such thy meek outset, with a crown, though frail,
Kept in perpetual verdure by the steam
Of thy soft breath !—Less vivid wreath entwined
Nemæan victor's brow ; less bright was worn,
Meed of some Roman chief—in triumph borne
With captives chained ; and shedding from his car
The sunset splendours of a finished war
Upon the proud enslavers of mankind !

"SURPRISED BY JOY—IMPATIENT AS THE WIND"

SURPRISED by joy—impatient as the Wind
I turned to share the transport—Oh ! with whom
But thee, deep buried in the silent tomb,
That spot which no vicissitude can find ?
Love, faithful love, recalled thee to my mind—
But how could I forget thee ?   Through what power,
Even for the least division of an hour,
Have I been so beguiled as to be blind
To my most grievous loss ?—That thought's return
Was the worst pang that sorrow ever bore,
Save one, one only, when I stood forlorn,
Knowing my heart's best treasure was no more :
That neither present time, nor years unborn
Could to my sight that heavenly face restore.

" IT IS A BEAUTEOUS EVENING, CALM AND FREE "

IT is a beauteous evening, calm and free,
The holy time is quiet as a Nun
Breathless with adoration ; the broad sun
Is sinking down in its tranquillity ;
The gentleness of heaven broods o'er the Sea :
Listen ! the mighty Being is awake,
And doth with his eternal motion make
A sound like thunder—everlastingly.
Dear Child ! dear Girl ! that walkest with me here,
If thou appear untouched by solemn thought,
Thy nature is not therefore less divine :
Thou liest in Abraham's bosom all the year ;
And worship'st at the Temple's inner shrine,
God being with thee when we know it not.

" WHERE LIES THE LAND TO WHICH YON SHIP MUST GO ? "

WHERE lies the Land to which yon Ship must go ?
Fresh as a lark mounting at break of day,
Festively she puts forth in trim array ;
Is she for tropic suns, or polar snow ?
What boots the inquiry ?—Neither friend nor foe
She cares for ; let her travel where she may,
She finds familiar names, a beaten way
Ever before her, and a wind to blow.
Yet still I ask, what haven is her mark ?
And, almost as it was when ships were rare,
(From time to time, like Pilgrims, here and there
Crossing the waters) doubt, and something dark,
Of the old Sea some reverential fear,
Is with me at thy farewell, joyous Bark !

" THE WORLD IS TOO MUCH WITH US ; LATE AND SOON "

THE world is too much with us ; late and soon,
Getting and spending, we lay waste our powers :
Little we see in Nature that is ours ;
We have given our hearts away, a sordid boon !
The Sea that bares her bosom to the moon ;
The winds that will be howling at all hours,
And are up-gathered now like sleeping flowers ;
For this, for everything, we are out of tune ;
It moves us not.—Great God ! I'd rather be
A Pagan suckled in a creed outworn ;
So might I, standing on this pleasant lea,
Have glimpses that would make me less forlorn ;
Have sight of Proteus rising from the sea ;
Or hear old Triton blow his wreathèd horn.

PERSONAL TALK

I AM not One who much or oft delight
To season my fireside with personal talk,—
Of friends, who live within an easy walk,
Or neighbours, daily, weekly, in my sight :
And, for my chance-acquaintance, ladies bright,
Sons, mothers, maidens withering on the stalk,
These all wear out of me, like Forms, with chalk
Painted on rich men's floors, for one feast-night.
Better than such discourse doth silence long,
Long, barren silence, square with my desire ;
To sit without emotion, hope, or aim,
In the loved presence of my cottage-fire,
And listen to the flapping of the flame,
Or kettle whispering its faint undersong.

" Yet life," you say, " is life ; we have seen and see,
And with a living pleasure we describe ;
And fits of sprightly malice do but bribe
The languid mind into activity.
Sound sense, and love itself, and mirth and glee
Are fostered by the comment and the gibe."
Even be it so ; yet still among your tribe,
Our daily world's true Worldlings, rank not me !
Children are blest, and powerful ; their world lies
More justly balanced ; partly at their feet
And part far from them ; sweetest melodies
Are those that are by distance made more sweet ;
Whose mind is but the mind of his own eyes,
He is a Slave ; the meanest we can meet !

Wings have we,—and as far as we can go
We may find pleasure : wilderness and wood,
Blank ocean and mere sky, support that mood
Which with the lofty sanctifies the low.
Dreams, books, are each a world ; and books, we know,
Are a substantial world, both pure and good :
Round these, with tendrils strong as flesh and blood,
Our pastime and our happiness will grow.
There find I personal themes, a plenteous store,
Matter wherein right voluble I am,
To which I listen with a ready ear ;
Two shall be named, pre-eminently dear,—
The gentle lady married to the Moor ;
And heavenly Una with her milk-white Lamb.

Nor can I not believe but that hereby
Great gains are mine ; for thus I live remote
From evil-speaking ; rancour, never sought,
Comes to me not ; malignant truth, or lie.
Hence have I genial seasons, hence have I
Smooth passions, smooth discourse, and joyous thought :
And thus from day to day my little boat
Rocks in its harbour, lodging peaceably.

Blessings be with them—and eternal praise,
Who gave us nobler loves, and nobler cares—
The Poets, who on earth have made us heirs
Of truth and pure delight by heavenly lays!
Oh! might my name be numbered among theirs,
Then gladly would I end my mortal days.

"SCORN NOT THE SONNET"

SCORN not the Sonnet; Critic, you have frowned,
Mindless of its just honours; with this key
Shakespeare unlocked his heart; the melody
Of this small lute gave ease to Petrarch's wound;
A thousand times this pipe did Tasso sound;
With it Camöens soothed an exile's grief;
The Sonnet glittered a gay myrtle leaf
Amid the cypress with which Dante crowned
His visionary brow: a glow-worm lamp
It cheered mild Spenser, called from Faeryland
To struggle through dark ways; and, when a damp
Fell round the path of Milton, in his hand
The Thing became a trumpet; whence he blew
Soul-animating strains—alas, too few!

COMPOSED UPON WESTMINSTER BRIDGE,
SEPTEMBER 3, 1802

EARTH has not anything to show more fair:
Dull would he be of soul who could pass by
A sight so touching in its majesty:
This City now doth, like a garment, wear
The beauty of the morning; silent, bare,
Ships, towers, domes, theatres, and temples lie
Open unto the fields, and to the sky;
All bright and glittering in the smokeless air.

Never did sun more beautifully steep
In his first splendour, valley, rock, or hill ;
Ne'er saw I, never felt, a calm so deep !
The river glideth at his own sweet will :
Dear God ! the very houses seem asleep ;
And all that mighty heart is lying still !

TO THE CUCKOO

NOT the whole warbling grove in concert heard
When sunshine follows shower, the breast can thrill
Like the first summons, Cuckoo ! of thy bill,
With its twin notes inseparably paired.
The captive 'mid damp vaults unsunned, unaired,
Measuring the periods of his lonely doom,
That cry can reach ; and to the sick man's room
Sends gladness, by no languid smile declared.
The lordly eagle-race through hostile search
May perish ; time may come when never more
The wilderness shall hear the lion roar ;
But, long as cock shall crow from household perch
To rouse the dawn, soft gales shall speed thy wing,
And thy erratic voice be faithful to the Spring !

TO ROTHA Q——

ROTHA, my Spiritual Child ! this head was grey
When at the sacred font for thee I stood ;
Pledged till thou reach the verge of womanhood,
And shalt become thy own sufficient stay :
Too late, I feel, sweet Orphan ! was the day
For stedfast hope the contract to fulfil ;
Yet shall my blessing hover o'er thee still,
Embodied in the music of this Lay,

Breathed forth beside the peaceful mountain Stream
Whose murmur soothed thy languid Mother's ear
After her throes, this Stream of name more dear
Since thou dost bear it,—a memorial theme
For others ; for thy future self, a spell
To summon fancies out of Time's dark cell.

COMPOSED BY THE SEA-SIDE, NEAR CALAIS,
AUGUST 1802

FAIR Star of evening, Splendour of the west,
Star of my Country !—on the horizon's brink
Thou hangest, stooping, as might seem, to sink
On England's bosom ; yet well pleased to rest,
Meanwhile, and be to her a glorious crest
Conspicuous to the Nations.   Thou, I think,
Should'st be my Country's emblem ; and should'st wink,
Bright Star ! with laughter on her banners, drest
In thy fresh beauty.   There ! that dusky spot
Beneath thee, that is England ; there she lies.
Blessings be on you both ! one hope, one lot,
One life, one glory !—I, with many a fear
For my dear Country, many heartfelt sighs,
Among men who do not love her, linger here.

CALAIS, AUGUST 1802

Is it a reed that's shaken by the wind ?
Or what is it that ye go forth to see ?
Lords, lawyers, statesmen, squires of low degree,
Men known, and men unknown, sick, lame, and blind,
Post forward all, like creatures of one kind,
With first-fruit offerings crowd to bend the knee
In France, before the new-born Majesty.
'Tis ever thus.   Ye men of prostrate mind,

A seemly reverence may be paid to power ;
But that's a loyal virtue, never sown
In haste, nor springing with a transient shower :
When truth, when sense, when liberty were flown,
What hardship had it been to wait an hour ?
Shame on you, feeble Heads, to slavery prone !

" I GRIEVED FOR BUONAPARTÉ "

I GRIEVED for Buonaparté, with a vain
And an unthinking grief !   The tenderest mood
Of that Man's mind—what can it be ? what food
Fed his first hopes ? what knowledge could *he* gain ?
'Tis not in battles that from youth we train
The Governor who must be wise and good,
And temper with the sternness of the brain
Thoughts motherly, and meek as womanhood.
Wisdom doth live with children round her knees :
Books, leisure, perfect freedom, and the talk
Man holds with week-day man in the hourly walk
Of the mind's business : these are the degrees
By which true Sway doth mount ; this is the stalk
True Power doth grow on ; and her rights are these.

ON THE EXTINCTION OF THE VENETIAN REPUBLIC

ONCE did She hold the gorgeous east in fee ;
And was the safeguard of the west : the worth
Of Venice did not fall below her birth,
Venice, the eldest Child of Liberty.
She was a maiden City, bright and free ;
No guile seduced, no force could violate ;
And, when she took unto herself a Mate,
She must espouse the everlasting Sea.

And what if she had seen those glories fade,
Those titles vanish, and that strength decay ;
Yet shall some tribute of regret be paid
When her long life hath reached its final day :
Men are we, and must grieve when even the Shade
Of that which once was great is passed away.

TO TOUSSAINT L'OUVERTURE

TOUSSAINT, the most unhappy man of men !
Whether the whistling Rustic tend his plough
Within thy hearing, or thy head be now
Pillowed in some deep dungeon's earless den ;—
O miserable Chieftain ! where and when
Wilt thou find patience ?   Yet die not ; do thou
Wear rather in thy bonds a cheerful brow :
Though fallen thyself, never to rise again,
Live, and take comfort.   Thou hast left behind
Powers that will work for thee ; air, earth, and skies ;
There's not a breathing of the common wind
That will forget thee ; thou hast great allies ;
Thy friends are exultations, agonies,
And love, and man's unconquerable mind.

SEPTEMBER 1, 1802

WE had a female Passenger who came
From Calais with us, spotless in array,—
A white-robed Negro, like a lady gay,
Yet downcast as a woman fearing blame ;
Meek, destitute, as seemed, of hope or aim
She sate, from notice turning not away,
But on all proffered intercourse did lay
A weight of languid speech, or to the same
No sign of answer made by word or face :
Yet still her eyes retained their tropic fire,
That, burning independent of the mind,

Joined with the lustre of her rich attire
To mock the Outcast.—O ye Heavens, be kind !
And feel, thou Earth, for this afflicted Race !

NEAR DOVER, September 1802

INLAND, within a hollow vale, I stood ;
And saw, while sea was calm and air was clear,
The coast of France—the coast of France how near !
Drawn almost into frightful neighbourhood.
I shrunk ; for verily the barrier flood
Was like a lake, or river bright and fair,
A span of waters ; yet what power is there !
What mightiness for evil and for good !
Even so doth God protect us if we be
Virtuous and wise.   Winds blow, and waters roll,
Strength to the brave, and Power, and Deity ;
Yet in themselves are nothing !   One decree
Spake laws to *them*, and said that by the soul
Only, the Nations shall be great and free.

THOUGHT OF A BRITON ON THE SUBJUGATION OF SWITZERLAND

Two Voices are there ; one is of the sea,
One of the mountains ; each a mighty Voice :
In both from age to age thou didst rejoice,
They were thy chosen music, Liberty !
There came a Tyrant, and with holy glee
Thou fought'st against him ; but hast vainly striven :
Thou from thy Alpine holds at length art driven,
Where not a torrent murmurs heard by thee.
Of one deep bliss thine ear hath been bereft :
Then cleave, O cleave to that which still is left ;
For, high-souled Maid, what sorrow would it be
That Mountain floods should thunder as before
And Ocean bellow from his rocky shore,
And neither awful Voice be heard by thee !

WRITTEN IN LONDON, SEPTEMBER 1802

O FRIEND ! I know not which way I must look
For comfort, being, as I am, opprest,
To think that now our life is only drest
For show ; mean handy-work of craftsman, cook,
Or groom !—We must run glittering like a brook
In the open sunshine, or we are unblest :
The wealthiest man among us is the best :
No grandeur now in nature or in book
Delights us.   Rapine, avarice, expense,
This is idolatry ; and these we adore :
Plain living and high thinking are no more :
The homely beauty of the good old cause
Is gone ; our peace, our fearful innocence,
And pure religion breathing household laws.

LONDON, 1802

MILTON ! thou should'st be living at this hour :
England hath need of thee : she is a fen
Of stagnant waters : altar, sword, and pen,
Fireside, the heroic wealth of hall and bower,
Have forfeited their ancient English dower
Of inward happiness.   We are selfish men ;
Oh ! raise us up, return to us again ;
And give us manners, virtue, freedom, power.
Thy soul was like a Star, and dwelt apart :
Thou hadst a voice whose sound was like the sea :
Pure as the naked heavens, majestic, free,
So didst thou travel on life's common way,
In cheerful godliness ; and yet thy heart
The lowliest duties on herself did lay.

"GREAT MEN HAVE BEEN AMONG US"

GREAT men have been among us; hands that penned
And tongues that uttered wisdom—better none:
The later Sidney, Marvel, Harrington,
Young Vane, and others who called Milton friend.
These moralists could act and comprehend:
They knew how genuine glory was put on;
Taught us how rightfully a nation shone
In splendour: what strength was, that would not bend
But in magnanimous meekness. France, 'tis strange,
Hath brought forth no such souls as we had then.
Perpetual emptiness! unceasing change!
No single volume paramount, no code,
No master spirit, no determined road;
But equally a want of books and men!

"IT IS NOT TO BE THOUGHT OF"

IT is not to be thought of that the Flood
Of British freedom, which, to the open sea
Of the world's praise, from dark antiquity
Hath flowed, "with pomp of waters, unwithstood,"
Roused though it be full often to a mood
Which spurns the check of salutary bands,
That this most famous Stream in bogs and sands
Should perish; and to evil and to good
Be lost for ever. In our halls is hung
Armoury of the invincible Knights of old:
We must be free or die, who speak the tongue
That Shakspeare spake; the faith and morals hold
Which Milton held.—In everything we are sprung
Of Earth's first blood, have titles manifold.

"WHEN I HAVE BORNE IN MEMORY"

WHEN I have borne in memory what has tamed
Great Nations, how ennobling thoughts depart
When men change swords for ledgers, and desert
The student's bower for gold, some fears unnamed
I had, my Country!—am I to be blamed?
Now, when I think of thee, and what thou art,
Verily, in the bottom of my heart,
Of those unfilial fears I am ashamed.
For dearly must we prize thee; we who find
In thee a bulwark for the cause of men:
And I by my affection was beguiled:
What wonder if a Poet now and then,
Among the many movements of his mind,
Felt for thee as a lover or a child!

TO THE MEN OF KENT

OCTOBER 1803

VANGUARD of Liberty, ye men of Kent,
Ye children of a Soil that doth advance
Her haughty brow against the coast of France,
Now is the time to prove your hardiment!
To France be words of invitation sent!
They from their fields can see the countenance
Of your fierce war, may ken the glittering lance
And hear you shouting forth your brave intent.
Left single, in bold parley, ye, of yore,
Did from the Norman win a gallant wreath;
Confirmed the charters that were yours before;—
No parleying now! In Britain is one breath;
We all are with you now from shore to shore:—
Ye men of Kent, 'tis victory or death!

ANTICIPATION, October 1803

SHOUT, for a mighty Victory is won !
On British ground the Invaders are laid low ;
The breath of Heaven has drifted them like snow,
And left them lying in the silent sun,
Never to rise again !—the work is done.
Come forth, ye old men, now in peaceful show
And greet your sons ! drums beat and trumpets blow !
Make merry, wives ! ye little children, stun
Your grandame's ears with pleasure of your noise !
Clap, infants, clap your hands !   Divine must be
That triumph, when the very worst, the pain,
And even the prospect of our brethren slain,
Hath something in it which the heart enjoys :—
In glory will they sleep and endless sanctity.

NOVEMBER 1806

ANOTHER year !—another deadly blow !
Another mighty Empire overthrown !
And We are left, or shall be left, alone ;
The last that dare to struggle with the Foe.
'Tis well ! from this day forward we shall know
That in ourselves our safety must be sought ;
That by our own right hands it must be wrought ;
That we must stand unpropped, or be laid low.
O dastard whom such foretaste doth not cheer !
We shall exult, if they who rule the land
Be men who hold its many blessings dear,
Wise, upright, valiant ; not a servile band,
Who are to judge of danger which they fear,
And honour which they do not understand.

OCCASIONED BY THE BATTLE OF WATERLOO

I

(The last six lines intended for an Inscription.)

INTREPID sons of Albion ! not by you
Is life despised ; ah no, the spacious earth
Ne'er saw a race who held, by right of birth,
So many objects to which love is due :
Ye slight not life—to God and Nature true ;
But death, becoming death, is dearer far,
When duty bids you bleed in open war :
Hence hath your prowess quelled that impious crew.
Heroes !—for instant sacrifice prepared ;
Yet filled with ardour and on triumph bent,
'Mid direst shocks of mortal accident—
To you who fell, and you whom slaughter spared
To guard the fallen, and consummate the event,
Your Country rears this sacred Monument !

II

THE Bard—whose soul is meek as dawning day,
Yet trained to judgments righteously severe ;
Fervid, yet conversànt with holy fear,
As recognising one Almighty sway :
He—whose experienced eye can pierce the array
Of past events ; to whom, in vision clear,
The aspiring heads of future things appear,
Like mountain-tops whose mists have rolled away—
Assoiled from all encumbrance of our time,
He only, if such breathe, in strains devout
Shall comprehend this victory sublime ;
Shall worthily rehearse the hideous rout,
The triumph hail, which from their peaceful clime
Angels might welcome with a choral shout !

" EMPERORS AND KINGS, HOW OFT HAVE TEMPLES RUNG "

EMPERORS and Kings, how oft have temples rung
With impious thanksgiving, the Almighty's scorn !
How oft above their altars have been hung
Trophies that led the good and wise to mourn
Triumphant wrong, battle of battle born,
And sorrow that to fruitless sorrow clung !
Now, from Heaven-sanctioned victory, Peace is sprung;
In this firm hour Salvation lifts her horn.
Glory to arms !   But, conscious that the nerve
Of popular reason, long mistrusted, freed
Your thrones, ye Powers, from duty fear to swerve !
Be just, be grateful ; nor, the oppressor's creed
Reviving, heavier chastisement deserve
Than ever forced unpitied hearts to bleed.

SCENERY BETWEEN NAMUR AND LIEGE

WHAT lovelier home could gentle Fancy choose ?
Is this the stream, whose cities, heights, and plains,
War's favourite playground, are with crimson stains
Familiar, as the Morn with pearly dews ?
The Morn, that now, along the silver MEUSE,
Spreading her peaceful ensigns, calls the swains
To tend their silent boats and ringing wains,
Or strip the bough whose mellow fruit bestrews
The ripening corn beneath it.   As mine eyes
Turn from the fortified and threatening hill,
How sweet the prospect of yon watery glade,
With its grey rocks clustering in pensive shade—
That, shaped like old monastic turrets, rise
From the smooth meadow-ground, serene and still !

COMPOSED AT RYDAL ON MAY MORNING,
1838

IF with old love of you, dear Hills ! I share
New love of many a rival image brought
From far, forgive the wanderings of my thought :
Nor art thou wronged, sweet May ! when I compare
Thy present birth-morn with thy last, so fair,
So rich to me in favours.   For my lot
Then was, within the famed Egerian Grot
To sit and muse, fanned by its dewy air
Mingling with thy soft breath !   That morning too,
Warblers I heard their joy unbosoming
Amid the sunny, shadowy, Colyseum ;
Heard them, unchecked by aught of saddening hue,
For victories there won by flower-crowned Spring,
Chant in full choir their innocent Te Deum.

SOLE LISTENER, DUDDON !

SOLE listener, Duddon ! to the breeze that played
With thy clear voice, I caught the fitful sound
Wafted o'er sullen moss and craggy mound—
Unfruitful solitudes, that seemed to upbraid
The sun in heaven !—but now, to form a shade
For Thee, green alders have together wound
Their foliage ; ashes flung their arms around ;
And birch-trees risen in silver colonnade.
And thou hast also tempted here to rise,
'Mid sheltering pines, this Cottage rude and grey ;
Whose ruddy children, by the mother's eyes
Carelessly watched, sport through the summer day,
Thy pleased associates :—light as endless May
On infant bosoms lonely Nature lies.

ON THE DEPARTURE OF SIR WALTER SCOTT FROM ABBOTSFORD, FOR NAPLES

A TROUBLE, not of clouds, or weeping rain,
Nor of the setting sun's pathetic light
Engendered, hangs o'er Eildon's triple height :
Spirits of Power, assembled there, complain
For kindred Power departing from their sight ;
While Tweed, best pleased in chanting a blithe
    strain,
Saddens his voice again, and yet again.
Lift up your hearts, ye Mourners ! for the might
Of the whole world's good wishes with him goes ;
Blessings and prayers, in nobler retinue
Than sceptred king or laurelled conqueror knows,
Follow this wondrous Potentate. Be true,
Ye winds of ocean, and the midland sea,
Wafting your Charge to soft Parthenope !

COMPOSED IN ROSLIN CHAPEL DURING A STORM

THE wind is now thy organist ;—a clank
(We know not whence) ministers for a bell
To mark some change of service. As the swell
Of music reached its height, and even when sank
The notes, in prelude, ROSLIN ! to a blank
Of silence, how it thrilled thy sumptuous roof,
Pillars, and arches,—not in vain time-proof,
Though Christian rites be wanting ! From what bank
Came those live herbs ? by what hand were they sown
Where dew falls not, where rain-drops seem unknown ?
Yet in the Temple they a friendly niche
Share with their sculptured fellows, that, green-grown,
Copy their beauty more and more, and preach,
Though mute, of all things blending into one.

THE TROSSACHS

THERE'S not a nook within this solemn Pass,
But were an apt confessional for One
Taught by his summer spent, his autumn gone,
That Life is but a tale of morning grass
Withered at eve.   From scenes of art which chase
That thought away, turn, and with watchful eyes
Feed it 'mid Nature's old felicities,
Rocks, rivers, and smooth lakes more clear than glass
Untouched, unbreathed upon.   Thrice happy quest,
If from a golden perch of aspen spray
(October's workmanship to rival May)
The pensive warbler of the ruddy breast
That moral sweeten by a heaven-taught lay,
Lulling the year, with all its cares, to rest !

COMPOSED ON A MAY MORNING, 1838

LIFE with yon Lambs, like day, is just begun,
Yet Nature seems to them a heavenly guide.
Does joy approach ? they meet the coming tide ;
And sullenness avoid, as now they shun
Pale twilight's lingering glooms,—and in the sun
Couch near their dams, with quiet satisfied ;
Or gambol—each with his shadow at his side,
Varying its shape wherever he may run.
As they from turf yet hoar with sleepy dew
All turn, and court the shining and the green,
Where herbs look up, and opening flowers are seen ;
Why to God's goodness cannot We be true,
And so, His gifts and promises between,
Feed to the last on pleasures ever new ?

IN SIGHT OF THE TOWN OF COCKERMOUTH

A POINT of life between my Parents' dust,
And yours, my buried Little-ones ! am I ;
And to those graves looking habitually
In kindred quiet I repose my trust.
Death to the innocent is more than just,
And, to the sinner, mercifully bent ;
So may I hope, if truly I repent
And meekly bear the ills which bear I must :
And You, my Offspring ! that do still remain,
Yet may outstrip me in the appointed race,
If e'er, through fault of mine, in mutual pain
We breathed together for a moment's space,
The wrong, by love provoked, let love arraign,
And only love keep in your hearts a place.

MARY QUEEN OF SCOTS

LANDING AT THE MOUTH OF THE DERWENT, WORKINGTON

DEAR to the Loves, and to the Graces vowed,
The Queen drew back the wimple that she wore ;
And to the throng, that on the Cumbrian shore
Her landing hailed, how touchingly she bowed !
And like a Star (that, from a heavy cloud
Of pine-tree foliage poised in air, forth darts,
When a soft summer gale at evening parts
The gloom that did its loveliness enshroud)
She smiled ; but Time, the old Saturnian seer,
Sighed on the wing as her foot pressed the strand,
With step prelusive to a long array
Of woes and degradations hand in hand—
Weeping captivity, and shuddering fear
Stilled by the ensanguined block of Fotheringay !

IN THE FRITH OF CLYDE, AILSA CRAG

DURING AN ECLIPSE OF THE SUN, JULY 17

SINCE risen from ocean, ocean to defy,
Appeared the crag of Ailsa, ne'er did morn
With gleaming lights more gracefully adorn
His sides, or wreathe with mist his forehead high :
Now, faintly darkening with the sun's eclipse,
Still is he seen, in lone sublimity,
Towering above the sea and little ships ;
For dwarfs the tallest seem while sailing by,
Each for her haven ; with her freight of Care,
Pleasure, or Grief, and Toil that seldom looks
Into the secret of to-morrow's fare ;
Though poor, yet rich, without the wealth of books,
Or aught that watchful Love to Nature owes
For her mute Powers, fixed Forms, or transient Shows.

ON THE FRITH OF CLYDE

IN A STEAMBOAT

ARRAN ! a single-crested Teneriffe,
A St. Helena next—in shape and hue,
Varying her crowded peaks and ridges blue ;
Who but must covet a cloud-seat, or skiff
Built for the air, or wingèd Hippogriff ?
That he might fly, where no one could pursue,
From this dull Monster and her sooty crew ;
And, as a God, light on thy topmost cliff.
Impotent wish ! which reason would despise
If the mind knew no union of extremes,
No natural bond between the boldest schemes,
Ambition frames, and heart-humilities.
Beneath stern mountains many a soft vale lies,
And lofty springs give birth to lowly streams.

CAVE OF STAFFA—I

WE saw, but surely, in the motley crowd,
Not One of us has felt the far-famed sight ;
How *could* we feel it ? each the other's blight,
Hurried and hurrying, volatile and loud.
O for those motions only that invite
The Ghost of Fingal to his tuneful Cave
By the breeze entered, and wave after wave
Softly embosoming the timid light !
And by *one* Votary who at will might stand
Gazing and take into his mind and heart,
With undistracted reverence, the effect
Of those proportions where the almighty hand
That made the worlds, the sovereign Architect,
Has deigned to work as if with human Art !

CAVE OF STAFFA—II

AFTER THE CROWD HAD DEPARTED

THANKS for the lessons of this Spot—fit school
For the presumptuous thoughts that would assign
Mechanic laws to agency divine ;
And, measuring heaven by earth, would overrule
Infinite Power.   The pillared vestibule,
Expanding yet precise, the roof embowed,
Might seem designed to humble man, when proud
Of his best workmanship by plan and tool.
Down-bearing with his whole Atlantic weight
Of tide and tempest on the Structure's base,
And flashing to that Structure's topmost height,
Ocean has proved its strength, and of its grace
In calms is conscious, finding for his freight
Of softest music some responsive place.

CAVE OF STAFFA—III

YE shadowy Beings, that have rights and claims
In every cell of Fingal's mystic Grot,
Where are ye ?   Driven or venturing to the spot,
Our fathers glimpses caught of your thin Frames,
And, by your mien and bearing knew your names ;
And they could hear *his* ghostly song who trod
Earth, till the flesh lay on him like a load,
While he struck his desolate harp without hopes or
     aims.
Vanished ye are, but subject to recall ;
Why keep *we* else the instincts whose dread law
Ruled here of yore, till what men felt they saw,
Not by black arts but magic natural !
If eyes be still sworn vassals of belief,
Yon light shapes forth a Bard, that shade a Chief.

FLOWERS ON THE TOP OF THE PILLARS
AT THE ENTRANCE OF THE CAVE

HOPE smiled when your nativity was cast,
Children of Summer !   Ye fresh Flowers that brave
What Summer here escapes not, the fierce wave,
And whole artillery of the western blast,
Battering the Temple's front, its long-drawn nave
Smiting, as if each moment were their last.
But ye, bright Flowers, on frieze and architrave
Survive, and once again the Pile stands fast :
Calm as the Universe, from specular towers
Of heaven contemplated by Spirits pure
With mute astonishment, it stands sustained
Through every part in symmetry, to endure,
Unhurt, the assault of Time with all his hours,
As the supreme Artificer ordained.

IONA—I

On to Iona !—What can she afford
To *us* save matter for a thoughtful sigh,
Heaved over ruin with stability
In urgent contrast ?   To diffuse the Word
(Thy Paramount, mighty Nature ! and Time's Lord)
Her Temples rose, 'mid pagan gloom ; but why,
Even for a moment, has our verse deplored
Their wrongs, since they fulfilled their destiny ?
And when, subjected to a common doom
Of mutability, those far-famed Piles
Shall disappear from both the sister Isles,
Iona's Saints, forgetting not past days,
Garlands shall wear of amaranthine bloom,
While heaven's vast sea of voices chants their praise.

IONA—II

UPON LANDING

How sad a welcome !   To each voyager
Some ragged child holds up for sale a store
Of wave-worn pebbles, pleading on the shore
Where once came monk and nun with gentle stir,
Blessings to give, news ask, or suit prefer.
Yet is yon neat trim church a grateful speck
Of novelty amid the sacred wreck
Strewn far and wide.   Think, proud Philosopher !
Fallen though she be, this Glory of the west,
Still on her sons, the beams of mercy shine ;
And " hopes, perhaps more heavenly bright than thine,
A grace by thee unsought and unpossest,
A faith more fixed, a rapture more divine,
Shall gild their passage to eternal rest."

THE BLACK STONES OF IONA

HERE on their knees men swore : the stones were black,
Black in the people's minds and words, yet they
Were at that time, as now, in colour grey.
But what is colour, if upon the rack
Of conscience souls are placed by deeds that lack
Concord with oaths ?   What differ night and day
Then, when before the Perjured on his way
Hell opens, and the heavens in vengeance crack
Above his head uplifted in vain prayer
To Saint, or Fiend, or to the Godhead whom
He had insulted—Peasant, King, or Thane ?
Fly where the culprit may, guilt meets a doom ;
And, from invisible worlds at need laid bare,
Come links for social order's awful chain.

"HOMEWARD WE TURN"

HOMEWARD we turn.   Isle of Columba's Cell,
Where Christian piety's soul-cheering spark
(Kindled from Heaven between the light and dark
Of time) shone like the morning-star, farewell !—
And fare thee well, to Fancy visible,
Remote St. Kilda, lone and loved sea-mark
For many a voyage made in her swift bark,
When with more hues than in the rainbow dwell
Thou a mysterious intercourse dost hold,
Extracting from clear skies and air serene,
And out of sun-bright waves, a lucid veil,
That thickens, spreads, and, mingling fold with fold,
Makes known, when thou no longer canst be seen,
Thy whereabout, to warn the approaching sail.

PART IV

ODES

ODES

COMPOSED UPON AN EVENING OF EXTRAORDINARY SPLENDOUR AND BEAUTY

HAD this effulgence disappeared
With flying haste, I might have sent,
Among the speechless clouds, a look
Of blank astonishment ;
But 'tis endued with power to stay,
And sanctify one closing day,
That frail Mortality may see—
What is ?—ah no, but what *can* be !
Time was when field and watery cove
With modulated echoes rang,
While choirs of fervent Angels sang
Their vespers in the grove ;
Or, crowning, star-like, each some sovereign height,
Warbled, for heaven above and earth below,
Strains suitable to both.—Such holy rite,
Methinks, if audibly repeated now
From hill or valley, could not move
Sublimer transport, purer love,
Than doth this silent spectacle—the gleam—
The shadow—and the peace supreme !

No sound is uttered,—but a deep
And solemn harmony pervades
The hollow vale from steep to steep,
And penetrates the glades.
Far-distant images draw nigh,
Called forth by wondrous potency
Of beamy radiance, that imbues,
Whate'er it strikes, with gem-like hues !
In vision exquisitely clear,
Herds range along the mountain side ;
And glistening antlers are descried ;
And gilded flocks appear.

Thine is the tranquil hour, purpureal Eve !
But long as god-like wish, or hope divine,
Informs my spirit, ne'er can I believe
That this magnificence is wholly thine !
—From worlds not quickened by the sun
A portion of the gift is won ;
An intermingling of Heaven's pomp is spread
On ground which British shepherds tread !

And, if there be whom broken ties
Afflict, or injuries assail,
Yon hazy ridges to their eyes
Present a glorious scale,
Climbing suffused with sunny air,
To stop—no record hath told where !
And tempting Fancy to ascend,
And with immortal Spirits blend !
—Wings at my shoulders seem to play ;
But, rooted here, I stand and gaze
On those bright steps that heavenward raise
Their practicable way.
Come forth, ye drooping old men, look abroad,
And see to what fair countries ye are bound !
And if some traveller, weary of his road,
Hath slept since noon-tide on the grassy ground,
Ye Genii ! to his covert speed ;
And wake him with such gentle heed
As may attune his soul to meet the dower
Bestowed on this transcendent hour !

Such hues from their celestial Urn
Were wont to stream before mine eye,
Where'er it wandered in the morn
Of blissful infancy.
This glimpse of glory, why renewed ?
Nay, rather speak with gratitude ;
For, if a vestige of those gleams
Survived, 'twas only in my dreams,

Dread Power ! whom peace and calmness serve
No less than Nature's threatening voice,
If aught unworthy be my choice,
From THEE if I would swerve ;
Oh, let thy grace remind me of the light
Full early lost, and fruitlessly deplored ;
Which, at this moment, on my waking sight
Appears to shine, by miracle restored ;
My soul, though yet confined to earth,
Rejoices in a second birth !
—'Tis past, the visionary splendour fades ;
And night approaches with her shades.

NOTE.—The multiplication of mountain ridges, described at the
commencement of the third Stanza of this Ode, as a kind of Jacob's
Ladder, leading to Heaven, is produced either by watery vapours, or
sunny haze ;—in the present instance by the latter cause. Allusions
to the Ode entitled "Intimations of Immortality" pervade the last
stanza of the foregoing Poem.

ODE

COMPOSED IN JANUARY 1816

——————— Carmina possumus
Donare, et pretium dicere muneri.
Non incisa notis marmora publicis,
Per quæ spiritus et vita redit bonis
Post mortem ducibus
——————— clarius indicant
Laudes, quam ——— Pierides ; neque,
Si chartæ sileant quod bene feceris,
Mercedem tuleris.—HOR. Car. 8, Lib. 4.

WHEN the soft hand of sleep had closed the latch
On the tired household of corporeal sense,
And Fancy, keeping unreluctant watch,
Was free her choicest favours to dispense ;
I saw, in wondrous pérspective displayed,
A landscape more august than happiest skill

Of pencil ever clothed with light and shade ;
An intermingled pomp of vale and hill,
City, and naval stream, suburban grove,
And stately forest where the wild deer rove ;
Nor wanted lurking hamlet, dusky towns,
And scattered rural farms of aspect bright ;
And, here and there, between the pastoral downs,
The azure sea upswelled upon the sight.
Fair prospect, such as Britain only shows !
But not a living creature could be seen
Through its wide circuit, that, in deep repose,
And, even to sadness, lonely and serene,
Lay hushed ; till—through a portal in the sky
Brighter than brightest loop-hole, in a storm,
Opening before the sun's triumphant eye—
Issued, to sudden view, a glorious Form !
Earthward it glided with a swift descent :
Saint George himself this Visitant must be ;
And, ere a thought could ask on what intent
He sought the regions of Humanity,
A thrilling voice was heard, that vivified
City and field and flood ;—aloud it cried—

" Though from my celestial home,
    Like a Champion, armed I come ;
    On my helm the dragon crest,
    And the red cross on my breast ;
    I, the Guardian of this Land,
    Speak not now of toilsome duty ;
    Well obeyed was that command—
    Whence bright days of festive beauty ;
Haste, Virgins, haste !—the flowers which summer gave
    Have perished in the field ;
But the green thickets plenteously shall yield
    Fit garlands for the brave,
That will be welcome, if by you entwined ;
Haste, Virgins, haste ; and you, ye Matrons grave,

Go forth with rival youthfulness of mind,
    And gather what ye find
Of hardy laurel and wild holly boughs—
To deck your stern Defenders' modest brows !
    Such simple gifts prepare,
Though they have gained a worthier meed ;
    And in due time shall share
Those palms and amaranthine wreaths
Unto their martyred Countrymen decreed,
In realms where everlasting freshness breathes ! "

    And lo ! with crimson banners proudly streaming,
And upright weapons innocently gleaming,
Along the surface of a spacious plain
Advance in order the redoubted Bands,
And there receive green chaplets from the hands
    Of a fair female train—
    Maids and Matrons, dight
    In robes of dazzling white ;
While from the crowd bursts forth a rapturous noise
    By the cloud-capt hills retorted ;
    And a throng of rosy boys
    In loose fashion tell their joys ;
And grey-haired sires, on staffs supported,
Look round, and by their smiling seem to say,
Thus strives a grateful Country to display
The mighty debt which nothing can repay !

    Anon before my sight a palace rose
Built of all precious substances,—so pure
And exquisite, that sleep alone bestows
Ability like splendour to endure :
Entered, with streaming thousands, through the gate,
I saw the banquet spread beneath a Dome of state,
A lofty Dome, that dared to emulate
    The heaven of sable night
With starry lustre ; yet had power to throw
Solemn effulgence, clear as solar light,

Upon a princely company below,
While the vault rang with choral harmony,
Like some Nymph-haunted grot beneath the roaring sea.
—No sooner ceased that peal, than on the verge
Of exultation hung a dirge
Breathed from a soft and lonely instrument,
    That kindled recollections
    Of agonised affections ;
And, though some tears the strain attended,
    The mournful passion ended
In peace of spirit, and sublime content !

    But garlands wither ; festal shows depart,
Like dreams themselves ; and sweetest sound—
    (Albeit of effect profound)
    It was—and it is gone !
Victorious England ! bid the silent Art
Reflect, in glowing hues that shall not fade,
Those high achievements ; even as she arrayed
With second life the deed of Marathon
    Upon Athenian walls ;
So may she labour for thy civic halls :
    And be the guardian spaces
    Of consecrated places,
As nobly graced by Sculpture's patient toil ;
And let imperishable Columns rise
Fixed in the depths of this courageous soil ;
Expressive signals of a glorious strife,
And competent to shed a spark divine
Into the torpid breast of daily life ;—
Records on which, for pleasure of all eyes,
    The morning sun may shine
With gratulation thoroughly benign !

    And ye, Pierian Sisters, sprung from Jove
And sage Mnemosyne,—full long debarred
From your first mansions, exiled all too long
From many a hallowed stream and grove,

Dear native regions where ye wont to rove,
Chanting for patriot heroes the reward
    Of never-dying song !
Now (for, though Truth descending from above
The Olympian summit hath destroyed for aye
Your kindred Deities, *Ye* live and move,
Spared for obeisance from perpetual love
For privilege redeemed of godlike sway)
Now, on the margin of some spotless fountain,
Or top serene of unmolested mountain,
Strike audibly the noblest of your lyres,
And for a moment meet the soul's desires !
That I, or some more favoured Bard, may hear
What ye, celestial Maids ! have often sung
Of Britain's acts,—may catch it with rapt ear,
And give the treasure to our British tongue !
So shall the characters of that proud page
Support their mighty theme from age to age ;
And, in the desert places of the earth,
When they to future empires have given birth,
So shall the people gather and believe
The bold report, transferred to every clime ;
And the whole world, not envious but admiring.
    And to the like aspiring,
Own—that the progeny of this fair Isle
Had power as lofty actions to achieve
As were performed in man's heroic prime ;
Nor wanted, when their fortitude had held
Its even tenor, and the foe was quelled,
A corresponding virtue to beguile
The hostile purpose of wide-wasting Time—
That not in vain they laboured to secure,
For their great deeds, perpetual memory,
And fame as largely spread as land and sea,
By Works of spirit high and passion pure !

VERNAL ODE

[Rerum Natura tota est nusquam magis quam in minimis.—PLIN. *Nat. Hist.*]

BENEATH the concave of an April sky,
When all the fields with freshest green were dight,
Appeared, in presence of the spiritual eye
That aids or supersedes our grosser sight,
The form and rich habiliments of One
Whose countenance bore resemblance to the sun,
When it reveals, in evening majesty,
Features half lost amid their own pure light.
Poised like a weary cloud, in middle air
He hung,—then floated with angelic ease
(Softening that bright effulgence by degrees)
Till he had reached a summit sharp and bare,
Where oft the venturous heifer drinks the noontide
        breeze.
Upon the apex of that lofty cone
Alighted, there the Stranger stood alone ;
Fair as a gorgeous Fabric of the east
Suddenly raised by some enchanter's power,
Where nothing was ; and firm as some old Tower
Of Britain's realm, whose leafy crest
Waves high, embellished by a gleaming shower !

Beneath the shadow of his purple wings
Rested a golden harp ;—he touched the strings ;
And, after prelude of unearthly sound
Poured through the echoing hills around,
He sang—
                " No wintry desolations,
Scorching blight or noxious dew,
Affect my native habitations ;
Buried in glory, far beyond the scope
Of man's inquiring gaze, but to his hope

Imaged, though faintly, in the hue
Profound of night's ethereal blue ;
And in the aspect of each radiant orb ;—
Some fixed, some wandering with no timid curb :
But wandering star and fixed, to mortal eye—
Blended in absolute serenity,
And free from semblance of decline ;—
Fresh as if Evening brought their natal hour,
Her darkness splendour gave, her silence power
To testify of Love and Grace divine.

" What if those bright fires
Shine subject to decay,
Sons haply of extinguished sires,
Themselves to lose their light, or pass away
Like clouds before the wind,
Be thanks poured out to Him whose hand bestows,
Nightly, on human kind
That vision of endurance and repose.
—And though to every draught of vital breath
Renewed throughout the bounds of earth or ocean,
The melancholy gates of Death
Respond with sympathetic motion ;
Though all that feeds on nether air,
Howe'er magnificent or fair,
Grows but to perish, and entrust
Its ruins to their kindred dust ;
Yet, by the Almighty's ever-during care,
Her procreant vigils Nature keeps
Amid the unfathomable deeps ;
And saves the peopled fields of earth
From dread of emptiness or dearth.
Thus, in their stations, lifting tow'rd the sky
The foliaged head in cloud-like majesty,
The shadow-casting race of trees survive :
Thus, in the train of Spring, arrive
Sweet flowers ;—what living eye hath viewed
Their myriads ?—endlessly renewed,

Wherever strikes the sun's glad ray ;
Where'er the subtle waters stray ;
Wherever sportive breezes bend
Their course, or genial showers descend !
Mortals, rejoice ! the very Angels quit
Their mansions unsusceptible of change,
Amid your pleasant bowers to sit,
And though your sweet vicissitudes to range ! "

Oh, nursed at happy distance from the cares
Of a too-anxious world, mild pastoral Muse !
That, to the sparkling crown Urania wears,
And to her sister Clio's laurel wreath,
Prefer'st a garland culled from purple heath,
Or blooming thicket moist with morning dews ;
Was such bright Spectacle vouchsafed to me ?
And was it granted to the simple ear
Of thy contented Votary
Such melody to hear !
Him rather suits it, side by side with thee—
Wrapped in a fit of pleasing indolence,
While thy tired lute hangs on the hawthorn-tree,
To lie and listen—till o'er-drowsèd sense
Sinks, hardly conscious of the influence—
To the soft murmur of the vagrant Bee.
—A slender sound ! yet hoary Time
Doth to the *Soul* exalt it with the chime
Of all his years ;—a company
Of ages coming, ages gone ;
(Nations from before them sweeping,
Regions in destruction steeping,)
But every awful note in unison
With that faint utterance, which tells
Of treasure sucked from buds and bells,
For the pure keeping of those waxen cells ;
Where She—a statist prudent to confer
Upon the common weal ; a warrior bold,
Radiant all over with unburnished gold,

And armed with living spear for mortal fight ;
        A cunning forager
That spreads no waste ; a social builder ; one
In whom all busy offices unite
With all fine functions that afford delight—
Safe through the winter storm in quiet dwells !

And is She brought within the power
Of vision ?—o'er this tempting flower
Hovering until the petals stay
Her flight, and take its voice away !—
Observe each wing !—a tiny van !
The structure of her laden thigh,
How fragile ! yet of ancestry
Mysteriously remote and high ;
High as the imperial front of man ;
The roseate bloom on woman's cheek ;
The soaring eagle's curvèd beak ;
The white plumes of the floating swan ;
Old as the tiger's paw, the lion's mane
Ere shaken by that mood of stern disdain
At which the desert trembles.—Humming Bee !
Thy sting was needless then, perchance unknown,
The seeds of malice were not sown ;
All creatures met in peace, from fierceness free,
And no pride blended with their dignity.
—Tears had not broken from their source ;
Nor Anguish strayed from her Tartarean den ;
The golden years maintained a course
Not undiversified though smooth and even ;
We were not mocked with glimpse and shadow then,
Bright Seraphs mixed familiarly with men ;
And earth and stars composed a universal heaven !

ODE TO LYCORIS

An age hath been when Earth was proud
Of lustre too intense
To be sustained ; and Mortals bowed
The front in self-defence.
Who *then*, if Dian's crescent gleamed,
Or Cupid's sparkling arrow streamed
While on the wing the Urchin played,
Could fearlessly approach the shade ?
—Enough for one soft vernal day,
If I, a bard of ebbing time,
And nurtured in a fickle clime,
May haunt this hornèd bay ;
Whose amorous water multiplies
The flitting halcyon's vivid dyes ;
And smooths her liquid breast—to show
These swan-like specks of mountain snow,
White as the pair that slid along the plains
Of heaven, when Venus held the reins !

In youth we love the darksome lawn
Brushed by the owlet's wing ;
Then, Twilight is preferred to Dawn
And Autumn to the Spring.
Sad fancies do we then affect,
In luxury of disrespect
To our own prodigal excess
Of too familiar happiness.
Lycoris (if such name befit
Thee, thee my life's celestial sign !)
When Nature marks the year's decline,
Be ours to welcome it ;
Pleased with the harvest hope that runs
Before the path of milder suns ;
Pleased while the sylvan world displays
Its ripeness to the feeding gaze ;

Pleased when the sullen winds resound the knell
Of the resplendent miracle.

But something whispers to my heart
That, as we downward tend,
Lycoris ! life requires an *art*
To which our souls must bend ;
A skill—to balance and supply ;
And, ere the flowing fount be dry,
As soon it must, a sense to sip,
Or drink, with no fastidious lip.
Then welcome, above all, the Guest
Whose smiles, diffused o'er land and sea,
Seem to recall the Deity
Of youth into the breast :
May pensive Autumn ne'er present
A claim to her disparagement !
While blossoms and the budding spray
Inspire us in our own decay ;
Still, as we nearer draw to life's dark goal,
Be hopeful Spring the favourite of the Soul !

TO THE SAME

ENOUGH of climbing toil !—Ambition treads
Here, as 'mid busier scenes, ground steep and rough,
Or slippery even to peril ! and each step,
As we for most uncertain recompense
Mount toward the empire of the fickle clouds,
Each weary step, dwarfing the world below,
Induces, for its old familiar sights,
Unacceptable feelings of contempt,
With wonder mixed—that Man could e'er be tied,
In anxious bondage, to such nice array
And formal fellowship of petty things !
—Oh ! 'tis the *heart* that magnifies this life,
Making a truth and beauty of her own ;

And moss-grown alleys, circumscribing shades,
And gurgling rills, assist her in the work
More efficaciously than realms outspread,
As in a map, before the adventurer's gaze—
Ocean and Earth contending for regard.

 The umbrageous woods are left—how far beneath !
But lo ! where darkness seems to guard the mouth
Of yon wild cave, whose jaggèd brows are fringed
With flaccid threads of ivy, in the still
And sultry air, depending motionless.
Yet cool the space within, and not uncheered
(As whoso enters shall ere long perceive)
By stealthy influx of the timid day
Mingling with night, such twilight to compose
As Numa loved ; when, in the Egerian grot,
From the sage Nymph appearing at his wish,
He gained whate'er a regal mind might ask,
Or need, of counsel breathed through lips divine.

 Long as the heat shall rage, let that dim cave
Protect us, there deciphering as we may
Diluvian records ; or the sighs of Earth
Interpreting ; or counting for old Time
His minutes, by reiterated drops,
Audible tears, from some invisible source
That deepens upon fancy—more and more
Drawn toward the centre whence those sighs creep forth
To awe the lightness of humanity :
Or, shutting up thyself within thyself,
There let me see thee sink into a mood
Of gentler thought, protracted till thine eye
Be calm as water when the winds are gone,
And no one can tell whither. Dearest Friend !
We two have known such happy hours together
That, were power granted to replace them (fetched
From out the pensive shadows where they lie)
In the first warmth of their original sunshine,
Loth should I be to use it : passing sweet
Are the domains of tender memory !

DION

(SEE PLUTARCH)

SERENE, and fitted to embrace,
Where'er he turned, a swan-like grace
Of haughtiness without pretence,
And to unfold a still magnificence,
Was princely Dion, in the power
And beauty of his happier hour.
And what pure homage *then* did wait
On Dion's virtues, while the lunar beam
Of Plato's genius, from its lofty sphere,
Fell round him in the grove of Academe,
Softening their inbred dignity austere—
    That he, not too elate
    With self-sufficing solitude,
But with majestic lowliness endued,
    Might in the universal bosom reign,
And from affectionate observance gain
Help, under every change of adverse fate.

Five thousand warriors—O the rapturous day !
Each crowned with flowers, and armed with spear and
        shield,
Or ruder weapon which their course might yield,
To Syracuse advance in bright array.
Who leads them on ?—The anxious people see
Long-exiled Dion marching at their head,
He also crowned with flowers of Sicily,
And in a white, far-beaming, corselet clad !
Pure transport undisturbed by doubt or fear
The gazers feel ; and, rushing to the plain,
Salute those strangers as a holy train
Or blest procession (to the Immortals dear)
That brought their precious liberty again.

Lo ! when the gates are entered, on each hand,
Down the long street, rich goblets filled with wine
     In seemly order stand,
On tables set, as if for rites divine ;—
And, as the great Deliverer marches by,
   He looks on festal ground with fruits bestrown ;
And flowers are on his person thrown
    In boundless prodigality ;
Nor doth the general voice abstain from prayer,
Invoking Dion's tutelary care,
As if a very Deity he were !

Mourn, hills and groves of Attica ! and mourn
Ilissus, bending o'er thy classic urn !
Mourn, and lament for him whose spirit dreads
Your once sweet memory, studious walks and shades !
For him who to divinity aspired,
Not on the breath of popular applause,
But through dependence on the sacred laws
Framed in the schools where Wisdom dwelt retired,
Intent to trace the ideal path of right
(More fair than heaven's broad causeway paved with
     stars)
Which Dion learned to measure with sublime delight ;—
But He hath overleaped the eternal bars ;
And, following guides whose craft holds no consent
With aught that breathes the ethereal element,
Hath stained the robes of civil power with blood,
Unjustly shed, though for the public good.
Whence doubts that came too late, and wishes vain,
Hollow excuses, and triumphant pain ;
And oft his cogitations sink as low
As, through the abysses of a joyless heart,
The heaviest plummet of despair can go—
But whence that sudden check ? that fearful start !
    He hears an uncouth sound—
    Anon his lifted eyes
Saw, at a long-drawn gallery's dusky bound,

A Shape of more than mortal size
And hideous aspect, stalking round and round!
   A woman's garb the Phantom wore,
   And fiercely swept the marble floor,—
   Like Auster whirling to and fro,
   His force on Caspian foam to try;
Or Boreas when he scours the snow
That skins the plains of Thessaly,
Or when aloft on Mænalus he stops
His flight, 'mid eddying pine-tree tops!

So, but from toil less sign of profit reaping,
The sullen Spectre to her purpose bowed,
   Sweeping—vehemently sweeping—
No pause admitted, no design avowed!
" Avaunt, inexplicable Guest!—avaunt,"
Exclaimed the Chieftain—" let me rather see
The coronal that coiling vipers make;
The torch that flames with many a lurid flake,
And the long train of doleful pageantry
Which they behold, whom vengeful Furies haunt;
Who, while they struggle from the scourge to flee,
Move where the blasted soil is not unworn,
And, in their anguish, bear what other minds have
     borne!"

But Shapes that come not at an earthly call,
Will not depart when mortal voices bid;
Lords of the visionary eye whose lid,
Once raised, remains aghast, and will not fall!
Ye Gods, thought He, that servile Implement
Obeys a mystical intent!
Your Minister would brush away
The spots that to my soul adhere;
But should she labour night and day,
They will not, cannot disappear;
Whence angry perturbations,—and that look
Which no Philosophy can brook!

Ill-fated Chief ! there are whose hopes are built
Upon the ruins of thy glorious name ;
Who, through the portal of one moment's guilt,
Pursue thee with their deadly aim !
O matchless perfidy ! portentous lust
Of monstrous crime !—that horror-striking blade,
Drawn in defiance of the Gods, hath laid
The noble Syracusan low in dust !
Shuddered the walls—the marble city wept—
And sylvan places heaved a pensive sigh ;
But in calm peace the appointed Victim slept,
As he had fallen in magnanimity ;
Of spirit too capacious to require
That Destiny her course should change ; too just
To his own native greatness to desire
That wretched boon, days lengthened by mistrust
So were the hopeless troubles, that involved
The soul of Dion, instantly dissolved.
Released from life and cares of princely state,
He left this moral grafted on his Fate ;
" Him only pleasure leads, and peace attends,
Him, only him, the shield of Jove defends,
Whose means are fair and spotless as his ends."

ODE TO DUTY

[" Jam non consilio bonus, sed more eò perductus, ut non tantum
rectè facere possim, sed nisi rectè facere non possim."]

Stern Daughter of the Voice of God !
O Duty ! if that name thou love
Who art a light to guide, a rod
To check the erring, and reprove ;
Thou, who art victory and law
When empty terrors overawe ;
From vain temptations dost set free ;
And calm'st the weary strife of frail humanity !

There are who ask not if thine eye
Be on them ; who, in love and truth,
Where no misgiving is, rely
Upon the genial sense of youth :
Glad Hearts ! without reproach or blot
Who do thy work, and know it not :
Oh ! if through confidence misplaced
They fail, thy saving arms, dread Power ! around them
  cast.

Serene will be our days and bright,
And happy will our nature be,
When love is an unerring light,
And joy its own security.
And they a blissful course may hold
Even now, who, not unwisely bold,
Live in the spirit of this creed ;
Yet seek thy firm support, according to their need.

I, loving freedom, and untried ;
No sport of every random gust,
Yet being to myself a guide,
Too blindly have reposed my trust :
And oft, when in my heart was heard
Thy timely mandate, I deferred
The task, in smoother walks to stray ;
But thee I now would serve more strictly, if I may.

Through no disturbance of my soul,
Or strong compunction in me wrought,
I supplicate for thy control ;
But in the quietness of thought :
Me this unchartered freedom tires ;
I feel the weight of chance-desires :
My hopes no more must change their name,
I long for a repose that ever is the same.

Stern Lawgiver ! yet thou dost wear
The Godhead's most benignant grace ;
Nor know we anything so fair
As is the smile upon thy face :
Flowers laugh before thee on their beds
And fragrance in thy footing treads ;
Thou dost preserve the stars from wrong ;
And the most ancient heavens, through Thee, are fresh
    and strong.

To humbler functions, awful Power !
I call thee : I myself commend
Unto thy guidance from this hour ;
Oh, let my weakness have an end !
Give unto me, made lowly wise,
The spirit of self-sacrifice ;
The confidence of reason give ;
And in the light of truth thy Bondman let me live !

ODE

INTIMATIONS OF IMMORTALITY FROM RECOL-LECTIONS OF EARLY CHILDHOOD

> "The Child is Father of the Man ;
>   And I could wish my days to be
>   Bound each to each by natural piety."

THERE was a time when meadow, grove, and stream,
The earth, and every common sight,
    To me did seem
    Apparelled in celestial light,
The glory and the freshness of a dream.
It is not now as it hath been of yore ;—
    Turn wheresoe'er I may,
    By night or day,
The things which I have seen I now can see no more.

The Rainbow comes and goes,
And lovely is the Rose,
The Moon doth with delight
Look round her when the heavens are bare,
Waters on a starry night
Are beautiful and fair ;
The sunshine is a glorious birth ;
But yet I know, where'er I go,
That there hath past away a glory from the earth.

Now, while the birds thus sing a joyous song,
And while the young lambs bound
As to the tabor's sound,
To me alone there came a thought of grief :
A timely utterance gave that thought relief,
And I again am strong :
The cataracts blow their trumpets from the steep ;
No more shall grief of mine the season wrong ;
I hear the Echoes through the mountains throng,
The Winds come to me from the fields of sleep,
And all the earth is gay ;
Land and sea
Give themselves up to jollity,
And with the heart of May
Doth every Beast keep holiday ;—
Thou Child of Joy,
Shout round me, let me hear thy shouts, thou happy
Shepherd-boy !

Ye blessèd Creatures, I have heard the call
Ye to each other make ; I see
The heavens laugh with you in your jubilee ;
My heart is at your festival,
My head hath its coronal,
The fulness of your bliss, I feel—I feel it all.
Oh evil day ! if I were sullen
While Earth herself is adorning,
This sweet May-morning,

And the Children are culling
    On every side,
In a thousand valleys far and wide,
Fresh flowers ; while the sun shines warm,
And the Babe leaps up on his Mother's arm :—
    I hear, I hear, with joy I hear !
    —But there's a Tree, of many, one,
A single Field which I have looked upon,
Both of them speak of something that is gone :
    The Pansy at my feet
    Doth the same tale repeat :
Whither is fled the visionary gleam ?
Where is it now, the glory and the dream ?

Our birth is but a sleep and a forgetting :
The Soul that rises with us, our life's Star,
    Hath had elsewhere its setting,
    And cometh from afar :
    Not in entire forgetfulness,
    And not in utter nakedness,
But trailing clouds of glory do we come
    From God, who is our home :
Heaven lies about us in our infancy !
Shades of the prison-house begin to close
    Upon the growing Boy,
But He beholds the light, and whence it flows,
    He sees it in his joy ;
The Youth, who daily farther from the east
    Must travel, still is Nature's Priest,
    And by the vision splendid
    Is on his way attended ;
At length the Man perceives it die away,
And fade into the light of common day.

Earth fills her lap with pleasures of her own ;
Yearnings she hath in her own natural kind,
And, even with something of a Mother's mind,
    And no unworthy aim,

The homely Nurse doth all she can
To make her Foster-child, her Inmate Man,
    Forget the glories he hath known,
And that imperial palace whence he came.

Behold the Child among his new-born blisses,
A six years' Darling of a pigmy size !
See, where 'mid work of his own hand he lies,
Fretted by sallies of his mother's kisses,
With light upon him from his father's eyes !
See, at his feet, some little plan or chart,
Some fragment from his dream of human life,
Shaped by himself with newly-learned art ;
    A wedding or a festival,
    A mourning or a funeral ;
        And this hath now his heart,
    And unto this he frames his song :
        Then will he fit his tongue
To dialogues of business, love, or strife ;
    But it will not be long
    Ere this be thrown aside,
    And with new joy and pride
The little Actor cons another part ;
Filling from time to time his " humorous stage "
With all the Persons, down to palsied Age,
That Life brings with her in her equipage ;
    As if his whole vocation
    Were endless imitation.

Thou, whose exterior semblance doth belie
    Thy Soul's immensity ;
Thou best Philosopher, who yet dost keep
Thy heritage, thou Eye among the blind,
That, deaf and silent, read'st the eternal deep,
Haunted for ever by the eternal mind,—
    Mighty Prophet ! Seer blest !
    On whom those truths do rest,
Which we are toiling all our lives to find

In darkness lost, the darkness of the grave ;
Thou, over whom thy Immortality
Broods like the Day, a Master o'er a Slave,
A Presence which is not to be put by ;
Thou, little Child, yet glorious in the might
Of heaven-born freedom on thy being's height,
Why with such earnest pains dost thou provoke
The years to bring the inevitable yoke,
Thus blindly with thy blessedness at strife ?
Full soon thy Soul shall have her earthly freight,
And custom lie upon thee with a weight,
Heavy as frost, and deep almost as life !

  O joy ! that in our embers
  Is something that doth live,
  That nature yet remembers
  What was so fugitive !
The thought of our past years in me doth breed
Perpetual benediction : not indeed
For that which is most worthy to be blest—
Delight and liberty, the simple creed
Of Childhood, whether busy or at rest,
With new-fledged hope still fluttering in his breast :—
  Not for these I raise
  The song of thanks and praise ;
 But for those obstinate questionings
 Of sense and outward things,
 Fallings from us, vanishings ;
 Blank misgivings of a Creature
Moving about in worlds not realised,
High instincts before which our mortal Nature
Did tremble like a guilty Thing surprised :
  But for those first affections,
  Those shadowy recollections,
 Which, be they what they may,
Are yet the fountain light of all our day,
Are yet a master light of all our seeing ;
 Uphold us, cherish, and have power to make

Our noisy years seem moments in the being
Of the eternal Silence : truths that wake,
　　To perish never ;
Which neither listlessness, nor mad endeavour,
　　Nor Man nor Boy,
Nor all that is at enmity with joy,
Can utterly abolish or destroy !
　　Hence in a season of calm weather
　　Though inland far we be,
Our Souls have sight of that immortal sea
　　Which brought us hither,
　　Can in a moment travel thither,
And see the Children sport upon the shore,
And hear the mighty waters rolling evermore.

Then sing, ye Birds, sing, sing a joyous song !
　　And let the young Lambs bound
　　As to the tabor's sound !
We in thought will join your throng,
　　Ye that pipe and ye that play,
　　Ye that through your hearts to-day
　　Feel the gladness of the May !
What though the radiance which was once so bright
Be now for ever taken from my sight,
　　Though nothing can bring back the hour
Of splendour in the grass, of glory in the flower ;
　　We will grieve not, rather find
　　Strength in what remains behind ;
　　In the primal sympathy
　　Which having been must ever be ;
　　In the soothing thoughts that spring
　　Out of human suffering ;
　　In the faith that looks through death,
In years that bring the philosophic mind.

And O, ye Fountains, Meadows, Hills, and Groves,
Forebode not any severing of our loves !
Yet in my heart of hearts I feel your might ;

I only have relinquished one delight
To live beneath your more habitual sway.
I love the Brooks which down their channels fret,
Even more than when I tripped lightly as they ;
The innocent brightness of a new-born Day
　　　　Is lovely yet ;
The Clouds that gather round the setting sun
Do take a sober colouring from an eye
That hath kept watch o'er man's mortality ;
Another race hath been, and other palms are won.
Thanks to the human heart by which we live,
Thanks to its tenderness, its joys, and fears,
To me the meanest flower that blows can give
Thoughts that do often lie too deep for tears.

ODE

COMPOSED ON MAY MORNING

WHILE from the purpling east departs
　　The star that led the dawn,
Blithe Flora from her couch upstarts,
　　For May is on the lawn.
A quickening hope, a freshening glee,
　　Foreran the expected Power
Whose first-drawn breath, from bush and tree,
　　Shakes off that pearly shower.

All Nature welcomes Her whose sway
　　Tempers the year's extremes ;
Who scattereth lustres o'er noon-day,
　　Like morning's dewy gleams ;
While mellow warble, sprightly trill,
　　The tremulous heart excite ;
And hums the balmy air to still
　　The balance of delight.

Time was, blest Power! when youths and maids
  At peep of dawn would rise,
And wander forth, in forest glades
  Thy birth to solemnize.
Though mute the song—to grace the rite
  Untouched the hawthorn bough,
Thy Spirit triumphs o'er the slight;
  Man changes, but not Thou!

Thy feathered Lieges bill and wings
  In love's disport employ;
Warmed by thy influence, creeping things
  Awake to silent joy:
Queen art thou still for each gay plant
  Where the slim wild deer roves;
And served in depths where fishes haunt
  Their own mysterious groves.

Cloud-piercing peak, and trackless heath,
  Instinctive homage pay;
Nor wants the dim-lit cave a wreath
  To honour thee, sweet May!
Where cities fanned by thy brisk airs
  Behold a smokeless sky,
Their puniest flower pot nursling dares
  To open a bright eye.

And if, on this thy natal morn,
  The pole, from which thy name
Hath not departed, stands forlorn
  Of song and dance and game;
Still from the village-green a vow
  Aspires to thee addrest,
Wherever peace is on the brow,
  Or love within the breast.

Yes! where Love nestles thou canst teach
  The soul to love the more;

Hearts also shall thy lessons reach
    That never loved before.
Stript is the haughty one of pride,
    The bashful freed from fear,
While rising, like the ocean-tide,
    In flows the joyous year.

Hush, feeble lyre ! weak words refuse
    The service to prolong !
To yon exulting thrush the Muse
    Entrusts the imperfect song ;
His voice shall chant, in accents clear,
    Throughout the live-long day,
Till the first silver star appear,
    The sovereignty of May.

PART V

SELECTIONS FROM "THE PRELUDE OR, GROWTH OF A POET'S MIND"

AN AUTOBIOGRAPHICAL POEM

ADVERTISEMENT

THE following Poem was commenced in the beginning of the year 1799, and completed in the summer of 1805.

The design and occasion of the work are described by the Author in his Preface to the EXCURSION, first published in 1814, where he thus speaks :—

" Several years ago, when the Author retired to his native mountains with the hope of being enabled to construct a literary work that might live, it was a reasonable thing that he should take a review of his own mind, and examine how far Nature and Education had qualified him for such an employment.

" As subsidiary to this preparation, he undertook to record, in verse, the origin and progress of his own powers, as far as he was acquainted with them.

" That work, addressed to a dear friend, most distinguished for his knowledge and genius, and to whom the Author's intellect is deeply indebted, has been long finished ; and the result of the investigation which gave rise to it, was a determination to compose a philosophical Poem, containing views of Man, Nature, and Society, and to be entitled the ' Recluse ' ; as having for its principal subject the sensations and opinions of a poet living in retirement.

" The preparatory poem is biographical, and conducts the history of the Author's mind to the point when he was emboldened to hope that his faculties were sufficiently matured for entering upon the arduous labour which he had proposed to himself ; and the two works have the same kind of relation to each other, if he may so express himself, as the Ante-chapel has to the body of a Gothic church. Continuing this allusion, he may be permitted to add, that his minor pieces, which have been long before the public, when they shall be properly arranged, will be found by the attentive reader to have such connection with the main work as may give them claim to be likened to the little cells, oratories, and sepulchral recesses, ordinarily included in those edifices."

Such was the Author's language in the year 1814.

It will thence be seen, that the present Poem was intended to be introductory to the RECLUSE, and that the RECLUSE, if completed, would have consisted of Three Parts. Of these, the Second Part alone, viz. the EXCURSION, was finished, and given to the world by the Author.

The First Book of the First Part of the RECLUSE still remains in manuscript ; but the Third Part was only planned. The materials of which it would have been formed have, however, been incorporated, for the most part, in the Author's other Publications, written subsequently to the EXCURSION.

The Friend, to whom the present Poem is addressed, was the late SAMUEL TAYLOR COLERIDGE, who was resident in Malta, for the restoration of his health, when the greater part of it was composed.

Mr. Coleridge read a considerable portion of the Poem while he was abroad ; and his feelings, on hearing it recited by the Author (after his return to his own country), are recorded in his Verses, addressed to Mr. Wordsworth, which will be found in the *Sibylline Leaves*, p. 197, ed. 1817, or *Poetical Works, by S. T. Coleridge*, vol. i. p. 206.

RYDAL MOUNT,
    July 13, 1850.

SELECTIONS FROM "THE PRELUDE"

CHILDHOOD AND SCHOOL-TIME

OH there is blessing in this gentle breeze,
A visitant that while it fans my cheek
Doth seem half-conscious of the joy it brings
From the green fields, and from yon azure sky.
Whate'er its mission, the soft breeze can come
To none more grateful than to me ; escaped
From the vast city, where I long had pined
A discontented sojourner : now free,
Free as a bird to settle where I will.
What dwelling shall receive me ? in what vale
Shall be my harbour ? underneath what grove
Shall I take up my home ? and what clear stream
Shall with its murmur lull me into rest ?
The earth is all before me. With a heart
Joyous, nor scared at its own liberty,
I look about ; and should the chosen guide
Be nothing better than a wandering cloud,
I cannot miss my way. I breathe again !
Trances of thought and mountings of the mind
Come fast upon me : it is shaken off,
That burthen of my own unnatural self,
The heavy weight of many a weary day
Not mine, and such as were not made for me.
Long months of peace (if such bold word accord
With any promises of human life),
Long months of ease and undisturbed delight
Are mine in prospect ; whither shall I turn,
By road or pathway, or through trackless field,
Up hill or down, or shall some floating thing
Upon the river point me out my course ?

Dear Liberty ! Yet what would it avail
But for a gift that consecrates the joy ?
For I, methought, while the sweet breath of heaven
Was blowing on my body, felt within
A corresponding breeze, that gently moved
With quickening virtue, but is now become
A tempest, a redundant energy,
Vexing its own creation.   Thanks to both,
And their congenial powers, that, while they join
In breaking up a long-continued frost,
Bring with them vernal promises, the hope
Of active days urged on by flying hours,—
Days of sweet leisure, taxed with patient thought
Abstruse, nor wanting punctual service high,
Matins and vespers of harmonious verse !

SKATING

AND in the frosty season, when the sun
Was set, and visible for many a mile
The cottage windows blazed through twilight gloom,
I heeded not their summons : happy time
It was indeed for all of us—for me
It was a time of rapture !   Clear and loud
The village clock tolled six,—I wheeled about,
Proud and exulting like an untired horse
That cares not for his home.   All shod with steel,
We hissed along the polished ice in games
Confederate, imitative of the chase
And woodland pleasures,—the resounding horn,
The pack loud chiming, and the hunted hare.
So through the darkness and the cold we flew,
And not a voice was idle ; with the din
Smitten, the precipices rang aloud ;
The leafless trees and every icy crag
Tinkled like iron ; while far distant hills
Into the tumult sent an alien sound

Of melancholy not unnoticed, while the stars
Eastward were sparkling clear, and in the west
The orange sky of evening died away.
Not seldom from the uproar I retired
Into a silent bay, or sportively
Glanced sideway, leaving the tumultuous throng,
To cut across the reflex of a star
That fled, and, flying still before me, gleamed
Upon the glassy plain ; and oftentimes,
When we had given our bodies to the wind,
And all the shadowy banks on either side
Came sweeping through the darkness, spinning still
The rapid line of motion, then at once
Have I, reclining back upon my heels,
Stopped short ; yet still the solitary cliffs
Wheeled by me—even as if the earth had rolled
With visible motion her diurnal round !
Behind me did they stretch in solemn train,
Feebler and feebler, and I stood and watched
Till all was tranquil as a dreamless sleep.

BOATING

          WHEN summer came,
Our pastime was, on bright half-holidays,
To sweep along the plain of Windermere
With rival oars ; and the selected bourne
Was now an Island musical with birds
That sang and ceased not ; now a Sister Isle
Beneath the oaks' umbrageous covert, sown
With lilies of the valley like a field ;
And now a third small Island, where survived
In solitude the ruins of a shrine
Once to Our Lady dedicate, and served
Daily with chaunted rites. In such a race
So ended, disappointment could be none,
Uneasiness, or pain, or jealousy :

We rested in the shade, all pleased alike,
Conquered and conqueror. Thus the pride of strength,
And the vain-glory of superior skill,
Were tempered ; thus was gradually produced
A quiet independence of the heart ;
And to my Friend who knows me I may add,
Fearless of blame, that hence for future days
Ensued a diffidence and modesty,
And I was taught to feel, perhaps too much,
The self-sufficing power of Solitude.

PLAIN LIVING

OUR daily meals were frugal, Sabine fare !
More than we wished we knew the blessing then
Of vigorous hunger—hence corporeal strength
Unsapped by delicate viands ; for, exclude
A little weekly stipend, and we lived
Through three divisions of the quartered year
In penniless poverty. But now to school
From the half-yearly holidays returned,
We came with weightier purses, that sufficed
To furnish treats more costly than the Dame
Of the old grey stone, from her scant board, supplied.
Hence rustic dinners on the cool green ground,
Or in the woods, or by a river side
Or shady fountains, while among the leaves
Soft airs were stirring, and the mid-day sun
Unfelt shone brightly round us in our joy.
Nor is my aim neglected if I tell
How sometimes, in the length of those half-years,
We from our funds drew largely ;—proud to curb,
And eager to spur on, the galloping steed ;
And with the courteous inn-keeper, whose stud
Supplied our want, we haply might employ
Sly subterfuge, if the adventure's bound

Were distant : some famed temple where of yore
The Druids worshipped, or the antique walls
Of that large abbey, where within the Vale
Of Nightshade, to St. Mary's honour built,
Stands yet a mouldering pile with fractured arch,
Belfry, and images, and living trees ;
A holy scene !—Along the smooth green turf
Our horses grazed. To more than inland peace,
Left by the west wind sweeping overhead
From a tumultuous ocean, trees and towers
In that sequestered valley may be seen,
Both silent and both motionless alike ;
Such the deep shelter that is there, and such
The safeguard for repose and quietness.

Our steeds remounted and the summons given,
With whip and spur we through the chauntry flew
In uncouth race, and left the cross-legged knight,
And the stone-abbot, and that single wren
Which one day sang so sweetly in the nave
Of the old church, that—though from recent showers
The earth was comfortless, and, touched by faint
Internal breezes, sobbings of the place
And respirations, from the roofless walls
The shuddering ivy dripped large drops—yet still
So sweetly 'mid the gloom the invisible bird
Sang to herself, that there I could have made
My dwelling-place, and lived for ever there
To hear such music. Through the walls we flew
And down the valley, and, a circuit made
In wantonness of heart, through rough and smooth
We scampered homewards. Oh, ye rocks and streams,
And that still spirit shed from evening air !
Even in this joyous time I sometimes felt
Your presence, when with slackened step we breathed
Along the sides of the steep hills, or when
Lighted by gleams of moonlight from the sea
We beat with thundering hoofs the level sand.

ST. JOHN'S COLLEGE, CAMBRIDGE

THE Evangelist St. John my patron was :
Three Gothic courts are his, and in the first
Was my abiding-place, a nook obscure ;
Right underneath, the College kitchens made
A humming sound, less tuneable than bees,
But hardly less industrious ; with shrill notes
Of sharp command and scolding intermixed.
Near me hung Trinity's loquacious clock,
Who never let the quarters, night or day,
Slip by him unproclaimed, and told the hours
Twice over with a male and female voice.
Her pealing organ was my neighbour too ;
And from my pillow, looking forth by light
Of moon or favouring stars, I could behold
The antechapel where the statue stood
Of Newton with his prism and silent face,
The marble index of a mind for ever
Voyaging through strange seas of Thought, alone.

UNIVERSITY LIFE

BESIDE the pleasant Mill of Trompington
I laughed with Chaucer in the hawthorn shade ;
Heard him, while birds were warbling, tell his tales
Of amorous passion. And that gentle Bard,
Chosen by the Muses for their Page of State—
Sweet Spenser, moving through his clouded heaven
With the moon's beauty and the moon's soft pace,
I called him Brother, Englishman, and Friend !
Yea, our blind Poet, who in his later day,
Stood almost single ; uttering odious truth—
Darkness before, and danger's voice behind,
Soul awful—if the earth has ever lodged

An awful soul—I seemed to see him here
Familiarly, and in his scholar's dress
Bounding before me, yet a stripling youth—
A boy, no better, with his rosy cheeks
Angelical, keen eye, courageous look,
And conscious step of purity and pride.
Among the band of my compeers was one
Whom chance had stationed in the very room
Honoured by Milton's name.   O temperate Bard!
Be it confest that, for the first time, seated
Within thy innocent lodge and oratory,
One of a festive circle, I poured out
Libations, to thy memory drank, till pride
And gratitude grew dizzy in a brain
Never excited by the fumes of wine
Before that hour, or since.   Then, forth I ran
From the assembly ; through a length of streets,
Ran, ostrich-like, to reach our chapel door
In not a desperate or opprobrious time,
Albeit long after the importunate bell
Had stopped, with wearisome Cassandra voice
No longer haunting the dark winter night.
Call back, O Friend! a moment to thy mind,
The place itself and fashion of the rites.
With careless ostentation shouldering up
My surplice, through the inferior throng I clove
Of the plain Burghers, who in audience stood
On the last skirts of their permitted ground,
Under the pealing organ.   Empty thoughts!
I am ashamed of them : and that great Bard,
And thou, O Friend! who in thy ample mind
Hast placed me high above my best deserts,
Ye will forgive the weakness of that hour,
In some of its unworthy vanities,
Brother to many more.

"A GRACIOUS SPIRIT"

A GRACIOUS spirit o'er this earth presides,
And o'er the heart of man ; invisibly
It comes, to works of unreproved delight,
And tendency benign, directing those
Who care not, know not, think not, what they do.
The tales that charm away the wakeful night
In Araby, romances ; legends penned
For solace by dim light of monkish lamps ;
Fictions, for ladies of their love, devised
By youthful squires ; adventures endless, spun
By the dismantled warrior in old age,
Out of the bowels of those very schemes
In which his youth did first extravagate ;
These spread like day, and something in the shape
Of these will live till man shall be no more.
Dumb yearnings, hidden appetites, are ours,
And *they must* have their food. Our childhood sits,
Our simple childhood, sits upon a throne
That hath more power than all the elements.
I guess not what this tells of Being past,
Nor what it augurs of the life to come ;
But so it is ; and, in that dubious hour—
That twilight—when we first begin to see
This dawning earth, to recognise, expect,
And, in the long probation that ensues,
The time of trial, ere we learn to live
In reconcilement with our stinted powers ;
To endure this state of meagre vassalage,
Unwilling to forego, confess, submit,
Uneasy and unsettled, yoke-fellows
To custom, mettlesome, and not yet tamed
And humbled down—oh ! then we feel, we feel,
We know where we have friends. Ye dreamers, then,
Forgers of daring tales ! we bless you then,

Impostors, drivellers, dotards, as the ape
Philosophy will call you : *then* we feel
With what, and how great might ye are in league,
Who make our wish, our power, our thought a deed,
An empire, a possession—ye whom time
And seasons serve ; all Faculties to whom
Earth crouches, the elements are potter's clay,
Space like a heaven filled up with northern lights,
Here, nowhere, there, and everywhere at once.

THE POET'S SOUL

THE Poet's soul was with me at that time ;
Sweet meditations, the still overflow
Of present happiness, while future years
Lacked not anticipations, tender dreams,
No few of which have since been realised ;
And some remain, hopes for my future life.
Four years and thirty, told this very week,
Have I been now a sojourner on earth,
By sorrow not unsmitten ; yet for me
Life's morning radiance hath not left the hills,
Her dew is on the flowers. Those were the days
Which also first emboldened me to trust
With firmness, hitherto but slightly touched
By such a daring thought, that I might leave
Some monument behind me which pure hearts
Should reverence. The instinctive humbleness,
Maintained even by the very name and thought
Of printed books and authorship, began
To melt away ; and further, the dread awe
Of mighty names was softened down and seemed
Approachable, admitting fellowship
Of modest sympathy. Such aspect now,
Though not familiarly, my mind put on,
Content to observe, to achieve, and to enjoy.

HOLIDAY

In summer, making quest for works of art,
Or scenes renowned for beauty, I explored
That streamlet whose blue current works its way
Between romantic Dovedale's spiry rocks ;
Pried into Yorkshire dales, or hidden tracts
Of my own native region, and was blest
Between these sundry wanderings with a joy
Above all joys, that seemed another morn
Risen on mid noon ; blest with the presence, Friend
Of that sole Sister, her who hath been long
Dear to thee also, thy true friend and mine,
Now, after separation desolate,
Restored to me—such absence that she seemed
A gift then first bestowed.   The varied banks
Of Emont, hitherto unnamed in song,
And that monastic castle, 'mid tall trees,
Low standing by the margin of the stream,
A mansion visited (as fame reports)
By Sidney, where, in sight of our Helvellyn,
Or stormy Cross-fell, snatches he might pen
Of his Arcadia, by fraternal love
Inspired ;—that river and those mouldering towers
Have seen us side by side, when, having clomb
The darksome windings of a broken stair,
And crept along a ridge of fractured wall,
Not without trembling, we in safety looked
Forth, through some Gothic window's open space,
And gathered with one mind a rich reward
From the far-stretching landscape, by the light
Of morning beautified, or purple eve ;
Or, not less pleased, lay on some turret's head,
Catching from tufts of grass and hare-bell flowers
Their faintest whisper to the passing breeze,
Given out while mid-day heat oppressed the plains.

LOVE OF NATURE LEADING TO LOVE OF MAN

WHAT sounds are those, Helvellyn, that are heard
Up to thy summit, through the depth of air
Ascending, as if distance had the power
To make the sounds more audible ?   What crowd
Covers, or sprinkles o'er, yon village green ?
Crowd seems it, solitary hill ! to thee,
Though but a little family of men,
Shepherds and tillers of the ground—betimes
Assembled with their children and their wives,
And here and there a stranger interspersed.
They hold a rustic fair—a festival,
Such as, on this side now, and now on that,
Repeated through his tributary vales,
Helvellyn, in the silence of his rest,
Sees annually, if clouds towards either ocean
Blown from their favourite resting-place, or mists
Dissolved, have left him an unshrouded head.
Delightful day it is for all who dwell
In this secluded glen, and eagerly
They give it welcome.   Long ere heat of noon,
From byre or field the kine were brought ; the sheep
Are penned in cotes ; the chaffering is begun.
The heifer lows, uneasy at the voice
Of a new master ; bleat the flocks aloud.
Booths are there none ; a stall or two is here ;
A lame man or a blind, the one to beg,
The other to make music ; hither, too,
From far, with basket, slung upon her arm,
Of hawker's wares—books, pictures, combs, and pins—
Some aged woman finds her way again,
Year after year, a punctual visitant !
There also stands a speech-maker by rote,
Pulling the strings of his boxed raree-show ;

And in the lapse of many years may come
Prouder itinerant, mountebank, or he
Whose wonders in a covered wain lie hid.
But one there is, the loveliest of them all,
Some sweet lass of the valley, looking out
For gains, and who that sees her would not buy ?
Fruits of her father's orchard are her wares,
And with the ruddy produce she walks round
Among the crowd, half pleased with, half ashamed
Of, her new office, blushing restlessly.
The children now are rich, for the old to-day
Are generous as the young ; and, if content
With looking on, some ancient wedded pair
Sit in the shade together ; while they gaze,
" A cheerful smile unbends the wrinkled brow,
The days departed start again to life,
And all the scenes of childhood reappear,
Faint, but more tranquil, like the changing sun
To him who slept at noon and wakes at eve." *
Thus gaiety and cheerfulness prevail,
Spreading from young to old, from old to young,
And no one seems to want his share.—Immense
Is the recess, the circumambient world
Magnificent, by which they are embraced :
They move about upon the soft green turf :
How little they, they and their doings, seem,
And all that they can further or obstruct !
Through utter weakness pitiably dear,
As tender infants are : and yet how great !
For all things serve them : them the morning light
Loves, as it glistens on the silent rocks ;
And them the silent rocks, which now from high
Look down upon them ; the reposing clouds ;
The wild brooks prattling from invisible haunts ;
And old Helvellyn, conscious of the stir
Which animates this day their calm abode.

* These lines are from a descriptive Poem—" Malvern Hills "—by one of Mr. Wordsworth's oldest friends, Mr. Joseph Cottle.

With deep devotion, Nature, did I feel,
In that enormous City's turbulent world
Of men and things, what benefit I owed
To thee, and those domains of rural peace,
Where to the sense of beauty first my heart
Was opened ; tract more exquisitely fair
Than that famed paradise of ten thousand trees,
Or Gehol's matchless gardens, for delight
Of the Tartarian dynasty composed
(Beyond that mighty wall, not fabulous,
China's stupendous mound) by patient toil
Of myriads and boon nature's lavish help ;
There, in a clime from widest empire chosen,
Fulfilling (could enchantment have done more ?)
A sumptuous dream of flowery lawns, with domes
Of pleasure sprinkled over, shady dells
For eastern monasteries, sunny mounts
With temples crested, bridges, gondolas,
Rocks, dens, and groves of foliage taught to melt
Into each other their obsequious hues,
Vanished and vanishing in subtle chase,
Too fine to be pursued ; or standing forth
In no discordant opposition, strong
And gorgeous as the colours side by side
Bedded among rich plumes of tropic birds ;
And mountains over all, embracing all ;
And all the landscape, endlessly enriched
With waters running, falling, or asleep.

But lovelier far than this, the paradise
Where I was reared ; in Nature's primitive gifts
Favoured no less, and more to every sense
Delicious, seeing that the sun and sky,
The elements, and seasons as they change,
Do find a worthy fellow-labourer there—
Man free, man working for himself, with choice
Of time, and place, and object ; by his wants,
His comforts, native occupations, cares,

Cheerfully led to individual ends
Or social, and still followed by a train
Unwooed, unthought-of even—simplicity,
And beauty, and inevitable grace.

Yea, when a glimpse of those imperial bowers
Would to a child be transport over-great,
When but a half-hour's roam through such a place
Would leave behind a dance of images,
That shall break in upon his sleep for weeks ;
Even then the common haunts of the green earth,
And ordinary interests of man,
Which they embosom, all without regard
As both may seem, are fastening on the heart
Insensibly, each with the other's help.
For me, when my affections first were led
From kindred, friends, and playmates, to partake
Love for the human creature's absolute self,
That noticeable kindliness of heart
Sprang out of fountains, there abounding most,
Where sovereign Nature dictated the tasks
And occupations which her beauty adorned,
And Shepherds were the men that pleased me first ;
Not such as Saturn ruled 'mid Latian wilds,
With arts and laws so tempered, that their lives
Left, even to us toiling in this late day,
A bright tradition of the golden age ;
Not such as, 'mid Arcadian fastnesses
Sequestered, handed down among themselves
Felicity, in Grecian song renowned ;
Nor such as—when an adverse fate had driven,
From house and home, the courtly band whose fortunes
Entered, with Shakspeare's genius, the wild woods
Of Arden—amid sunshine or in shade
Culled the best fruits of Time's uncounted hours.
Ere Phœbe sighed for the false Ganymede ;
Or there where Perdita and Florizel
Together danced, Queen of the feast, and King ;

Nor such as Spenser fabled.   True it is,
That I had heard (what he perhaps had seen)
Of maids at sunrise bringing in from far
Their May-bush, and along the streets in flocks
Parading with a song of taunting rhymes,
Aimed at the laggards slumbering within doors ;
Had also heard, from those who yet remembered,
Tales of the May-pole dance, and wreaths that decked
Porch, door-way, or kirk-pillar ; and of youths,
Each with his maid, before the sun was up,
By annual custom, issuing forth in troops,
To drink the waters of some sainted well,
And hang it round with garlands.   Love survives ;
But, for such purpose, flowers no longer grow :
The times, too sage, perhaps too proud, have dropped
These lighter graces ; and the rural ways
And manners which my childhood looked upon
Were the unluxuriant produce of a life
Intent on little but substantial needs,
Yet rich in beauty, beauty that was felt.
But images of danger and distress,
Man suffering among awful Powers and Forms ;
Of this I heard, and saw enough to make
Imagination restless ; nor was free
Myself from frequent perils ; nor were tales
Wanting,—the tragedies of former times,
Hazards and strange escapes, of which the rocks
Immutable, and everflowing streams,
Where'er I roamed, were speaking monuments.

Smooth life had flock and shepherd in old time,
Long springs and tepid winters, on the banks
Of delicate Galesus ; and no less
Those scattered along Adria's myrtle shores :
Smooth life had herdsman, and his snow-white herd
To triumphs and to sacrificial rites
Devoted, on the inviolable stream
Of rich Clitumnus ; and the goat-herd lived

As calmly, underneath the pleasant brows
Of cool Lucretilis, where the pipe was heard
Of Pan, Invisible God, thrilling the rocks
With tutelary music, from all harm
The fold protecting.   I myself, mature
In manhood then, have seen a pastoral tract
Like one of these, where Fancy might run wild,
Though under skies less generous, less serene :
There, for her own delight had Nature framed
A pleasure-ground, diffused a fair expanse
Of level pasture, islanded with groves
And banked with woody risings ; but the Plain
Endless, here opening widely out, and there
Shut up in lesser lakes or beds of lawn
And intricate recesses, creek or bay
Sheltered within a shelter, where at large
The shepherd strays, a rolling hut his home.
Thither he comes with spring-time, there abides
All summer, and at sunrise ye may hear
His flageolet to liquid notes of love
Attuned, or sprightly fife resounding far.
Nook is there none, nor tract of that vast space
Where passage opens, but the same shall have
In turn its visitant, telling there his hours
In unlaborious pleasure, with no task
More toilsome than to carve a beechen bowl
For spring or fountain, which the traveller finds,
When through the region he pursues at will
His devious course.   A glimpse of such sweet life
I saw when, from the melancholy walls
Of Goslar, once imperial, I renewed
My daily walk along that wide champaign,
That, reaching to her gates, spreads east and west,
And northwards, from beneath the mountainous verge
Of the Hercynian forest.   Yet, hail to you
Moors, mountains, headlands, and ye hollow vales,
Ye long deep channels for the Atlantic's voice,
Powers of my native region !   Ye that seize

The heart with firmer grasp ! Your snows and streams
Ungovernable, and your terrifying winds,
That howl so dismally for him who treads
Companionless your awful solitudes !
There, 'tis the shepherd's task the winter long
To wait upon the storms : of their approach
Sagacious, into sheltering coves he drives
His flock, and thither from the homestead bears
A toilsome burden up the craggy ways,
And deals it out, their regular nourishment
Strewn on the frozen snow.   And when the spring
Looks out, and all the pastures dance with lambs,
And when the flock, with warmer weather, climbs
Higher and higher, him his office leads
To watch their goings, whatsoever track
The wanderers choose.   For this he quits his home
At day-spring, and no sooner doth the sun
Begin to strike him with a fire-like heat,
Than he lies down upon some shining rock,
And breakfasts with his dog.   When they have stolen,
As is their wont, a pittance from strict time,
For rest not needed or exchange of love,
Then from his couch he starts ; and now his feet
Crush out a livelier fragrance from the flowers
Of lowly thyme, by Nature's skill enwrought
In the wild turf : the lingering dews of morn
Smoke round him, as from hill to hill he hies,
His staff protending like a hunter's spear,
Or by its aid leaping from crag to crag,
And o'er the brawling beds of unbridged streams.
Philosophy, methinks, at Fancy's call,
Might deign to follow him through what he does
Or sees in his day's march ; himself he feels,
In those vast regions where his service lies,
A freeman, wedded to his life of hope
And hazard, and hard labour interchanged
With that majestic indolence so dear
To native man.   A rambling schoolboy, thus,

I felt his presence in his own domain,
As of a lord and master, or a power,
Or genius, under Nature, under God,
Presiding ; and severest solitude
Had more commanding looks when he was there.
When up the lonely brooks on rainy days
Angling I went, or trod the trackless hills
By mists bewildered, suddenly mine eyes
Have glanced upon him distant a few steps,
In size a giant, stalking through thick fog,
His sheep like Greenland bears ; or, as he stepped
Beyond the boundary line of some hill-shadow,
His form hath flashed upon me, glorified
By the deep radiance of the setting sun :
Or him have I descried in distant sky,
A solitary object and sublime,
Above all height ! like an aerial cross
Stationed alone upon a spiry rock
Of the Chartreuse, for worship.   Thus was man
Ennobled outwardly before my sight,
And thus my heart was early introduced
To an unconscious love and reverence
Of human nature ; hence the human form
To me became an index of delight,
Of grace and honour, power and worthiness.
Meanwhile this creature—spiritual almost
As those of books, but more exalted far ;
Far more of an imaginative form
Than the gay Corin of the groves, who lives
For his own fancies, or to dance by the hour,
In coronal, with Phyllis in the midst—
Was, for the purposes of kind, a man
With the most common ; husband, father ; learned,
Could teach, admonish ; suffered with the rest
From vice and folly, wretchedness and fear ;
Of this I little saw, cared less for it,
But something must have felt.
                              Call ye these appearances—

Which I beheld of shepherds in my youth,
This sanctity of Nature given to man—
A shadow, a delusion, ye who pore
On the dead letter, miss the spirit of things ;
Whose truth is not a motion or a shape
Instinct with vital functions, but a block
Or waxen image which yourselves have made
And ye adore !   But blessèd be the God
Of Nature and of Man that this was so ;
That men before my inexperienced eyes
Did first present themselves thus purified,
Removed, and to a distance that was fit :
And so we all of us in some degree
Are led to knowledge, wheresoever led,
And howsoever ; were it otherwise,
And we found evil fast as we find good
In our first years, or think that it is found,
How could the innocent heart bear up and live !
But doubly fortunate my lot ; not here
Alone, that something of a better life
Perhaps was round me than it is the privilege
Of most to move in, but that first I looked
At Man through objects that were great or fair ;
First communed with him by their help.   And thus
Was founded a sure safeguard and defence
Against the weight of meanness, selfish cares,
Coarse manners, vulgar passions, that beat in
On all sides from the ordinary world
In which we traffic.   Starting from this point
I had my face turned toward the truth, began
With an advantage furnished by that kind
Of prepossession, without which the soul
Receives no knowledge that can bring forth good,
No genuine insight ever comes to her.
From the restraint of over-watchful eyes
Preserved, I moved about, year after year,
Happy, and now most thankful that my walk
Was guarded from too early intercourse

With the deformities of crowded life,
And those ensuing laughters and contempts,
Self-pleasing, which, if we would wish to think
With a due reverence on earth's rightful lord,
Here placed to be the inheritor of heaven,
Will not permit us ; but pursue the mind,
That to devotion willingly would rise,
Into the temple and the temple's heart.

THE "TERROR" IN FRANCE

DOMESTIC carnage now filled the whole year
With feast-days ; old men from the chimney-nook,
The maiden from the bosom of her love,
The mother from the cradle of her babe,
The warrior from the field—all perished, all—
Friends, enemies, of all parties, ages, ranks,
Head after head, and never heads enough
For those that bade them fall.   They found their joy,
They made it proudly, eager as a child,
(If like desires of innocent little ones
May with such heinous appetites be compared),
Pleased in some open field to exercise
A toy that mimics with revolving wings
The motion of a wind-mill ; though the air
Do of itself blow fresh, and make the vanes
Spin in his eyesight, *that* contents him not,
But with the plaything at arm's length, he sets
His front against the blast, and runs amain,
That it may whirl the faster.

                      Amid the depth
Of those enormities, even thinking minds
Forgot, at seasons, whence they had their being ;
Forgot that such a sound was ever heard
As Liberty upon earth : yet all beneath
Her innocent authority was wrought,
Nor could have been, without her blessed name.

The illustrious wife of Roland, in the hour
Of her composure, felt that agony,
And gave it vent in her last words.   O Friend !
It was a lamentable time for man,
Whether a hope had e'er been his or not :
A woful time for them whose hopes survived
The shock ; most woful for those few who still
Were flattered, and had trust in human kind :
They had the deepest feeling of the grief.
Meanwhile the Invaders fared as they deserved :
The Herculean Commonwealth had put forth her arms,
And throttled with an infant godhead's might
The snakes about her cradle ; that was well,
And as it should be ; yet no cure for them
Whose souls were sick with pain of what would be
Hereafter brought in charge against mankind.
Most melancholy at that time, O Friend !
Were my day-thoughts,—my nights were miserable ;
Through months, through years, long after the last beat
Of those atrocities, the hour of sleep
To me came rarely charged with natural gifts,
Such ghastly visions had I of despair
And tyranny, and implements of death ;
And innocent victims sinking under fear,
And momentary hope, and worn-out prayer,
Each in his separate cell, or penned in crowds
For sacrifice, and struggling with fond mirth
And levity in dungeons, where the dust
Was laid with tears.   Then suddenly the scene
Changed, and the unbroken dream entangled me
In long orations, which I strove to plead
Before unjust tribunals,—with a voice
Labouring, a brain confounded, and a sense,
Death-like, of treacherous desertion, felt
In the last place of refuge—my own soul.

AFTER THE "TERROR"

FROM that time forth, Authority in France
Put on a milder face ; Terror had ceased,
Yet everything was wanting that might give
Courage to them who looked for good by light
Of rational Experience, for the shoots
And hopeful blossoms of a second spring :
Yet, in me, confidence was unimpaired ;
The Senate's language, and the public acts
And measures of the Government, though both
Weak, and of heartless omen, had not power
To daunt me ; in the People was my trust :
And, in the virtues which mine eyes had seen,
I knew that wound external could not take
Life from the young Republic ; that new foes
Would only follow, in the path of shame,
Their brethren, and her triumphs be in the end
Great, universal, irresistible.
This intuition led me to confound
One victory with another, higher far,—
Triumphs of unambitious peace at home,
And noiseless fortitude. Beholding still
Resistance strong as heretofore, I thought
That what was in degree the same was likewise
The same in quality,—that, as the worse
Of the two spirits then at strife remained
Untired, the better, surely, would preserve
The heart that first had roused him.   Youth maintains,
In all conditions of society,
Communion more direct and intimate
With nature,—hence, ofttimes, with reason too—
Than age or manhood, even.   To Nature then,
Power had reverted : habit, custom, law,
Had left an interregnum's open space
For *her* to move about in, uncontrolled.

Hence could I see how Babel-like their task,
Who, by the recent deluge stupefied,
With their whole souls went culling from the day
Its petty promises, to build a tower
For their own safety ; laughed with my compeers
At gravest heads, by enmity to France
Distempered, till they found, in every blast
Forced from the street-disturbing news man's horn,
For her great cause record or prophecy
Of utter ruin.   How might we believe
That wisdom could, in any shape, come near
Men clinging to delusions so insane ?
And thus, experience proving that no few
Of our opinions had been just, we took
Like credit to ourselves where less was due.
And thought that other notions were as sound,
Yea, could not but be right, because we saw
That foolish men opposed them.

                    To a strain
More animated I might here give way,
And tell, since juvenile errors are my theme,
What in those days, through Britain, was performed
To turn *all* judgments out of their right course ;
But this is passion over-near ourselves,
Reality too close and too intense,
And intermixed with something, in my mind,
Of scorn and condemnation personal,
That would profane the sanctity of verse.
Our Shepherds, this say merely, at that time
Acted, or seemed at least to act, like men
Thirsting to make the guardian crook of law
A tool of murder ; they who ruled the State—
Though with such awful proof before their eyes
That he, who would sow death, reaps death, or worse,
And can reap nothing better—child-like longed
To imitate, not wise enough to avoid ;
Or left (by mere timidity betrayed)
The plain straight road, for one no better chosen

Than if their wish had been to undermine
Justice, and make an end of Liberty.

But from these bitter truths I must return
To my own history.   It hath been told
That I was led to take an eager part
In arguments of civil polity,
Abruptly, and indeed before my time :
I had approached, like other youths, the shield
Of human nature from the golden side,
And would have fought, even to the death, to attest
The quality of the metal which I saw.
What there is best in individual man,
Of wise in passion, and sublime in power,
Benevolent in small societies,
And great in large ones, I had oft revolved,
Felt deeply, but not thoroughly understood
By reason : nay, far from it ; they were yet,
As cause was given me afterwards to learn,
Not proof against the injuries of the day ;
Lodged only at the sanctuary's door,
Not safe within its bosom.   Thus prepared,
And with such general insight into evil,
And of the bounds which sever it from good,
As books and common intercourse with life
Must needs have given—to the inexperienced mind,
When the world travels in a beaten road,
Guide faithful as is needed—I began
To meditate with ardour on the rule
And management of nations ; what it is
And ought to be ; and strove to learn how far
Their power or weakness, wealth or poverty,
Their happiness or misery, depends
Upon their laws, and fashion of the State.

O pleasant exercise of hope and joy !
For mighty were the auxiliars which then stood
Upon our side, us who were strong in love !

Bliss was it in that dawn to be alive,
But to be young was very Heaven ! O times,
In which the meagre, stale, forbidding ways
Of custom, law, and statute, took at once
The attraction of a country in romance !
When Reason seemed the most to assert her rights
When most intent on making of herself
A prime enchantress—to assist the work,
Which then was going forward in her name !
Not favoured spots alone, but the whole Earth,
The beauty wore of promise—that which sets
(As at some moments might not be unfelt
Among the bowers of Paradise itself)
The budding rose above the rose full blown.
What temper at the prospect did not wake
To happiness unthought of ? The inert
Were roused, and lively natures rapt away !
They who had fed their childhood upon dreams,
The play-fellows of fancy, who had made
All powers of swiftness, subtilty, and strength
Their ministers,—who in lordly wise had stirred
Among the grandest objects of the sense,
And dealt with whatsoever they found there
As if they had within some lurking right
To wield it ;—they, too, who of gentle mood
Had watched all gentle motions, and to these
Had fitted their own thoughts, schemers more mild,
And in the region of their peaceful selves ;—
Now was it that *both* found, the meek and lofty
Did both find, helpers to their hearts' desire,
And stuff at hand, plastic as they could wish,—
Were called upon to exercise their skill,
Not in Utopia,—subterranean fields,—
Or some secreted island, Heaven knows where !
But in the very world, which is the world
Of all of us,—the place where, in the end,
We find our happiness, or not at all !

HEALING NATURE

FROM Nature doth emotion come, and moods
Of calmness equally are Nature's gift :
This is her glory ; these two attributes
Are sister horns that constitute her strength.
Hence Genius, born to thrive by interchange
Of peace and excitation, finds in her
His best and purest friend ; from her receives
That energy by which he seeks the truth,
From her that happy stillness of the mind
Which fits him to receive it when unsought.

   Such benefit the humblest intellects
Partake of, each in their degree ; 'tis mine
To speak, what I myself have known and felt ;
Smooth task ! for words find easy way, inspired
By gratitude, and confidence in truth.
Long time in search of knowledge did I range
The field of human life, in heart and mind
Benighted ; but, the dawn beginning now
To reappear, 'twas proved that not in vain
I had been taught to reverence a Power
That is the visible quality and shape
And image of right reason ; that matures
Her processes by stedfast laws ; gives birth
To no impatient or fallacious hopes,
No heat of passion or excessive zeal,
No vain conceits ; provokes to no quick turns
Of self-applauding intellect ; but trains
To meekness, and exalts by humble faith ;
Holds up before the mind intoxicate
With present objects, and the busy dance
Of things that pass away, a temperate show
Of objects that endure ; and by this course
Disposes her, when over-fondly set

On throwing off incumbrances, to seek
In man, and in the frame of social life,
Whate'er there is desirable and good
Of kindred permanence, unchanged in form
And function, or, through strict vicissitude
Of life and death, revolving. Above all
Were re-established now those watchful thoughts
Which, seeing little worthy or sublime
In what the Historian's pen so much delights
To blazon—power and energy detached
From moral purpose—early tutored me
To look with feelings of fraternal love
Upon the unassuming things that hold
A silent station in this beauteous world.

Thus moderated, thus composed, I found
Once more in Man an object of delight,
Of pure imagination, and of love ;
And, as the horizon of my mind enlarged,
Again I took the intellectual eye
For my instructor, studious more to see
Great truths, than touch and handle little ones.
Knowledge was given accordingly ; my trust
Became more firm in feelings that had stood
The test of such a trial ; clearer far
My sense of excellence—of right and wrong :
The promise of the present time retired
Into its true proportion ; sanguine schemes,
Ambitious projects, pleased me less ; I sought
For present good in life's familiar face,
And built thereon my hopes of good to come.

GENUINE LIBERTY

OH ! who is he that hath his whole life long
Preserved, enlarged, this freedom in himself ?
For this alone is genuine liberty :

Where is the favoured being who hath held
That course unchecked, unerring, and untired,
In one perpetual progress smooth and bright ?—
A humbler destiny have we retraced,
And told of lapse and hesitating choice,
And backward wanderings along thorny ways :
Yet—compassed round by mountain solitudes,
Within whose solemn temple I received
My earliest visitations, careless then
Of what was given me ; and which now I range,
A meditative, oft a suffering, man—
Do I declare—in accents which, from truth
Deriving cheerful confidence, shall blend
Their modulation with these vocal streams—
That, whatsoever falls my better mind,
Revolving with the accidents of life,
May have sustained, that, howsoe'er misled,
Never did I, in quest of right and wrong,
Tamper with conscience from a private aim ;
Nor was in any public hope the dupe
Of selfish passions ; nor did ever yield
Wilfully to mean cares or low pursuits,
But shrunk with apprehensive jealousy
From every combination which might aid
The tendency, too potent in itself,
Of use and custom to bow down the soul
Under a growing weight of vulgar sense,
And substitute a universe of death
For that which moves with light and life informed,
Actual, divine, and true.   To fear and love,
To love as prime and chief, for there fear ends,
Be this ascribed ; to early intercourse,
In presence of sublime or beautiful forms,
With the adverse principles of pain and joy—
Evil as one is rashly named by men
Who know not what they speak.   By love subsists
All lasting grandeur, by pervading love ;
That gone, we are as dust.—Behold the fields

In balmy spring-time full of rising flowers
And joyous creatures ; see that pair, the lamb
And the lamb's mother, and their tender ways
Shall touch thee to the heart ; thou callest this love,
And not inaptly so, for love it is,
Far as it carries thee.   In some green bower
Rest, and be not alone, but have thou there
The One who is thy choice of all the world :
There linger, listening, gazing, with delight
Impassioned, but delight how pitiable !
Unless this love by a still higher love
Be hallowed, love that breathes not without awe ;
Love that adores, but on the knees of prayer,
By heaven inspired ; that frees from chains the soul,
Lifted, in union with the purest, best,
Of earth-born passions, on the wings of praise
Bearing a tribute to the Almighty's Throne.

PART VI

SELECTIONS FROM
"THE EXCURSION"

PREFACE TO THE EDITION OF 1814

THE Title-page announces that this is only a portion of a poem ; and the Reader must be here apprised that it belongs to the second part of a long and laborious Work, which is to consist of three parts.—The Author will candidly acknowledge that, if the first of these had been completed, and in such a manner as to satisfy his own mind, he should have preferred the natural order of publication, and have given that to the world first ; but, as the second division of the Work was designed to refer more to passing events, and to an existing state of things, than the others were meant to do, more continuous exertion was naturally bestowed upon it, and greater progress made here than in the rest of the poem ; and as this part does not depend upon the preceding to a degree which will materially injure its own peculiar interest, the Author, complying with the earnest entreaties of some valued Friends, presents the following pages to the Public.

It may be proper to state whence the poem, of which " The Excursion " is a part, derives its Title of THE RECLUSE.—Several years ago, when the Author retired to his native mountains, with the hope of being enabled to construct a literary Work that might live, it was a reasonable thing that he should take a review of his own mind, and examine how far Nature and Education had qualified him for such employment.   As subsidiary to this preparation, he undertook to record, in verse, the origin and progress of his own powers, as far as he was acquainted with them.   That Work,* addressed to a dear Friend, most distinguished for his knowledge and genius, and to whom the Author's Intellect is deeply indebted, has been long finished ; and the result of the investigation which gave rise to it was a determination to compose a philosophical poem, containing views of

* The Prelude.

Man, Nature, and Society ; and to be entitled, " The Recluse " ; as having for its principal subject the sensations and opinions of a poet living in retirement.— The preparatory poem * is biographical, and conducts the history of the Author's mind to the point when he was emboldened to hope that his faculties were sufficiently matured for entering upon the arduous labour which he had proposed to himself ; and the two Works have the same kind of relation to each other, if he may so express himself, as the ante-chapel has to the body of a Gothic church.　Continuing this allusion, he may be permitted to add, that his minor Pieces, which have been long before the Public, when they shall be properly arranged, will be found by the attentive Reader to have such connection with the main Work as may give them claim to be likened to the little cells, oratories, and sepulchral recesses, ordinarily included in those edifices.

The Author would not have deemed himself justified in saying, upon this occasion, so much of performances either unfinished or unpublished, if he had not thought that the labour bestowed by him upon what he has heretofore and now laid before the Public entitled him to candid attention for such a statement as he thinks necessary to throw light upon his endeavours to please and, he would hope, to benefit his countrymen.—Nothing further need be added, than that the first and third parts of " The Recluse " will consist chiefly of meditations in the Author's own person ; and that in the intermediate part (" The Excursion ") the intervention of characters speaking is employed, and something of a dramatic form adopted.

It is not the Author's intention formally to announce a system ; it was more animating to him to proceed in a different course ; and if he shall succeed in conveying to the mind clear thoughts, lively images, and strong feelings, the Reader will have no difficulty in extracting the system for himself.　And in the meantime the fol-

* The Prelude.

lowing passage, taken from the conclusion of the first
book of " The Recluse," may be acceptable as a kind
of *Prospectus* of the design and scope of the whole Poem.

"ON MAN, ON NATURE, AND ON HUMAN LIFE "

On Man, on Nature, and on Human Life,
Musing in solitude, I oft perceive
Fair trains of imagery before me rise,
Accompanied by feelings of delight
Pure, or with no unpleasing sadness mixed ;
And I am conscious of affecting thoughts
And dear remembrances, whose presence soothes
Or elevates the Mind, intent to weigh
The good and evil of our mortal state.
—To these emotions, whencesoe'er they come,
Whether from breath of outward circumstance,
Or from the Soul—an impulse to herself—
I would give utterance in numerous verse.
Of Truth, of Grandeur, Beauty, Love, and Hope,
And melancholy Fear subdued by Faith ;
Of blessèd consolations in distress ;
Of moral strength, and intellectual Power ;
Of joy in widest commonalty spread ;
Of the individual Mind that keeps her own
Inviolate retirement, subject there
To Conscience only, and the law supreme
Of that Intelligence which governs all—
I sing :—" fit audience let me find though few ! "
    So prayed, more gaining than he asked, the Bard—
In holiest mood. Urania, I shall need
Thy guidance, or a greater Muse, if such
Descend to earth or dwell in highest heaven !
For I must tread on shadowy ground, must sink
Deep—and, aloft ascending, breathe in worlds
To which the heaven of heavens is but a veil.
All strength—all terror, single or in bands,

That ever was put forth in personal form—
Jehovah—with his thunder, and the choir
Of shouting Angels, and the empyreal thrones—
I pass them unalarmed.   Not Chaos, not
The darkest pit of lowest Erebus,
Nor aught of blinder vacancy, scooped out
By help of dreams—can breed such fear and awe
As fall upon us often when we look
Into our Minds, into the Mind of Man—
My haunt, and the main region of my song
—Beauty—a living Presence of the earth,
Surpassing the most fair ideal Forms
Which craft of delicate Spirits hath composed
From earth's materials—waits upon my steps ;
Pitches her tents before me as I move,
An hourly neighbour.   Paradise, and groves
Elysian, Fortunate Fields—like those of old
Sought in the Atlantic Main—why should they be
A history only of departed things,
Or a mere fiction of what never was ?
For the discerning intellect of Man,
When wedded to this goodly universe
In love and holy passion, shall find these
A simple produce of the common day.
—I, long before the blissful hour arrives,
Would chant, in lonely peace, the spousal verse
Of this great consummation :—and, by words
Which speak of nothing more than what we are,
Would I arouse the sensual from their sleep
Of Death, and win the vacant and the vain
To noble raptures ; while my voice proclaims
How exquisitely the individual Mind
(And the progressive powers perhaps no less
Of the whole species) to the external World
Is fitted :—and how exquisitely, too—
Theme this but little heard of among men—
The external World is fitted to the Mind ;
And the creation (by no lower name

Can it be called) which they with blended might
Accomplish :—this is our high argument.
—Such grateful haunts foregoing, if I oft
Must turn elsewhere—to travel near the tribes
And fellowships of men, and see ill sights
Of madding passions mutually inflamed ;
Must hear Humanity in fields and groves
Pipe solitary anguish ; or must hang
Brooding above the fierce confederate storm
Of sorrow, barricadoed evermore
Within the walls of cities—may these sounds
Have their authentic comment ; that even these
Hearing, I be not downcast or forlorn !—
Descend, prophetic Spirit ! that inspir'st
The human Soul of universal earth,
Dreaming on things to come ; and dost possess
A metropolitan temple in the hearts
Of mighty Poets ; upon me bestow
A gift of genuine insight ; that my Song
With star-like virtue in its place may shine,
Shedding benignant influence, and secure
Itself from all malevolent effect
Of those mutations that extend their sway
Throughout the nether sphere !—And if with this
I mix more lowly matter ; with the thing
Contemplated, describe the Mind and Man
Contemplating ; and who, and what he was—
The transitory Being that beheld
This Vision ;—when and where, and how he lived ;
Be not this labour useless. If such theme
May sort with highest objects, then—dread Power !
Whose gracious favour is the primal source
Of all illumination—may my Life
Express the image of a better time,
More wise desires, and simpler manners ;—nurse
My Heart in genuine freedom :—all pure thoughts
Be with me ;—so shall thy unfailing love
Guide, and support, and cheer me to the end !

SELECTIONS FROM "THE EXCURSION"

THE WANDERER

[A summer forenoon—The Author reaches a ruined Cottage upon a Common, and there meets with a revered Friend, the Wanderer, of whose education and course of life he gives an account—The Wanderer, while resting under the shade of the Trees that surround the Cottage, relates the History of its last Inhabitant.]

'Twas summer, and the sun had mounted high :
Southward the landscape indistinctly glared
Through a pale steam ; but all the northern downs,
In clearest air ascending, showed far off
A surface dappled o'er with shadows flung
From brooding clouds ; shadows that lay in spots
Determined and unmoved, with steady beams
Of bright and pleasant sunshine interposed ;
To him most pleasant who on soft cool moss
Extends his careless limbs along the front
Of some huge cave, whose rocky ceiling casts
A twilight of its own, an ample shade,
Where the wren warbles, while the dreaming man,
Half conscious of the soothing melody,
With side-long eye looks out upon the scene,
By power of that impending covert, thrown
To finer distance.   Mine was at that hour
Far other lot, yet with good hope that soon
Under a shade as grateful I should find
Rest, and be welcomed there to livelier joy.
Across a bare wide Common I was toiling
With languid steps that by the slippery turf
Were baffled ; nor could my weak arm disperse
The host of insects gathering round my face,
And ever with me as I paced along.

Upon that open moorland stood a grove,
The wished-for port to which my course was bound.
Thither I came, and there, amid the gloom

Spread by a brotherhood of lofty elms,
Appeared a roofless Hut ; four naked walls
That stared upon each other !—I looked round,
And to my wish and to my hope espied
The Friend I sought ; a Man of reverend age,
But stout and hale, for travel unimpaired.
There was he seen upon the cottage-bench,
Recumbent in the shade, as if asleep ;
An iron-pointed staff lay at his side.

Him had I marked the day before—alone
And stationed in the public way, with face
Turned toward the sun then setting, while that staff
Afforded, to the figure of the man
Detained for contemplation or repose,
Graceful support ; his countenance as he stood
Was hidden from my view, and he remained
Unrecognised ; but, stricken by the sight,
With slackened footsteps I advanced, and soon
A glad congratulation we exchanged
At such unthought-of meeting.—For the night
We parted, nothing willingly ; and now
He by appointment waited for me here,
Under the covert of these clustering elms.

We were tried Friends : amid a pleasant vale,
In the antique market-village where was passed
My school-time, an apartment he had owned,
To which at intervals the Wanderer drew,
And found a kind of home or harbour there.
He loved me ; from a swarm of rosy boys
Singled out me, as he in sport would say,
For my grave looks, too thoughtful for my years.
As I grew up, it was my best delight
To be his chosen comrade. Many a time,
On holidays, we rambled through the woods :
We sate—we walked ; he pleased me with report
Of things which he had seen ; and often touched
Abstrusest matter, reasonings of the mind

Turned inward ; or at my request would sing
Old songs, the product of his native hills ;
A skilful distribution of sweet sounds,
Feeding the soul, and eagerly imbibed
As cool refreshing water, by the care
Of the industrious husbandman, diffused
Through a parched meadow-ground, in time of drought.
Still deeper welcome found his pure discourse ;
How precious, when in riper days I learned
To weigh with care his words, and to rejoice
In the plain presence of his dignity !

Oh ! many are the Poets that are sown
By Nature ; men endowed with highest gifts,
The vision and the faculty divine ;
Yet wanting the accomplishment of verse,
(Which, in the docile season of their youth,
It was denied them to acquire, through lack
Of culture and the inspiring aid of books,
Or haply by a temper too severe,
Or a nice backwardness afraid of shame)
Nor having e'er, as life advanced, been led
By circumstance to take unto the height
The measure of themselves, these favoured Beings,
All but a scattered few, live out their time,
Husbanding that which they possess within,
And go to the grave, unthought of.   Strongest minds
Are often those of whom the noisy world
Hears least ; else surely this Man had not left
His graces unrevealed and unproclaimed.
But, as the mind was filled with inward light,
So not without distinction had he lived,
Beloved and honoured—far as he was known.
And some small portion of his eloquent speech,
And something that may serve to set in view
The feeling pleasures of his loneliness,
His observations, and the thoughts his mind
Had dealt with—I will here record in verse ;

Which, if with truth it correspond, and sink
Or rise as venerable Nature leads,
The high and tender Muses shall accept
With gracious smile, deliberately pleased,
And listening Time reward with sacred praise.

Among the hills of Athol he was born ;
Where, on a small hereditary farm,
An unproductive slip of rugged ground,
His Parents, with their numerous offspring, dwelt ;
A virtuous household, though exceeding poor !
Pure livers were they all, austere and grave,
And fearing God ; the very children taught
Stern self-respect, a reverence for God's word,
And an habitual piety, maintained
With strictness scarcely known on English ground.

From his sixth year, the Boy of whom I speak,
In summer, tended cattle on the hills ;
But, through the inclement and the perilous days
Of long-continuing winter, he repaired,
Equipped with satchel, to a school, that stood
Sole building on a mountain's dreary edge,
Remote from view of city spire, or sound
Of minster clock ! From that bleak tenement
He, many an evening, to his distant home
In solitude returning, saw the hills
Grow larger in the darkness ; all alone
Beheld the stars come out above his head,
And travelled through the wood, with no one near
To whom he might confess the things he saw.

So the foundations of his mind were laid.
In such communion, not from terror free,
While yet a child, and long before his time,
Had he perceived the presence and the power
Of greatness ; and deep feelings had impressed
So vividly great objects that they lay

Upon his mind like substances, whose presence
Perplexed the bodily sense.   He had received
A precious gift ; for, as he grew in years,
With these impressions would he still compare
All his remembrances, thoughts, shapes, and forms ;
And, being still unsatisfied with aught
Of dimmer character, he thence attained
An active power to fasten images
Upon his brain ; and on their pictured lines
Intensely brooded, even till they acquired
The liveliness of dreams.   Nor did he fail,
While yet a child, with a child's eagerness
Incessantly to turn his ear and eye
On all things which the moving seasons brought
To feed such appetite—nor this alone
Appeased his yearning ;—in the after-day
Of boyhood, many an hour in caves forlórn,
And 'mid the hollow depths of naked crags
He sate, and even in their fixed lineaments,
Or from the power of a peculiar eye,
Or by creative feeling overborne,
Or by predominance of thought oppressed,
Even in their fixed and steady lineaments
He traced an ebbing and a flowing mind,
Expression ever varying !
                              Thus informed,
He had small need of books ; for many a tale
Traditionary, round the mountains hung,
And many a legend, peopling the dark woods,
Nourished Imagination in her growth,
And gave the Mind that apprehensive power
By which she is made quick to recognise
The moral properties and scope of things.
But eagerly he read, and read again,
Whate'er the minister's old shelf supplied ;
The life and death of martyrs, who sustained,
With will inflexible, those fearful pangs
Triumphantly displayed in records left

Of persecution, and the Covenant—times
Whose echo rings through Scotland to this hour !
And there, by lucky hap, had been preserved
A straggling volume, torn and incomplete,
That left half-told the preternatural tale,
Romance of giants, chronicle of fiends,
Profuse in garniture of wooden cuts
Strange and uncouth ; dire faces, figures dire,
Sharp-kneed, sharp-elbowed, and lean-ankled too,
With long and ghostly shanks—forms which once seen
Could never be forgotten !
                In his heart,
Where Fear sate thus, a cherished visitant,
Was wanting yet the pure delight of love
By sound diffused, or by the breathing air,
Or by the silent looks of happy things,
Or flowing from the universal face
Of earth and sky. But he had felt the power
Of Nature, and already was prepared,
By his intense conceptions, to receive
Deeply the lesson deep of love which he,
Whom Nature, by whatever means, has taught
To feel intensely, cannot but receive.

Such was the Boy—but for the growing Youth
What soul was his, when from the naked top
Of some bold headland, he beheld the sun
Rise up, and bathe the world in light ! He looked—
Ocean and earth, the solid frame of earth
And ocean's liquid mass, in gladness lay
Beneath him :—Far and wide the clouds were touched,
And in their silent faces could he read
Unutterable love. Sound needed none,
Nor any voice of joy ; his spirit drank
The spectacle : sensation, soul, and form,
All melted into him ; they swallowed up
His animal being ; in them did he live,
And by them did he live ; they were his life.

In such access of mind, in such high hour
Of visitation from the living God,
Thought was not ; in enjoyment it expired.
No thanks he breathed, he proffered no request ;
Rapt into still communion that transcends
The imperfect offices of prayer and praise,
His mind was a thanksgiving to the power
That made him ; it was blessedness and love !

A Herdsman on the lonely mountain tops,
Such intercourse was his, and in this sort
Was his existence oftentimes *possessed*.
O then how beautiful, how bright, appeared
The written promise ! Early had he learned
To reverence the volume that displays
The mystery, the life which cannot die ;
But in the mountains did he *feel* his faith.
All things, responsive to the writing, there
Breathed immortality, revolving life,
And greatness still revolving ; infinite :
There littleness was not ; the least of things
Seemed infinite ; and there his spirit shaped
Her prospects, nor did he believe,—he *saw*.
What wonder if his being thus became
Sublime and comprehensive ! Low desires,
Low thoughts had there no place ; yet was his heart
Lowly ; for he was meek in gratitude,
Oft as he called those ecstasies to mind,
And whence they flowed ; and from them he acquired
Wisdom, which works through patience ; thence he
          learned
In oft-recurring hours of sober thought
To look on Nature with a humble heart.
Self-questioned where it did not understand,
And with a superstitious eye of love.

So passed the time ; yet to the nearest town
He duly went with what small overplus

His earnings might supply, and brought away
The book that most had tempted his desires
While at the stall he read.   Among the hills
He gazed upon that mighty orb of song,
The divine Milton.   Lore of different kind,
The annual savings of a toilsome life,
His Schoolmaster supplied ; books that explain
The purer elements of truth involved
In lines and numbers, and, by charm severe,
(Especially perceived where nature droops
And feeling is suppressed) preserve the mind
Busy in solitude and poverty.
These occupations oftentimes deceived
The listless hours, while in the hollow vale,
Hollow and green, he lay on the green turf
In pensive idleness.   What could he do,
Thus daily thirsting, in that lonesome life,
With blind endeavours ?   Yet, still uppermost,
Nature was at his heart as if he felt,
Though yet he knew not how, a wasting power
In all things that from her sweet influence
Might tend to wean him.   Therefore with her hues,
Her forms, and with the spirit of her forms,
He clothed the nakedness of austere truth.
While yet he lingered in the rudiments
Of science, and among her simplest laws,
His triangles—they were the stars of heaven,
The silent stars !   Oft did he take delight
To measure the altitude of some tall crag
That is the eagle's birth-place, or some peak
Familiar with forgotten years, that shows,
Inscribed upon its visionary sides,
The history of many a winter storm,
Or obscure records of the path of fire.

And thus before his eighteenth year was told,
Accumulated feelings pressed his heart
With still increasing weight ; he was o'erpowered

By Nature ; by the turbulence subdued
Of his own mind ; by mystery and hope,
And the first virgin passion of a soul
Communing with the glorious universe.
Full often wished he that the winds might rage
When they were silent : far more fondly now
Than in his earlier season did he love
Tempestuous nights—the conflict and the sounds
That live in darkness.   From his intellect
And from the stillness of abstracted thought
He asked repose ; and, failing oft to win
The peace required, he scanned the laws of light
Amid the roar of torrents, where they send
From hollow clefts up to the clearer air
A cloud of mist that, smitten by the sun,
Varies its rainbow hues.   But vainly thus,
And vainly by all other means, he strove
To mitigate the fever of his heart.

In dreams, in study, and in ardent thought,
Thus was he reared ; much wanting to assist
The growth of intellect, yet gaining more,
And every moral feeling of his soul
Strengthened and braced, by breathing in content
The keen, the wholesome, air of poverty,
And drinking from the well of homely life.
—But, from past liberty, and tried restraints,
He now was summoned to select the course
Of humble industry that promised best
To yield him no unworthy maintenance.
Urged by his Mother, he essayed to teach
A village-school—but wandering thoughts were then
A misery to him ; and the Youth resigned
A task he was unable to perform.

That stern yet kindly Spirit, who constrains
The Savoyard to quit his naked rocks,
The free-born Swiss to leave his narrow vales,

(Spirit attached to regions mountainous
Like their own stedfast clouds) did now impel
His restless mind to look abroad with hope.
—An irksome drudgery seems it to plod on,
Through hot and dusty ways, or pelting storm,
A vagrant Merchant under a heavy load,
Bent as he moves, and needing frequent rest ;
Yet do such travellers find their own delight ;
And their hard service, deemed debasing now,
Gained merited respect in simpler times ;
When squire, and priest, and they who round them dwelt
In rustic sequestration—all dependent
Upon the PEDLAR'S toil—supplied their wants,
Or pleased their fancies, with the wares he brought.
Not ignorant was the Youth that still no few
Of his adventurous countrymen were led
By perseverance in this track of life
To competence and ease :—to him it offered
Attractions manifold ;—and this he chose.
—His Parents on the enterprise bestowed
Their farewell benediction, but with hearts
Foreboding evil.   From his native hills
He wandered far ; much did he see of men,
Their manners, their enjoyments, and pursuits,
Their passions and their feelings ; chiefly those
Essential and eternal in the heart,
That, 'mid the simpler forms of rural life,
Exist more simple in their elements,
And speak a plainer language.   In the woods,
A lone Enthusiast, and among the fields,
Itinerant in this labour, he had passed
The better portion of his time ; and there
Spontaneously had his affections thriven
Amid the bounties of the year, the peace
And liberty of nature ; there he kept
In solitude and solitary thought
His mind in a just equipoise of love.
Serene it was, unclouded by the cares

Of ordinary life ; unvexed, unwarped
By partial bondage.   In his steady course,
No piteous revolutions had he felt,
No wild varieties of joy and grief.
Unoccupied by sorrow of its own,
His heart lay open ; and, by nature tuned
And constant disposition of his thoughts
To sympathy with man, he was alive
To all that was enjoyed where'er he went,
And all that was endured ; for, in himself
Happy, and quiet in his cheerfulness,
He had no painful pressure from without
That made him turn aside from wretchedness
With coward fears.   He could *afford* to suffer
With those whom he saw suffer.   Hence it came
That in our best experience he was rich,
And in the wisdom of our daily life.
For hence, minutely, in his various rounds,
He had observed the progress and decay
Of many minds, of minds and bodies too ;
The history of many families ;
How they had prospered ; how they were o'erthrown
By passion or mischance, or such misrule
Among the unthinking masters of the earth
As makes the nations groan.

                                This active course
He followed till provision for his wants
Had been obtained ;—the Wanderer then resolved
To pass the remnant of his days, untasked
With needless services, from hardship free.
His calling laid aside, he lived at ease :
But still he loved to pace the public roads
And the wild paths ; and, by the summer's warmth
Invited, often would he leave his home
And journey far, revisiting the scenes
That to his memory were most endeared.
—Vigorous in health, of hopeful spirits, undamped
By worldly-mindedness or anxious care ;

Observant, studious, thoughtful, and refreshed
By knowledge gathered up from day to day ;
Thus had he lived a long and innocent life.

The Scottish Church, both on himself and those
With whom from childhood he grew up, had held
The strong hand of her purity ; and still
Had watched him with an unrelenting eye.
This he remembered in his riper age
With gratitude, and reverential thoughts.
But by the native vigour of his mind,
By his habitual wanderings out of doors,
By loneliness, and goodness, and kind works,
Whate'er, in docile childhood or in youth,
He had imbibed of fear or darker thought
Was melted all away ; so true was this,
That sometimes his religion seemed to me
Self-taught, as of a dreamer in the woods ;
Who to the model of his own pure heart
Shaped his belief, as grace divine inspired,
And human reason dictated with awe.
—And surely never did there live on earth
A man of kindlier nature.   The rough sports
And teasing ways of children vexed not him ;
Indulgent listener was he to the tongue
Of garrulous age ; nor did the sick man's tale,
To his fraternal sympathy addressed,
Obtain reluctant hearing.
                           Plain his garb ;
Such as might suit a rustic Sire, prepared
For sabbath duties ; yet he was a man
Whom no one could have passed without remark.
Active and nervous was his gait ; his limbs
And his whole figure breathed intelligence.
Time had compressed the freshness of his cheek
Into a narrower circle of deep red,
But had not tamed his eye ; that, under brows
Shaggy and grey, had meanings which it brought

From years of youth ; which, like a Being made
Of many Beings, he had wondrous skill
To blend with knowledge of the years to come,
Human, or such as lie beyond the grave.

———

So was He framed ; and such his course of life
Who now, with no appendage but a staff,
The prized memorial of relinquished toils,
Upon that cottage-bench reposed his limbs,
Screened from the sun.   Supine the Wanderer lay,
His eyes as if in drowsiness half shut,
The shadows of the breezy elms above
Dappling his face.   He had not heard the sound
Of my approaching steps, and in the shade
Unnoticed did I stand some minutes' space.
At length I hailed him, seeing that his hat
Was moist with water-drops, as if the brim
Had newly scooped a running stream.   He rose,
And ere our lively greeting into peace
Had settled, " 'Tis," said I, " a burning day :
My lips are parched with thirst, but you, it seems,
Have somewhere found relief."   He, at the word,
Pointing towards a sweet-briar, bade me climb
The fence where that aspiring shrub looked out
Upon the public way.   It was a plot
Of garden ground run wild, its matted weeds
Marked with the steps of those, whom, as they passed,
The gooseberry trees that shot in long lank slips,
Or currants, hanging from their leafless stems,
In scanty strings, had tempted to o'erleap
The broken wall.   I looked around, and there,
Where two tall hedge-rows of thick alder boughs
Joined in a cold damp nook, espied a well
Shrouded with willow-flowers and plumy fern.
My thirst I slaked, and, from the cheerless spot
Withdrawing, straightway to the shade returned
Where sate the old Man on the cottage-bench ;
And, while, beside him, with uncovered head,

I yet was standing, freely to respire,
And cool my temples in the fanning air,
Thus did he speak. " I see around me here
Things which you cannot see : we die, my Friend,
Nor we alone, but that which each man loved
And prized in his peculiar nook of earth
Dies with him, or is changed ; and very soon
Even of the good is no memorial left.
—The Poets, in their elegies and songs
Lamenting the departed, call the groves,
They call upon the hills and streams, to mourn,
And senseless rocks ; nor idly ; for they speak,
In these their invocations, with a voice
Obedient to the strong creative power
Of human passion. Sympathics there are
More tranquil, yet perhaps of kindred birth,
That steal upon the meditative mind,
And grow with thought. Beside yon spring I stood,
And eyed its waters till we seemed to feel
One sadness, they and I. For them a bond
Of brotherhood is broken : time has been
When, every day, the touch of human hand
Dislodged the natural sleep that binds them up
In mortal stillness ; and they ministered
To human comfort. Stooping down to drink,
Upon the slimy foot-stone I espied
The useless fragment of a wooden bowl,
Green with the moss of years, and subject only
To the soft handling of the elements :
There let it lie—how foolish are such thoughts !
Forgive them ;—never—never did my steps
Approach this door but she who dwelt within
A daughter's welcome gave me, and I loved her
As my own child. Oh, Sir ! the good die first,
And they whose hearts are dry as summer dust
Burn to the socket. Many a passenger
Hath blessed poor Margaret for her gentle looks,
When she upheld the cool refreshment drawn

From that forsaken spring ; and no one came
But he was welcome ; no one went away
But that it seemed she loved him.   She is dead,
The light extinguished of her lonely hut,
The hut itself abandoned to decay,
And she forgotten in the quiet grave.

I speak," continued he, " of One whose stock
Of virtues bloomed beneath this lonely roof.
She was a Woman of a steady mind,
Tender and deep in her excess of love ;
Not speaking much, pleased rather with the joy
Of her own thoughts : by some especial care
Her temper had been framed, as if to make
A Being, who by adding love to peace
Might live on earth a life of happiness.
Her wedded Partner lacked not on his side
The humble worth that satisfied her heart :
Frugal, affectionate, sober, and withal
Keenly industrious.   She with pride would tell
That he was often seated at his loom,
In summer, ere the mower was abroad
Among the dewy grass,—in early spring,
Ere the last star had vanished.—They who passed
At evening, from behind the garden fence
Might hear his busy spade, which he would ply,
After his daily work, until the light
Had failed, and every leaf and flower were lost
In the dark hedges.   So their days were spent
In peace and comfort ; and a pretty boy
Was their best hope, next to the God in heaven.

Not twenty years ago, but you I think
Can scarcely bear it now in mind, there came
Two blighting seasons, when the fields were left
With half a harvest.   It pleased Heaven to add
A worse affliction in the plague of war :
This happy Land was stricken to the heart !

A Wanderer then among the cottages,
I, with my freight of winter raiment, saw
The hardships of that season : many rich
Sank down, as in a dream, among the poor ;
And of the poor did many cease to be,
And their place knew them not. Meanwhile, abridged
Of daily comforts, gladly reconciled
To numerous self-denials, Margaret
Went struggling on through those calamitous years
With cheerful hope, until the second autumn,
When her life's Helpmate on a sick-bed lay,
Smitten with perilous fever.   In disease
He lingered long ; and, when his strength returned,
He found the little he had stored, to meet
The hour of accident or crippling age,
Was all consumed.   A second infant now
Was added to the troubles of a time
Laden, for them and all of their degree,
With care and sorrow ; shoals of artisans
From ill-requited labour turned adrift
Sought daily bread from public charity,
They, and their wives and children—happier far
Could they have lived as do the little birds
That peck along the hedge-rows, or the kite
That makes her dwelling on the mountain rocks !

A sad reverse it was for him who long
Had filled with plenty, and possessed in peace,
This lonely Cottage.   At the door he stood,
And whistled many a snatch of merry tunes
That had no mirth in them ; or with his knife
Carved uncouth figures on the heads of sticks—
Then, not less idly, sought, through every nook
In house or garden, any casual work
Of use or ornament ; and with a strange,
Amusing, yet uneasy, novelty,
He mingled, where he might, the various tasks
Of summer, autumn, winter, and of spring.

But this endured not ; his good humour soon
Became a weight in which no pleasure was :
And poverty brought on a petted mood
And a sore temper : day by day he drooped,
And he would leave his work—and to the town
Would turn without an errand his slack steps ;
Or wander here and there among the fields.
One while he would speak lightly of his babes,
And with a cruel tongue : at other times
He tossed them with a false unnatural joy :
And 'twas a rueful thing to see the looks
Of the poor innocent children. ' Every smile,'
Said Margaret to me, here beneath these trees,
' Made my heart bleed.' "

       At this the Wanderer paused ;
And, looking up to those enormous elms,
He said, " 'Tis now the hour of deepest noon.
At this still season of repose and peace,
This hour when all things which are not at rest
Are cheerful ; while this multitude of flies
With tuneful hum is filling all the air ;
Why should a tear be on an old Man's cheek ?
Why should we thus, with an untoward mind,
And in the weakness of humanity,
From natural wisdom turn our hearts away ;
To natural comfort shut our eyes and ears ;
And, feeding on disquiet, thus disturb
The calm of nature with our restless thoughts ? "

     —————

HE spake with somewhat of a solemn tone :
But, when he ended, there was in his face
Such easy cheerfulness, a look so mild,
That for a little time it stole away
All recollection ; and that simple tale
Passed from my mind like a forgotten sound.
A while on trivial things we held discourse,
To me soon tasteless.   In my own despite,
I thought of that poor Woman as of one

Whom I had known and loved.   He had rehearsed
Her homely tale with such familiar power,
With such an active countenance, an eye
So busy, that the things of which he spake
Seemed present ; and, attention now relaxed,
A heart-felt chillness crept along my veins.
I rose ; and, having left the breezy shade,
Stood drinking comfort from the warmer sun,
That had not cheered me long—ere, looking round
Upon that tranquil Ruin, I returned,
And begged of the old Man that, for my sake,
He would resume his story.

                              He replied,
" It were a wantonness, and would demand
Severe reproof, if we were men whose hearts
Could hold vain dalliance with the misery
Even of the dead ; contented thence to draw
A momentary pleasure, never marked
By reason, barren of all future good.
But we have known that there is often found
In mournful thoughts, and always might be found,
A power to virtue friendly ; were 't not so,
I am a dreamer among men, indeed
An idle dreamer ! 'Tis a common tale,
An ordinary sorrow of man's life,
A tale of silent suffering, hardly clothed
In bodily form.—But without further bidding
I will proceed.

                        While thus it fared with them,
To whom this cottage, till those hapless years,
Had been a blessèd home, it was my chance
To travel in a country far remote ;
And when these lofty elms once more appeared
What pleasant expectations lured me on
O'er the flat Common !—With quick step I reached
The threshold, lifted with light hand the latch ;
But, when I entered, Margaret looked at me

A little while ; then turned her head away
Speechless,—and, sitting down upon a chair,
Wept bitterly.   I wist not what to do,
Nor how to speak to her.   Poor Wretch ! at last
She rose from off her seat, and then,—O Sir !
I cannot *tell* how she pronounced my name :—
With fervent love, and with a face of grief
Unutterably helpless, and a look
That seemed to cling upon me, she enquired
If I had seen her husband.   As she spake
A strange surprise and fear came to my heart,
Nor had I power to answer ere she told
That he had disappeared—not two months gone.
He left his house : two wretched days had past,
And on the third, as wistfully she raised
Her head from off her pillow, to look forth,
Like one in trouble, for returning light,
Within her chamber-casement she espied
A folded paper, lying as if placed
To meet her waking eyes.   This tremblingly
She opened—found no writing, but beheld
Pieces of money carefully enclosed,
Silver and gold.   ' I shuddered at the sight,'
Said Margaret, ' for I knew it was his hand
That must have placed it there ; and ere that day
Was ended, that long anxious day, I learned,
From one who by my husband had been sent
With the sad news, that he had joined a troop
Of soldiers, going to a distant land.
—He left me thus—he could not gather heart
To take a farewell of me ; for he feared
That I should follow with my babes, and sink
Beneath the misery of that wandering life.'

This tale did Margaret tell with many tears :
And, when she ended, I had little power
To give her comfort, and was glad to take
Such words of hope from her own mouth as served

To cheer us both. But long we had not talked
Ere we built up a pile of better thoughts,
And with a brighter eye she looked around
As if she had been shedding tears of joy.
We parted.—'Twas the time of early spring ;
I left her busy with her garden tools ;
And well remember, o'er that fence she looked,
And, while I paced along the foot-way path,
Called out, and sent a blessing after me,
With tender cheerfulness, and with a voice
That seemed the very sound of happy thoughts.

I roved o'er many a hill and many a dale,
With my accustomed load ; in heat and cold,
Through many a wood and many an open ground,
In sunshine and in shade, in wet and fair,
Drooping or blithe of heart, as might befall ;
My best companions now the driving winds,
And now the ' trotting brooks ' and whispering trees,
And now the music of my own sad steps,
With many a short-lived thought that passed between,
And disappeared.
                          I journeyed back this way,
When, in the warmth of midsummer, the wheat
Was yellow ; and the soft and bladed grass,
Springing afresh, had o'er the hay-field spread
Its tender verdure. At the door arrived,
I found that she was absent. In the shade,
Where now we sit, I waited her return.
Her cottage, then a cheerful object, wore
Its customary look,—only, it seemed,
The honeysuckle, crowding round the porch,
Hung down in heavier tufts ; and that bright weed,
The yellow stone-crop, suffered to take root
Along the window's edge, profusely grew,
Blinding the lower panes. I turned aside,
And strolled into her garden. It appeared
To lag behind the season, and had lost

Its pride of neatness.   Daisy-flowers and thrift
Had broken their trim border-lines, and straggled
O'er paths they used to deck : carnations, once
Prized for surpassing beauty, and no less
For the peculiar pains they had required,
Declined their languid heads, wanting support.
The cumbrous bind-weed, with its wreaths and bells,
Had twined about her two small rows of peas,
And dragged them to the earth.

                       Ere this an hour
Was wasted.—Back I turned my restless steps ;
A stranger passed ; and, guessing whom I sought,
He said that she was used to ramble far.—
The sun was sinking in the west ; and now
I sate with sad impatience.   From within
Her solitary infant cried aloud ;
Then, like a blast that dies away self-stilled,
The voice was silent.   From the bench I rose ;
But neither could divert nor soothe my thoughts.
The spot, though fair, was very desolate—
The longer I remained, more desolate :
And, looking round me, now I first observed
The corner stones, on either side the porch,
With dull red stains discoloured, and stuck o'er
With tufts and hairs of wool, as if the sheep,
That fed upon the Common, thither came
Familiarly, and found a couching-place
Even at her threshold.   Deeper shadows fell
From these tall elms ; the cottage-clock struck eight ;—
I turned, and saw her distant a few steps.
Her face was pale and thin—her figure, too,
Was changed.   As she unlocked the door, she said,
' It grieves me you have waited here so long,
But, in good truth, I've wandered much of late ;
And sometimes—to my shame I speak—have need
Of my best prayers to bring me back again.
While on the board she spread our evening meal,
She told me—interrupting not the work

Which gave employment to her listless hands—
That she had parted with her elder child ;
To a kind master on a distant farm
Now happily apprenticed.—' I perceive
You look at me, and you have cause ; to-day
I have been travelling far ; and many days
About the fields I wander, knowing this
Only, that what I seek I cannot find ;
And so I waste my time : for I am changed ;
And to myself,' said she, ' have done much wrong
And to this helpless infant.   I have slept
Weeping, and weeping have I waked ; my tears
Have flowed as if my body were not such
As others are ; and I could never die.
But I am now in mind and in my heart
More easy ; and I hope,' said she, ' that God
Will give me patience to endure the things
Which I behold at home.'

                       It would have grieved
Your very soul to see her.   Sir, I feel
The story linger in my heart ; I fear
'Tis long and tedious ; but my spirit clings
To that poor Woman :—so familiarly
Do I perceive her manner, and her look,
And presence ; and so deeply do I feel
Her goodness, that, not seldom, in my walks
A momentary trance comes over me ;
And to myself I seem to muse on One
By sorrow laid asleep ; or borne away,
A human being destined to awake
To human life, or something very near
To human life, when he shall come again
For whom she suffered.   Yes, it would have grieved
Your very soul to see her : evermore
Her eyelids drooped, her eyes downward were cast ;
And, when she at her table gave me food,
She did not look at me.   Her voice was low,
Her body was subdued.   In every act

Pertaining to her house-affairs, appeared
The careless stillness of a thinking mind
Self-occupied ; to which all outward things
Are like an idle matter.   Still she sighed,
But yet no motion of the breast was seen,
No heaving of the heart.   While by the fire
We sate together, sighs came on my ear,
I knew not how, and hardly whence they came.

　　Ere my departure, to her care I gave,
For her son's use, some tokens of regard,
Which with a look of welcome she received ;
And I exhorted her to place her trust
In God's good love, and seek his help by prayer.
I took my staff, and, when I kissed her babe,
The tears stood in her eyes.   I left her then
With the best hope and comfort I could give :
She thanked me for my wish ;—but for my hope
It seemed she did not thank me.

　　　　　　　　　　　　I returned,
And took my rounds along this road again
When on its sunny bank the primrose flower
Peeped forth, to give an earnest of the Spring.
I found her sad and drooping : she had learned
No tidings of her husband ; if he lived,
She knew not that he lived ; if he were dead,
She knew not he was dead.   She seemed the same
In person and appearance ; but her house
Bespake a sleepy hand of negligence ;
The floor was neither dry nor neat, the hearth
Was comfortless, and her small lot of books,
Which, in the cottage-window, heretofore
Had been piled up against the corner panes
In seemly order, now, with straggling leaves,
Lay scattered here and there, open or shut,
As they had chanced to fall.   Her infant Babe
Had from his Mother caught the trick of grief,
And sighed among its playthings.   I withdrew,

And once again entering the garden saw,
More plainly still, that poverty and grief
Were now come nearer to her : weeds defaced
The hardened soil, and knots of withered grass :
No ridges there appeared of clear black mould,
No winter greenness ; of her herbs and flowers,
It seemed the better part was gnawed away
Or trampled into earth ; a chain of straw,
Which had been twined about the slender stem
Of a young apple-tree, lay at its root ;
The bark was nibbled round by truant sheep.
—Margaret stood near, her infant in her arms,
And, noting that my eye was on the tree,
She said, " I fear it will be dead and gone
Ere Robert come again." When to the House
We had returned together, she enquired
If I had any hope :—but for her babe
And for her little orphan boy, she said,
She had no wish to live, that she must die
Of sorrow. Yet I saw the idle loom
Still in its place ; his Sunday garments hung
Upon the self-same nail ; his very staff
Stood undisturbed behind the door.

                      And when,
In bleak December, I retraced this way,
She told me that her little babe was dead,
And she was left alone. She now, released
From her maternal cares, had taken up
The employment common through these wilds, and
    gained,
By spinning hemp, a pittance for herself ;
And for this end had hired a neighbour's boy
To give her needful help. That very time
Most willingly she put her work aside,
And walked with me along the miry road,
Heedless how far ; and, in such piteous sort
That any heart had ached to hear her, begged
That, whereso'er I went, I still would ask

For him whom she had lost. We parted then—
Our final parting ; for from that time forth
Did many seasons pass ere I returned
Into this tract again.
                Nine tedious years ;
From their first separation, nine long years,
She lingered in unquiet widowhood ;
A Wife and Widow. Needs must it have been
A sore heart-wasting ! I have heard, my Friend,
That in yon arbour oftentimes she sate
Alone, through half the vacant sabbath day ;
And, if a dog passed by, she still would quit
The shade, and look abroad. On this old bench
For hours she sate ; and evermore her eye
Was busy in the distance, shaping things
That made her heart beat quick. You see that path,
Now faint,—the grass has crept o'er its grey line ;
There, to and fro, she paced through many a day
Of the warm summer, from a belt of hemp
That girt her waist, spinning the long-drawn thread
With backward steps. Yet ever as there passed
A man whose garments showed the soldier's red,
Or crippled mendicant in sailor's garb,
The little child who sate to turn the wheel
Ceased from his task ; and she with faltering voice
Made many a fond enquiry ; and when they,
Whose presence gave no comfort, were gone by,
Her heart was still more sad. And by yon gate,
That bars the traveller's road, she often stood,
And when a stranger horseman came, the latch
Would lift, and in his face look wistfully ;
Most happy, if, from aught discovered there
Of tender feeling, she might dare repeat
The same sad question. Meanwhile her poor Hut
Sank to decay ; for he was gone, whose hand,
At the first nipping of October frost,
Closed up each chink, and with fresh bands of straw
Chequered the green-grown thatch. And so she lived

Through the long winter, reckless and alone ;
Until her house by frost, and thaw, and rain,
Was sapped ; and while she slept, the nightly damps
Did chill her breast ; and in the stormy day
Her tattered clothes were ruffled by the wind,
Even at the side of her own fire.   Yet still
She loved this wretched spot, nor would for worlds
Have parted hence ; and still that length of road,
And this rude bench, one torturing hope endeared,
Fast rooted at her heart : and here, my Friend,—
In sickness she remained ; and here she died ;
Last human tenant of these ruined walls ! "

The old Man ceased : he saw that I was moved ;
From that low bench, rising instinctively
I turned aside in weakness, nor had power
To thank him for the tale which he had told.
I stood, and leaning o'er the garden wall
Reviewed that Woman's sufferings ; and it seemed
To comfort me while with a brother's love
I blessed her in the impotence of grief.
Then towards the cottage I returned ; and traced
Fondly, though with an interest more mild,
That secret spirit of humanity
Which, 'mid the calm oblivious tendencies
Of nature, 'mid her plants, and weeds, and flowers,
And silent overgrowings, still survived.
The old Man, noting this, resumed, and said,
" My Friend ! enough to sorrow you have given,
The purposes of wisdom ask no more :
Nor more would she have craved as due to One
Who, in her worst distress, had ofttimes felt
The unbounded might of prayer ; and learned, with soul
Fixed on the Cross, that consolation springs,
From sources deeper far than deepest pain,
For the meek Sufferer.   Why then should we read
The forms of things with an unworthy eye ?
She sleeps in the calm earth, and peace is here.

I well remember that those very plumes,
Those weeds, and the high spear-grass on that wall,
By mist and silent rain-drops silvered o'er,
As once I passed, into my heart conveyed
So still an image of tranquillity,
So calm and still, and looked so beautiful
Amid the uneasy thoughts which filled my mind,
That what we feel of sorrow and despair
From ruin and from change, and all the grief
That passing shows of Being leave behind,
Appeared an idle dream, that could maintain,
Nowhere, dominion o'er the enlightened spirit
Whose meditative sympathies repose
Upon the breast of Faith. I turned away,
And walked along my road in happiness."

He ceased. Ere long the sun declining shot
A slant and mellow radiance, which began
To fall upon us, while, beneath the trees,
We sate on that low bench: and now we felt,
Admonished thus, the sweet hour coming on.
A linnet warbled from those lofty elms,
A thrush sang loud, and other melodies,
At distance heard, peopled the milder air.
The old Man rose, and, with a sprightly mien
Of hopeful preparation, grasped his staff;
Together casting then a farewell look
Upon those silent walls, we left the shade;
And, ere the stars were visible, had reached
A village-inn—our evening resting-place.

THE SOLITARY

ARGUMENT

[The Author describes his travels with the Wanderer, whose character is further illustrated—Morning scene, and View of a Village Wake—Wanderer's account of a Friend whom he purposes to visit—View, from an eminence, of the Valley which his Friend had chosen for his retreat —Sound of singing from below—A funeral procession—Descent into the Valley—Observations drawn from the Wanderer at sight of a book accidentally discovered in a recess in the Valley—Meeting with the Wanderer's friend, the Solitary—Wanderer's description of the mode of burial in this mountainous district—Solitary contrasts with this, that of the individual carried a few minutes before from the cottage—The cottage entered—Description of the Solitary's apartment—Repast there—View, from the window, of two mountain summits ; and the Solitary's description of the companionship they afford him—Account of the departed inmate of the cottage—Description of a grand spectacle upon the mountains, with its effect upon the Solitary's mind—Leave the house.]

In days of yore how fortunately fared
The Minstrel ! wandering on from hall to hall,
Baronial court or royal : cheered with gifts
Munificent, and love, and ladies' praise ;
Now meeting on his road an armèd knight,
Now resting with a pilgrim by the side
Of a clear brook ;—beneath an abbey's roof
One evening sumptuously lodged ; the next,
Humbly in a religious hospital ;
Or with some merry outlaws of the wood ;
Or haply shrouded in a hermit's cell.
Him, sleeping or awake, the robber spared ;
He walked—protected from the sword of war
By virtue of that sacred instrument
His harp, suspended at the traveller's side ;
His dear companion wheresoe'er he went
Opening from land to land an easy way
By melody, and by the charm of verse.
Yet not the noblest of that honoured Race
Drew happier, loftier, more empassioned, thoughts

From his long journeyings and eventful life,
Than this obscure Itinerant had skill
To gather, ranging through the tamer ground
Of these our unimaginative days ;
Both while he trod the earth in humblest guise
Accoutred with his burthen and his staff ;
And now, when free to move with lighter pace.

What wonder, then, if I, whose favourite school
Hath been the fields, the roads, and rural lanes,
Looked on this guide with reverential love ?
Each with the other pleased, we now pursued
Our journey, under favourable skies.
Turn wheresoe'er we would, he was a light
Unfailing : not a hamlet could we pass,
Rarely a house, that did not yield to him
Remembrances ; or from his tongue call forth
Some way-beguiling tale.   Nor less regard
Accompanied those strains of apt discourse,
Which nature's various objects might inspire ;
And in the silence of his face I read
His overflowing spirit.   Birds and beasts,
And the mute fish that glances in the stream,
And harmless reptile coiling in the sun,
And gorgeous insect hovering in the air,
The fowl domestic, and the household dog—
In his capacious mind, he loved them all :
Their rights acknowledging he felt for all.
Oft was occasion given me to perceive
How the calm pleasures of the pasturing herd
To happy contemplation soothed his walk ;
How the poor brute's condition, forced to run
Its course of suffering in the public road,
Sad contrast ! all too often smote his heart
With unavailing pity.   Rich in love
And sweet humanity, he was, himself,
To the degree that he desired, beloved.
Smiles of good-will from faces that he knew

Greeted us all day long ; we took our seats
By many a cottage-hearth, where he received
The welcome of an Inmate from afar,
And I at once forgot, I was a Stranger.
—Nor was he loth to enter raggèd huts,
Huts where his charity was blest ; his voice
Heard as the voice of an experienced friend.
And, sometimes—where the poor man held dispute
With his own mind, unable to subdue
Impatience through inaptness to perceive
General distress in his particular lot ;
Or cherishing resentment, or in vain
Struggling against it ; with a soul perplexed,
And finding in herself no steady power
To draw the line of comfort that divides
Calamity, the chastisement of Heaven,
From the injustice of our brother men—
To him appeal was made as to a judge ;
Who, with an understanding heart, allayed
The perturbation ; listened to the plea ;
Resolved the dubious point ; and sentence gave
So grounded, so applied, that it was heard
With softened spirit, even when it condemned.

Such intercourse I witnessed, while we roved,
Now as his choice directed, now as mine ;
Or both, with equal readiness of will,
Our course submitting to the changeful breeze
Of accident.   But when the rising sun
Had three times called us to renew our walk,
My Fellow-traveller, with earnest voice,
As if the thought were but a moment old,
Claimed absolute dominion for the day.
We started—and he led me toward the hills,
Up through an ample vale, with higher hills
Before us, mountains stern and desolate ;
But, in the majesty of distance, now
Set off, and to our ken appearing fair

Of aspect, with aërial softness clad,
And beautified with morning's purple beams.

The wealthy, the luxurious, by the stress
Of business roused, or pleasure, ere their time,
May roll in chariots, or provoke the hoofs
Of the fleet coursers they bestride, to raise
From earth the dust of morning, slow to rise ;
And they, if blest with health and hearts at ease,
Shall lack not their enjoyment :—but how faint
Compared with ours ! who, pacing side by side,
Could, with an eye of leisure, look on all
That we beheld ; and lend the listening sense
To every grateful sound of earth and air ;
Pausing at will—our spirits braced, our thoughts
Pleasant as roses in the thickets blown,
And pure as dew bathing their crimson leaves.

Mount slowly, sun ! that we may journey long,
By this dark hill protected from thy beams !
Such is the summer pilgrim's frequent wish ;
But quickly from among our morning thoughts
'Twas chased away : for, toward the western side
Of the broad vale, casting a casual glance,
We saw a throng of people ; wherefore met ?
Blithe notes of music, suddenly let loose
On the thrilled ear, and flags uprising, yield
Prompt answer ; they proclaim the annual Wake,
Which the bright season favours.—Tabor and pipe
In purpose join to hasten or reprove
The laggard Rustic ; and repay with boons
Of merriment a party-coloured knot,
Already formed upon the village-green.
—Beyond the limits of the shadow cast
By the broad hill, glistened upon our sight
That gay assemblage.   Round them and above,
Glitter, with dark recesses interposed,
Casement, and cottage-roof, and stems of trees

Half-veiled in vapoury cloud, the silver steam
Of dews fast melting on their leafy boughs
By the strong sunbeams smitten.   Like a mast
Of gold, the Maypole shines ; as if the rays
Of morning, aided by exhaling dew,
With gladsome influence could re-animate
The faded garlands dangling from its sides.

Said I, " The music and the sprightly scene
Invite us ; shall we quit our road, and join
These festive matins ? "—He replied, " Not loth
To linger I would here with you partake,
Not one hour merely, but till evening's close,
The simple pastimes of the day and place.
By the fleet Racers, ere the sun be set,
The turf of yon large pasture will be skimmed ;
There, too, the lusty Wrestlers shall contend :
But know we not that he, who intermits
The appointed task and duties of the day,
Untunes full oft the pleasures of the day ;
Checking the finer spirits that refuse
To flow when purposes are lightly changed ?
A length of journey yet remains untraced :
Let us proceed."   Then, pointing with his staff
Raised toward those craggy summits, his intent
He thus imparted :—
                    " In a spot that lies
Among yon mountain fastnesses concealed,
You will receive, before the hour of noon,
Good recompense, I hope, for this day's toil,
From sight of One who lives secluded there,
Lonesome and lost : of whom, and whose past life,
(Not to forestall such knowledge as may be
More faithfully collected from himself)
This brief communication shall suffice.

Though now sojourning there, he, like myself,
Sprang from a stock of lowly parentage

Among the wilds of Scotland, in a tract
Where many a sheltered and well-tended plant
Bears, on the humblest ground of social life,
Blossoms of piety and innocence.
Such grateful promises his youth displayed :
And, having shown in study forward zeal,
He to the Ministry was duly called ;
And straight, incited by a curious mind
Filled with vague hopes, he undertook the charge
Of Chaplain to a military troop
Cheered by the Highland bagpipe, as they marched
In plaided vest,—his fellow-countrymen.
This office filling, yet by native power
And force of native inclination made
An intellectual ruler in the haunts
Of social vanity, he walked the world,
Gay, and affecting graceful gaiety ;
Lax, buoyant—less a pastor with his flock
Than a soldier among soldiers—lived and roamed
Where Fortune led :—and Fortune, who oft proves
The careless wanderer's friend, to him made known
A blooming Lady—a conspicuous flower,
Admired for beauty, for her sweetness praised ;
Whom he had sensibility to love,
Ambition to attempt, and skill to win.

For this fair Bride, most rich in gifts of mind,
Nor sparingly endowed with worldly wealth,
His office he relinquished ; and retired
From the world's notice to a rural home.
Youth's season yet with him was scarcely past,
And she was in youth's prime.   How free their love,
How full their joy !   'Till, pitiable doom !
In the short course of one undreaded year
Death blasted all.   Death suddenly o'erthrew
Two lovely Children—all that they possessed !
The Mother followed :—miserably bare
The one Survivor stood : he wept, he prayed

For his dismissal, day and night, compelled
To hold communion with the grave, and face
With pain the regions of eternity.
An uncomplaining apathy displaced
This anguish ; and, indifferent to delight,
To aim and purpose, he consumed his days,
To private interest dead, and public care.
So lived he ; so he might have died.

                       But now,
To the wide world's astonishment, appeared
A glorious opening, the unlooked-for dawn,
That promised everlasting joy to France !
Her voice of social transport reached even him !
He broke from his contracted bounds, repaired
To the great City, an emporium then
Of golden expectations, and receiving
Freights every day from a new world of hope.
Thither his popular talents he transferred ;
And, from the pulpit, zealously maintained
The cause of Christ and civil liberty,
As one, and moving to one glorious end.
Intoxicating service ! I might say
A happy service ; for he was sincere
As vanity and fondness for applause,
And new and shapeless wishes, would allow.

    That righteous cause (such power hath freedom)
      bound,
For one hostility, in friendly league,
Ethereal natures and the worst of slaves ;
Was served by rival advocates that came
From regions opposite as heaven and hell.
One courage seemed to animate them all :
And, from the dazzling conquests daily gained
By their united efforts, there arose
A proud and most presumptuous confidence
In the transcendent wisdom of the age,
And her discernment ; not alone in rights,

And in the origin and bounds of power
Social and temporal ; but in laws divine,
Deduced by reason, or to faith revealed.
An overweening trust was raised ; and fear
Cast out, alike of person and of thing.
Plague from this union spread, whose subtle bane
The strongest did not easily escape ;
And He, what wonder ! took a mortal taint.
How shall I trace the change, how bear to tell
That he broke faith with them whom he had laid
In earth's dark chambers, with a Christian's hope !
An infidel contempt of holy writ
Stole by degrees upon his mind ; and hence
Life, like that Roman Janus, double-faced ;
Vilest hypocrisy—the laughing, gay
Hypocrisy, not leagued with fear, but pride.
Smooth words he had to wheedle simple souls ;
But, for disciples of the inner school,
Old freedom was old servitude, and they
The wisest whose opinions stooped the least
To known restraints ; and who most boldly drew
Hopeful prognostications from a creed,
That, in the light of false philosophy,
Spread like a halo round a misty moon,
Widening its circle as the storms advance.

His sacred function was at length renounced ;
And every day and every place enjoyed
The unshackled layman's natural liberty ;
Speech, manners, morals, all without disguise.
I do not wish to wrong him ; though the course
Of private life licentiously displayed
Unhallowed actions—planted like a crown
Upon the insolent aspiring brow
Of spurious notions—worn as open signs
Of prejudice subdued—still he retained,
'Mid much abasement, what he had received
From nature, an intense and glowing mind.
Wherefore, when humbled Liberty grew weak,

And mortal sickness on her face appeared,
He coloured objects to his own desire
As with a lover's passion.   Yet his moods
Of pain were keen as those of better men,
Nay keener, as his fortitude was less :
And he continued, when worse days were come,
To deal about his sparkling eloquence,
Struggling against the strange reverse with zeal
That showed like happiness.   But, in despite
Of all this outside bravery, within,
He neither felt encouragement nor hope :
For moral dignity, and strength of mind,
Were wanting ; and simplicity of life ;
And reverence for himself ; and, last and best,
Confiding thoughts, through love and fear of Him
Before whose sight the troubles of this world
Are vain, as billows in a tossing sea.

The glory of the times fading away—
The splendour, which had given a festal air
To self-importance, hallowed it, and veiled
From his own sight—this gone, he forfeited
All joy in human nature ; was consumed,
And vexed, and chafed, by levity and scorn,
And fruitless indignation ; galled by pride ;
Made desperate by contempt of men who throve
Before his sight in power or fame, and won,
Without desert, what he desired ; weak men,
Too weak even for his envy or his hate !
Tormented thus, after a wandering course
Of discontent, and inwardly opprest
With malady—in part, I fear, provoked
By weariness of life—he fixed his home,
Or, rather say, sate down by very chance,
Among these rugged hills ; where now he dwells,
And wastes the sad remainder of his hours,
Steeped in a self-indulging spleen, that wants not
Its own voluptuousness ;—on this resolved,

With this content, that he will live and die
Forgotten,—at safe distance from ' a world
Not moving to his mind.' "
                                        These serious words
Closed the preparatory notices
That served my Fellow-traveller to beguile
The way, while we advanced up that wide vale.
Diverging now (as if his quest had been
Some secret of the mountains, cavern, fall
Of water, or some lofty eminence,
Renowned for splendid prospect far and wide)
We scaled, without a track to ease our steps,
A steep ascent ; and reached a dreary plain,
With a tumultuous waste of huge hill tops
Before us ; savage region ! which I paced
Dispirited : when, all at once, behold !
Beneath our feet, a little lowly vale,
A lowly vale, and yet uplifted high
Among the mountains ; even as if the spot
Had been from eldest time by wish of theirs
So placed, to be shut out from all the world !
Urn-like it was in shape, deep as an urn ;
With rocks encompassed, save that to the south
Was one small opening, where a heath-clad ridge
Supplied a boundary less abrupt and close ;
A quiet treeless nook, with two green fields,
A liquid pool that glittered in the sun,
And one bare dwelling ; one abode, no more !
It seemed the home of poverty and toil,
Though not of want : the little fields, made green
By husbandry of many thrifty years,
Paid cheerful tribute to the moorland house.
—There crows the cock, single in his domain :
The small birds find in spring no thicket there
To shroud them ; only from the neighbouring
        vales
The cuckoo, straggling up to the hill tops,
Shouteth faint tidings of some gladder place.

Ah ! what a sweet Recess, thought I, is here !
Instantly throwing down my limbs at ease
Upon a bed of heath ;—full many a spot
Of hidden beauty have I chanced to espy
Among the mountains ; never one like this ;
So lonesome, and so perfectly secure ;
Not melancholy—no, for it is green,
And bright, and fertile, furnished in itself
With the few needful things that life requires.
—In rugged arms how softly does it lie,
How tenderly protected !   Far and near
We have an image of the pristine earth,
The planet in its nakedness : were this
Man's only dwelling, sole appointed seat,
First, last, and single, in the breathing world,
It could not be more quiet ; peace is here
Or nowhere ; days unruffled by the gale
Of public news or private ; years that pass
Forgetfully ; uncalled upon to pay
The common penalties of mortal life,
Sickness, or accident, or grief, or pain.

On these and kindred thoughts intent I lay
In silence musing by my Comrade's side,
He also silent ; when from out the heart
Of that profound abyss a solemn voice,
Or several voices in one solemn sound,
Was heard ascending ; mournful, deep, and slow
The cadence, as of psalms—a funeral dirge !
We listened, looking down upon the hut,
But seeing no one : meanwhile from below
The strain continued, spiritual as before ;
And now distinctly could I recognise
These words :—" *Shall in the grave thy love be known,
In death thy faithfulness ?* " —" God rest his soul ! "
Said the old man, abruptly breaking silence,—
" He is departed, and finds peace at last ! "

This scarcely spoken, and those holy strains

Not ceasing, forth appeared in view a band
Of rustic persons, from behind the hut
Bearing a coffin in the midst, with which
They shaped their course along the sloping side
Of that small valley, singing as they moved ;
A sober company and few, the men
Bare-headed, and all decently attired !
Some steps when they had thus advanced, the dirge
Ended ; and, from the stillness that ensued
Recovering, to my Friend I said, " You spake,
Methought, with apprehension that these rites
Are paid to Him upon whose shy retreat
This day we purposed to intrude."—" I did so,
But let us hence, that we may learn the truth :
Perhaps it is not he but some one else
For whom this pious service is performed ;
Some other tenant of the solitude."

So, to a steep and difficult descent
Trusting ourselves, we wound from crag to crag,
Where passage could be won ; and, as the last
Of the mute train, behind the heathy top
Of that off-sloping outlet, disappeared,
I, more impatient in my downward course,
Had landed upon easy ground ; and there
Stood waiting for my Comrade.   When behold
An object that enticed my steps aside !
A narrow, winding, entry opened out
Into a platform—that lay, sheepfold-wise,
Enclosed between an upright mass of rock
And one old moss-grown wall ;—a cool recess,
And fanciful !   For where the rock and wall
Met in an angle, hung a penthouse, framed
By thrusting two rude staves into the wall
And overlaying them with mountain sods ;
To weather-fend a little turf-built seat
Whereon a full-grown man might rest, nor dread
The burning sunshine, or a transient shower ;

But the whole plainly wrought by children's hands !
Whose skill had thronged the floor with a proud show
Of baby-houses, curiously arranged ;
Nor wanting ornament of walks between,
With mimic trees inserted in the turf,
And gardens interposed.   Pleased with the sight,
I could not choose but beckon to my Guide,
Who, entering, round him threw a careless glance,
Impatient to pass on, when I exclaimed,
" Lo ! what is here ? " and, stooping down, drew forth
A book, that, in the midst of stones and moss
And wreck of party-coloured earthen-ware,
Aptly disposed, had lent its help to raise
One of those petty structures.   " His it must be ! "
Exclaimed the Wanderer, " cannot but be his,
And he is gone ! "   The book, which in my hand
Had opened of itself (for it was swoln
With searching damp, and seemingly had lain
To the injurious elements exposed
From week to week,) I found to be a work
In the French tongue, a Novel of Voltaire,
His famous Optimist.   " Unhappy Man ! "
Exclaimed my Friend : " here then has been to him
Retreat within retreat, a sheltering-place
Within how deep a shelter !   He had fits,
Even to the last, of genuine tenderness,
And loved the haunts of children : here, no doubt,
Pleasing and pleased, he shared their simple sports,
Or sate companionless ; and here the book,
Left and forgotten in his careless way,
Must by the cottage-children have been found :
Heaven bless them, and their inconsiderate work !
To what odd purpose have the darlings turned
This sad memorial of their hapless friend ! "

   " Me," said I, " most doth it surprise, to find
Such book in such a place ! "—" A book it is,"
He answered, " to the Person suited well,

Though little suited to surrounding things :
'Tis strange, I grant ; and stranger still had been
To see the Man who owned it, dwelling here,
With one poor shepherd, far from all the world !—
Now, if our errand hath been thrown away,
As from these intimations I forebode,
Grieved shall I be—less for my sake than yours,
And least of all for him who is no more."

By this, the book was in the old Man's hand ;
And he continued, glancing on the leaves
An eye of scorn :—" The lover," said he, " doomed
To love when hope hath failed him—whom no depth
Of privacy is deep enough to hide,
Hath yet his bracelet or his lock of hair,
And that is joy to him.   When change of times
Hath summoned kings to scaffolds, do but give
The faithful servant, who must hide his head
Henceforth in whatsoever nook he may,
A kerchief sprinkled with his master's blood,
And he too hath his comforter.   How poor,
Beyond all poverty how destitute,
Must that Man have been left, who, hither driven,
Flying or seeking, could yet bring with him
No dearer relique, and no better stay,
Than this dull product of a scoffer's pen,
Impure conceits discharging from a heart
Hardened by impious pride !—I did not fear
To tax you with this journey ; "—mildly said
My venerable Friend, as forth we stepped
Into the presence of the cheerful light—
" For I have knowledge that you do not shrink
From moving spectacles ;—but let us on."

So speaking, on he went, and at the word
I followed, till he made a sudden stand :
For full in view, approaching through a gate
That opened from the enclosure of green fields

Into the rough uncultivated ground,
Behold the Man whom he had fancied dead !
I knew from his deportment, mien, and dress,
That it could be no other ; a pale face,
A meagre person, tall, and in a garb
Not rustic—dull and faded like himself !
He saw us not, though distant but few steps ;
For he was busy, dealing, from a store
Upon a broad leaf carried, choicest strings
Of red ripe currants ; gift by which he strove,
With intermixture of endearing words,
To soothe a Child, who walked beside him, weeping
As if disconsolate.—" They to the grave
Are bearing him, my Little-one," he said,
" To the dark pit ; but he will feel no pain ;
His body is at rest, his soul in heaven."

More might have followed—but my honoured Friend
Broke in upon the Speaker with a frank
And cordial greeting.—Vivid was the light
That flashed and sparkled from the other's eyes ;
He was all fire : no shadow on his brow
Remained, nor sign of sickness on his face.
Hands joined he with his Visitant,—a grasp,
An eager grasp ; and many moments' space—
When the first glow of pleasure was no more,
And, of the sad appearance which at once
Had vanished, much was come and coming back—
An amicable smile retained the life
Which it had unexpectedly received,
Upon his hollow cheek. " How kind," he said,
" Nor could your coming have been better timed ;
For this, you see, is in our narrow world
A day of sorrow. I have here a charge "—
And, speaking thus, he patted tenderly
The sun-burnt forehead of the weeping child—
" A little mourner, whom it is my task
To comfort :—but how came ye ?—if yon track

(Which doth at once befriend us and betray)
Conducted hither your most welcome feet,
Ye could not miss the funeral train—they yet
Have scarcely disappeared." " This blooming Child,"
Said the old Man, " is of an age to weep
At any grave or solemn spectacle,
Inly distressed or overpowered with awe,
He knows not wherefore ;—but the boy to-day,
Perhaps is shedding orphan's tears ; you also
Must have sustained a loss."—" The hand of Death,"
He answered, " has been here ; but could not well
Have fallen more lightly, if it had not fallen
Upon myself."—The other left these words
Unnoticed, thus continuing—

                              " From yon crag,
Down whose steep sides we dropped into the vale,
We heard the hymn they sang—a solemn sound
Heard anywhere ; but in a place like this
'Tis more than human ! Many precious rites
And customs of our rural ancestry
Are gone, or stealing from us ; this, I hope,
Will last for ever. Oft on my way have I
Stood still, though but a casual passenger,
So much I felt the awfulness of life,
In that one moment when the corse is lifted
In silence, with a hush of decency ;
Then from the threshold moves with song of peace,
And confidential yearnings, towards its home,
Its final home on earth. What traveller—who—
(How far soe'er a stranger) does not own
The bond of brotherhood, when he sees them go,
A mute procession on the houseless road ;
Or passing by some single tenement
Or clustered dwellings, where again they raise
The monitory voice ? But most of all
It touches, it confirms, and elevates,
Then, when the body, soon to be consigned
Ashes to ashes, dust bequeathed to dust,

Is raised from the church-aisle, and forward borne
Upon the shoulders of the next in love,
The nearest in affection or in blood ;
Yea, by the very mourners who had knelt
Beside the coffin, resting on its lid
In silent grief their unuplifted heads,
And heard meanwhile the Psalmist's mournful plaint,
And that most awful scripture which declares
We shall not sleep, but we shall all be changed !
—Have I not seen—ye likewise may have seen—
Son, husband, brothers—brothers side by side,
And son and father also side by side,
Rise from that posture :—and in concert move,
On the green turf following the vested Priest,
Four dear supporters of one senseless weight,
From which they do not shrink, and under which
They faint not, but advance towards the open grave
Step after step—together, with their firm
Unhidden faces : he that suffers most,
He outwardly, and inwardly perhaps,
The most serene, with most undaunted eye !—
Oh ! blest are they who live and die like these,
Loved with such love, and with such sorrow mourned ! "

" That poor Man taken hence to-day," replied
The Solitary, with a faint sarcastic smile
Which did not please me, " must be deemed, I fear,
Of the unblest ; for he will surely sink
Into his mother earth without such pomp
Of grief, depart without occasion given
By him for such array of fortitude.
Full seventy winters hath he lived, and mark !
This simple Child will mourn his one short hour,
And I shall miss him : scanty tribute ! yet,
This wanting, he would leave the sight of men,
If love were his sole claim upon their care,
Like a ripe date which in the desert falls
Without a hand to gather it."

                                        At this
I interposed, though loth to speak, and said,
" Can it be thus among so small a band
As ye must needs be here ? in such a place
I would not willingly, methinks, lose sight
Of a departing cloud."—" 'Twas not for love "—
Answered the sick Man with a careless voice—
" That I came hither ; neither have I found
Among associates who have power of speech,
Nor in such other converse as is here,
Temptation so prevailing as to change
That mood, or undermine my first resolve."
Then, speaking in like careless sort, he said
To my benign Companion,—" Pity 'tis
That fortune did not guide you to this house
A few days earlier ; then would you have seen
What stuff the Dwellers in a solitude,
That seems by Nature hollowed out to be
The seat and bosom of pure innocence,
Are made of ; an ungracious matter this !
Which, for truth's sake, yet in remembrance too
Of past discussions with this zealous friend
And advocate of humble life, I now
Will force upon his notice ; undeterred
By the example of his own pure course,
And that respect and deference which a soul
May fairly claim, by niggard age enriched
In what she most doth value, love of God
And his frail creature Man ;—but ye shall hear.
I talk—and ye are standing in the sun
Without refreshment ! "
                                Quickly had he spoken,
And, with light steps still quicker than his words,
Led toward the Cottage.   Homely was the spot ;
And, to my feeling, ere we reached the door,
Had almost a forbidding nakedness ;
Less fair, I grant, even painfully less fair,
Than it appeared when from the beetling rock

We had looked down upon it.   All within,
As left by the departed company,
Was silent ; save the solitary clock
That on mine ear ticked with a mournful sound.—
Following our Guide we clomb the cottage-stairs
And reached a small apartment dark and low,
Which was no sooner entered than our Host
Said gaily, " This is my domain, my cell,
My hermitage, my cabin, what you will—
I love it better than a snail his house.
But now ye shall be feasted with our best."

So, with more ardour than an unripe girl
Left one day mistress of her mother's stores,
He went about his hospitable task.
My eyes were busy, and my thoughts no less,
And pleased I looked upon my grey-haired Friend,
As if to thank him ; he returned that look,
Cheered, plainly, and yet serious.   What a wreck
Had we about us ! scattered was the floor,
And, in like sort, chair, window-seat, and shelf,
With books, maps, fossils, withered plants and flowers,
And tufts of mountain moss.   Mechanic tools
Lay intermixed with scraps of paper, some
Scribbled with verse : a broken angling-rod
And shattered telescope, together linked
By cobwebs, stood within a dusty nook ;
And instruments of music, some half-made,
Some in disgrace, hung dangling from the walls.
But speedily the promise was fulfilled ;
A feast before us, and a courteous Host
Inviting us in glee to sit and eat.
A napkin, white as foam of that rough brook
By which it had been bleached, o'erspread the board ;
And was itself half-covered with a store
Of dainties,—oaten bread, curd, cheese, and cream ;
And cakes of butter curiously embossed,
Butter that had imbibed from meadow-flowers

A golden hue, delicate as their own
Faintly reflected in a lingering stream.
Nor lacked, for more delight on that warm day,
Our table, small parade of garden fruits,
And whortle-berries from the mountain side.
The Child, who long ere this had stilled his sobs,
Was now a help to his late comforter,
And moved, a willing Page, as he was bid,
Ministering to our need.

                In genial mood,
While at our pastoral banquet thus we sate
Fronting the window of that little cell,
I could not, ever and anon, forbear
To glance an upward look on two huge Peaks
That from some other vale peered into this.
" Those lusty twins," exclaimed our host, " if here
It were your lot to dwell, would soon become
Your prized companions.—Many are the notes
Which, in his tuneful course, the wind draws forth
From rocks, woods, caverns, heaths, and dashing shores ;
And well those lofty brethren bear their part
In the wild concert—chiefly when the storm
Rides high ; then all the upper air they fill
With roaring sound, that ceases not to flow,
Like smoke, along the level of the blast,
In mighty current ; theirs, too, is the song
Of stream and headlong flood that seldom fails ;
And, in the grim and breathless hour of noon,
Methinks that I have heard them echo back
The thunder's greeting. Nor have nature's laws
Left them ungifted with a power to yield
Music of finer tone ; a harmony,
So do I call it, though it be the hand
Of silence, though there be no voice ;—the clouds,
The mist, the shadows, light of golden suns,
Motions of moonlight, all come thither—touch,
And have an answer—thither come, and shape
A language not unwelcome to sick hearts

And idle spirits :—there the sun himself,
At the calm close of summer's longest day,
Rests his substantial orb ;—between those heights
And on the top of either pinnacle,
More keenly than elsewhere in night's blue vault,
Sparkle the stars, as of their station proud.
Thoughts are not busier in the mind of man
Than the mute agents stirring there :—alone
Here do I sit and watch——"

                                    A fall of voice,
Regretted like the nightingale's last note,
Had scarcely closed this high-wrought strain of rapture
Ere with inviting smile the Wanderer said :
" Now for the tale with which you threatened us ! "
" In truth the threat escaped me unawares :
Should the tale tire you, let this challenge stand
For my excuse.   Dissevered from mankind,
As to your eyes and thoughts we must have seemed
When ye looked down upon us from the crag,
Islanders 'mid a stormy mountain sea,
We are not so ;—perpetually we touch
Upon the vulgar ordinances of the world ;
And he, whom this our cottage hath to-day
Relinquished, lived dependent for his bread
Upon the laws of public charity.
The Housewife, tempted by such slender gains
As might from that occasion be distilled,
Opened, as she before had done for me,
Her doors to admit this homeless Pensioner ;
The portion gave of coarse but wholesome fare
Which appetite required—a blind dull nook,
Such as she had, the *kennel* of his rest !
This, in itself not ill, would yet have been
Ill borne in earlier life ; but his was now
The still contentedness of seventy years.
Calm did he sit under the wide-spread tree
Of his old age ; and yet less calm and meek,
Winningly meek or venerably calm,

Than slow and torpid ; paying in this wise
A penalty, if penalty it were,
For spendthrift feats, excesses of his prime.
I loved the old Man, for I pitied him !
A task it was, I own, to hold discourse
With one so slow in gathering up his thoughts,
But he was a cheap pleasure to my eyes ;
Mild, inoffensive, ready in *his* way,
And helpful to his utmost power : and there
Our housewife knew full well what she possessed !
He was her vassal of all labour, tilled
Her garden, from the pasture fetched her kine ;
And, one among the orderly array
Of hay-makers, beneath the burning sun
Maintained his place ; or heedfully pursued
His course, on errands bound, to other vales,
Leading sometimes an inexperienced child
Too young for any profitable task.
So moved he like a shadow that performed
Substantial service.   Mark me now, and learn
For what reward !—The moon her monthly round
Hath not completed since our dame, the queen
Of this one cottage and this lonely dale,
Into my little sanctuary rushed—
Voice to a rueful treble humanized,
And features in deplorable dismay.
I treat the matter lightly, but, alas !
It is most serious : persevering rain
Had fallen in torrents ; all the mountain tops
Were hidden, and black vapours coursed their sides ;
This had I seen, and saw ; but, till she spake,
Was wholly ignorant that my ancient Friend—
Who at her bidding, early and alone,
Had clomb aloft to delve the moorland turf
For winter fuel—to his noontide meal
Returned not, and now, haply, on the heights
Lay at the mercy of this raging storm.
' Inhuman ! '—said I, ' was an old Man's life

Not worth the trouble of a thought ?—alas !
This notice comes too late.'   With joy I saw
Her husband enter—from a distant vale.
We sallied forth together ; found the tools
Which the neglected veteran had dropped,
But through all quarters looked for him in vain.
We shouted—but no answer !   Darkness fell
Without remission of the blast or shower,
And fears for our own safety drove us home.

I, who weep little, did, I will confess,
The moment I was seated here alone,
Honour my little cell with some few tears
Which anger and resentment could not dry.
All night the storm endured ; and, soon as help
Had been collected from the neighbouring vale,
With morning we renewed our quest : the wind
Was fallen, the rain abated, but the hills
Lay shrouded in impenetrable mist ;
And long and hopelessly we sought in vain :
Till, chancing on that lofty ridge to pass
A heap of ruin—almost without walls
And wholly without roof (the bleached remains
Of a small chapel, where, in ancient time,
The peasants of these lonely valleys used
To meet for worship on that central height)—
We there espied the object of our search,
Lying full three parts buried among tufts
Of heath-plant, under and above him strewn,
To baffle, as he might, the watery storm :
And there we found him breathing peaceably,
Snug as a child that hides itself in sport
'Mid a green hay-cock in a sunny field.
We spake—he made reply, but would not stir
At our entreaty ; less from want of power
Than apprehension and bewildering thoughts.

So was he lifted gently from the ground,

And with their freight homeward the shepherds
    moved
Through the dull mist, I following—when a step,
A single step, that freed me from the skirts
Of the blind vapour, opened to my view
Glory beyond all glory ever seen
By waking sense or by the dreaming soul !
The appearance, instantaneously disclosed,
Was of a mighty city—boldly say
A wilderness of building, sinking far
And self-withdrawn into a boundless depth,
Far sinking into splendour—without end !
Fabric it seemed of diamond and of gold,
With alabaster domes, and silver spires,
And blazing terrace upon terrace, high
Uplifted ; here, serene pavilions bright,
In avenues disposed ; there, towers begirt
With battlements that on their restless fronts
Bore stars—illumination of all gems !
By earthly nature had the effect been wrought
Upon the dark materials of the storm
Now pacified ; on them, and on the coves
And mountain-steeps and summits, whereunto
The vapours had receded, taking there
Their station under a cerulean sky.
Oh, 'twas an unimaginable sight !
Clouds, mists, streams, watery rocks and emerald
    turf,
Clouds of all tincture, rocks and sapphire sky,
Confused, commingled, mutually inflamed,
Molten together, and composing thus,
Each lost in each, that marvellous array
Of temple, palace, citadel, and huge
Fantastic pomp of structure without name,
In fleecy folds voluminous, enwrapped.
Right in the midst, where interspace appeared
Of open court, an object like a throne
Under a shining canopy of state

Stood fixed ; and fixed resemblances were seen
To implements of ordinary use,
But vast in size, in substance glorified ;
Such as by Hebrew Prophets were beheld
In vision—forms uncouth of mightiest power
For admiration and mysterious awe.
This little Vale, a dwelling-place of Man,
Lay low beneath my feet ; 'twas visible—
I saw not, but I felt that it was there.
That which I *saw* was the revealed abode
Of Spirits in beatitude : my heart
Swelled in my breast—' I have been dead,' I cried,
' And now I live !   Oh ! wherefore *do* I live ? '
And with that pang I prayed to be no more !—
—But I forget our Charge, as utterly
I then forgot him :—there I stood and gazed :
The apparition faded not away,
And I descended.

          Having reached the house,
I found its rescued inmate safely lodged,
And in serene possession of himself,
Beside a fire whose genial warmth seemed met
By a faint shining from the heart, a gleam,
Of comfort, spread over his pallid face.
Great show of joy the housewife made, and truly
Was glad to find her conscience set at ease ;
And not less glad, for sake of her good name,
That the poor Sufferer had escaped with life.
But, though he seemed at first to have received
No harm, and uncomplaining as before
Went through his usual tasks, a silent change
Soon showed itself : he lingered three short weeks ;
And from the cottage hath been borne to-day.

   So ends my dolorous tale, and glad I am
That it is ended." At these words he turned—
And, with blithe air of open fellowship,
Brought from the cupboard wine and stouter cheer,

Like one who would be merry. Seeing this,
My grey-haired Friend said courteously—" Nay, nay,
You have regaled us as a hermit ought ;
Now let us forth into the sun ! "—Our Host
Rose, though reluctantly, and forth we went.

THE END.

PRINTED IN GREAT BRITAIN AT
THE PRESS OF THE PUBLISHERS